INDIANS, NOT ALIENS

STORY OF TWO SISTERS

A LITERARY FICTION

INDIANS, NOT ALIENS

STORY OF TWO SISTERS

SWAPAN K. CHAUDHURI

White Falcon Publishing
www.whitefalconpublishing.com

Indians, Not Aliens - Story of Two Sisters

Swapan K. Chaudhuri

www.whitefalconpublishing.com

First Edition, 2022

Cover design by White Falcon Publishing, 2022
Cover image source freepik.com
Illustrations by Priyadarshi

Requests for permission should be addressed to
twosistersthebook@gmail.com

ISBN - 978-1-63640-705-0

To all refugees from East Bengal,
struggling for recognition as Indians.

Foreword

For the people of India, the acronyms NRC and CAA have aroused acrimonious debates during the last ten years. People have passionately argued for or against these legal strategies. Finally, when the exercise of registration of citizens was taken up in a small state, more than 1.9 million people, who believed themselves to be Indians for decades, could not qualify for inclusion of their names in the National Register for Citizens. The people who came to India from East Pakistan or Bangladesh on or after 25.03.1971, during the peak of genocide against the Bengalis, or thereafter, were not in the zone of consideration.

India was divided under the British law, without a plebiscite and people's participation in the decision. The leaders of different political formats and hues compromised their position in order not to delay the transfer of power. Although the Muslim League demanded the creation of Pakistan for all Muslims of British India, many Muslims in the provinces (except East Punjab) that formed the new India did not migrate en masse to Pakistan. But most of the Hindus in the provinces of Pakistan were insinuated to leave Pakistan at the time of partition, as zealous Muslims tagged their land 'Only for Muslims'. A large number of Bengali Hindus and Buddhists left their homeland in subsequent years to settle in India. A fraction of the Hindu population continued to stay in Pakistan, as they were averse to leaving their motherland. They had fought for her independence, not to leave their land behind.

When he was six or seven years old, this author had seen innumerable refugees living in the concourse of Sealdah station in wretched condition. Treated as unwanted aliens, they came over to India to take refuge in her lap. Those days, the concept of citizenship, passport, visa, etc., had no meaning to the homeless, uprooted people. The government was busy with their rehabilitation schemes for the refugees but did not do anything to offer them citizenship instantly. The die was cast with the passage of the Citizenship Act in 1955, making no major concession for the refugees who arrived and were still arriving. The refugees subsequently followed the tortuous route of securing a ration card for enlisting their names in the electoral roll. Many refugees continued to live without a valid citizenship certificate. Their unauthorized colonies were not legalized for decades, leaving the refugees with no documentary proof of their residence.

For historical reasons, many people originating from Nepal, Tibet, China, Myanmar, Sri Lanka, Iran, and Afghanistan are living in this country. Some of these groups, namely Parsis, Nepalese, Ahom, etc., have mixed with the local people and professed themselves as Indians. On the other hand, the indigenous people who have inhabited this country from time immemorial and speak one of the languages commonly spoken in India are subjected to proofs of birth, legacy, land ownership, legal migration, and residing in this land for several years. An immigrant from Pakistan or Bangladesh is needed to produce the same documents as a person from Somalia, and face many more questions, for sure.

On the one hand, every year, about 1.3 lakh people detach themselves from this country, forsaking Indian citizenship. They express absolute loyalty to countries like the USA, the UK, Canada, and Australia before courting their citizenship. Such people are held in high esteem by the authorities in India and are even offered the Overseas Citizen of India card. On the other hand, the refugees who escaped to India being persecuted in Pakistan or those people of Indian origin who migrated to India legally or clandestinely for permanent settlement, ready to vouchsafe full allegiance and loyalty to this country, are subjected to legal scrutiny, and if certain criteria are not satisfied, they get branded as non-citizens, illegal migrants or foreigners. The contradiction between these two situations has not been resolved. More than 1.9 million applicants, despite being people of Indian origin, were refused citizenship in 2018 and left high and dry.

The *story of two sisters is a literary fiction that* presents this tragedy in the life of a trade union leader and a teacher and propagates the need for empathy toward the cross-border migrants of Indian origin. Though set in a historical milieu, the protagonists in the novel are fictitious, and events imaginary. The story is expected to evoke compassion for human suffering without casting any aspersion on any community or blaming the people of any region. Jai Hind.

SKC, 20 July 2022.

PART ONE

INDIANS, ALIENATED

Chapter One

1.1 Birth of a girl

The family did not welcome her by blowing loud a conch-shell horn three times, nor did any female neighbour produce the peculiar '*ulu, ulu*' sound using their wagging tongue, as was customary to do on an auspicious occasion to dispel the evil forces. She was just born in a Hindu family on an island named Sandwip in the Bay of Bengal in 1931. As the *dhai* (midwife) announced that the second *bahu* (wife) had given birth to a female baby, the senior members of the family received the news with a shrug, and the gathering neighbours dispersed silently. Nayantara, the lady of the house, was waiting at the door of the improvised labour room. She returned to her room without a word after Sabina dhai confirmed that the newborn baby and her mother were doing fine.

The *dhai* did not insist on extra tips, and the visitors did not ask for sweetmeats.

No, not everybody was unhappy. The parents were happy to have a healthy baby. True, a son would have been more welcomed in their agrarian society. But theirs was an educated family, having regular income from white-collar jobs like teaching, trading, or drafting legal papers, supplemented by seasonal income from agriculture. The head of the family, Shakticharan Nandy, had his sons educated in colleges at Chittagong and at the University of Calcutta. Having received a liberal education in big cities, Suresh and Sisir came out of the traditional patriarchal masculine mould. The female education movement had already gathered momentum in these cities, and even in Chittagong, a few exclusive high-standard girls' schools had come up. Sisir promised his wife that he would provide the best education to his daughter. He named the baby Aparajita.

Madhuri, the young mother, was suckling the baby. Without raising her head, she said, "Blue flower! I shall call her 'Opu'." Sisir smiled and left.

A young girl of four peeped in from the window.

Madhuri spotted her and called out, "Come in, Sagar. Why are you standing over there? You have a sister now."

"But Granny told me not to enter the labour room."

"Oh, I see. That is why you are standing there. But do you want to see the baby?"

Sagarika nodded. Madhuri turned the newborn towards her, and she cried out, *'Onga, Onga.'*

Sagar was overjoyed. She shouted, "My little sister, my little sister!"

Sisir returned with his *boudi* (sister-in-law), Kanaklata; she brought milk and fruits for her fatigued sister-in-law. Then she lit up an incense burner to repel mosquitos. Sisir started to blow the conch-shell horn she had brought with her. Kanak did solo *'ulu, ulu'*. They prayed for the long life of the newly born baby, and Kanak gave a drop of honey in the baby's mouth.

Kanak remembered the day when Sagar was born four years ago in the same improvised labour room. At that time, the parents-in-law were not so openly unhappy. They knew more babies would follow, and they could wait for male children. They welcomed the baby and expressed their happiness. Her father-in-law was a poet of sorts and named the girl Sagarika, meaning the daughter of the sea, since the sea surrounded the island. The blue waters and the azure dome of the sky used to get reflected in all songs, music, and ballads of the island.

After two years, Kanak conceived once again. Her mother-in-law kept on praying to God for a male child. She even crossed the sea in a country boat and offered puja to Lord Chandranath on Sitakund Hill. But Kanak had a miscarriage due to an accidental fall and lost her fecundity.

"You need not recount that episode, boudi! It will make her sad on this day," said Sisir. "I was only trying to tell Madhuri why our parents-in-law were reacting in a subdued manner," said Kanak apologetically. "Perhaps I am responsible for this."

"Kanak!" the voice of Nayantara roared. "What are you doing in the labour room? Is it not time for lunch?"

"Yes, Mom!" Kanak came out hurriedly.

"Take a bath before you enter the kitchen."

Shakticharan was talking to his two sons, sitting cross-legged on a wooden seat laid on the floor. The two sons sat on his every side. They sprinkled a little water on the hard floor before them to prevent dust from getting carried by air to their food. Kanak placed the brass plates in front of them and served rice and five preparations of pulse, vegetables, and fish curry in separate bowls. Nayantara sat a little away on a low stool with a hand fan made of palm leaf. They offered a prayer to their family god, thanking him for the day's food, and dropped a few grains of rice by the side of the plate for the inferior creatures.

"The elder bahu will not bear a child anymore. I had hoped that the younger bahu would give you a son, but that has not happened. I am worried that our lineage will end with us. Married women do not inherit the property of their fathers. Your cousins will appropriate the ancestral land in our share."

"Papa, things are changing in our society quite fast. You see, the custom of *suttee* has been abolished, widow remarriage has been legalised, and schools have been set up for girls. That day is not far when married or unmarried women will inherit the ancestral property in equal share with men," said Sisir.

"I cannot foresee that far. But we shall bring up our daughters just like sons. Sagar will go to school in the coming session," Suresh, the elder brother, commented.

Nayantara said, "Your wives are also literate. They studied up to class six. Unlike me, they can read and write Bengali. But they cannot work outside the home."

"No, these girls will go to college and university and will at least be a teacher, if not a lawyer or a doctor," Suresh stated emphatically. As the lunch was about to be over, he added, "Papa, I have got an offer from Rauzan High School for the post of assistant headmaster. This is a high school, and I am to teach English in classes nine and ten. They will give me the government-approved scale. As I am a postgraduate teacher, they will raise me to the position of headmaster very soon. But I must join before another PG teacher joins. I need to move to the mainland for better prospects."

"But Kanak and Sagar will stay here. I will not allow them to leave the house," Nayantara said firmly.

"The question does not arise," Shakticharan confirmed.

"Don't worry. They will remain here. Chittagong is just a sail away. I shall come once in a fortnight."

Suresh felt happy that his ambition to become the headmaster of a high school would be fulfilled in the near future. He was teaching as an assistant teacher for the last six years in Sandwip Middle English School, although he was an M.A. – a rare accomplishment those days.

"Sisir, what name have you chosen for your daughter?"

"Brother, she may be called Aparajita after the blue flower if you and papa agree."

Shakticharan said, "I had expected a grandson, and I would have named him after Lord Shiva, my Chandranath. You have selected a beautiful name for my granddaughter. Do you know that Aparajita is the name of Devi Durga, the unvanquished goddess? She will fight to the end and will not surrender."

1.2 Ambience of Sandwip

The island of Sandwip, located at the estuary of River Meghna, off the coast of Chittagong, is a place of idyllic beauty. The fertility of her sedimentary soil made this place a granary and an easy target for the Portuguese pirates in yesteryears. Coconut and palm trees surround the island with the pristine beauty of nature to make her picturesque as well as romantic.

There were several houses of Nandys in the village on the fringe of Harishpur town. There were several other Hindu families in the vicinity. But the Muslims outnumbered the Hindus by a huge margin. Out of twelve Aaulias who came to Bengal for the propagation of Islam in the thirteenth century, one *Aaulia*[1] named Bakhtiar Maisuri set up his *Astana* in Sandwip at Rohini. His task was made easy by the heads of the Bengali Hindu society practising casteism to the point that most of the people in the lower rungs of the community used to fume with mute anger. Even many upper-caste Hindus were subjected to a strict code of conduct, and if they violated the norms, they would face castigation from the society – equally from their family. Many such Hindus, unable to bear the social persecution, had embraced Islam. These renegades led the conversion brigade of Islam subsequently.

On the island of Sandwip, about eighty per cent of the population was Muslim. Chittagong, the divisional headquarter, was the hub of Islamic propagation and Noakhali, the then district headquarters, had the maximum number of Islamic seminaries. Overall, Muslims were in the majority in the entire land east of the Bhagirathi, which used to be known as East Bengal.

Sagar was blissfully unaware of the communal heat around her. This island was so beautiful! The fields surrounding their village were either green or golden throughout the year. When paddy was

[1] Arabian preachers of Islam

harvested, the stubbles would weave a zig-zag pattern across the fields. Harishpur had about two or three hundred houses; mostly thatched huts with bamboo walls; only a few had brick walls and tin sheds on timber frames.

Sagar was growing up in the lap of nature; the green meadows overlooking the cluster of houses used to call her out. While playing with her friends, she would suddenly look at the waves in the paddy fields caused by the winds from the bay and clap her little hands in sheer joy. The roaring sound of breaking waves of the Bay of Bengal, audible from their home during the high tide or more distinctly at night, invited her. She used to persuade her uncle to take her on a bicycle to the seaside, which was only a mile away from her home. Sometimes, when he was unoccupied in the evening, Suresh would take her to the beach where Sagarika could have some idea of the huge expanse of the sea, sky, and universe. She was fond of her uncle, who played with her on the beach, frolicking with the frothy white bubbles of dashing water encroaching on the coastline. As their house was on the south-western part of the island, they had the advantage of watching the sunset in its full glory. Sagar used to cling to her father when he took her in the water. But after her father had left for the mainland, she would sit on the shore to keep watch on her sister. Later, as they grew up, Sagar used to lay flat on her belly on the sand, waiting for a wave to come over her and push her up. Her toddling sister would screech in excitement and run up the shore. Older still, the two sisters used to gather oyster shells from the seashore or make hillocks and sand statues. By the time they returned, the entire dome of the sky would be studded with scintillating stars. Sisir would show them different constellations and zodiac signs in the sky. Opu could see that her elder sister was already aware of some of these names from her schoolbook and wondered when she would grow as big as her sister.

When Sagar completed her studies up to class six, Suresh decided to put her in a boarding school in Chittagong. Opu was then in class two. At first, she did not understand what it meant for her, but within a few days of her sister's first voyage, she realised the pain of parting from her elder sister. Since her birth, she was totally ensconced by her sister, more than her mother; she had acted like a nurse, a babysitter, a playmate, and a teacher. Opu felt so safe and secure in her company that she did not feel any need to make friends with other children of the locality.

Her didi used to sing the lullaby when sometimes she would sleep with her. Later, she would pester her for a fairy tale. Didi used to teach her Bengali rhymes, then the Bengali alphabet and number counting. Didi would do all these after coming back from school. For the last two years, Opu had been going to the same mixed primary school where didi was also studying in upper primary. After her senior uncle got her admitted to Dr. Khastagir's High School for Girls in Chittagong, she used to come to Sandwip during vacations, every time smarter than earlier. Opu noticed that Sagar didi was talking differently, in a distinct accent. Opu began to adore her. But the vacations were short, and being without her sister's loving company, Opu grew up as a cheerless, sullen girl.

1.3 The Chittagong uprising

Sisir used to go to Chittagong to escort Sagar on her voyage to and from Sandwip. Earlier, he used to go to Chittagong when he studied B.Sc. at Ashutosh College. One day, when Sisir was coming to Sadarghat, he remembered how he came across his schoolmate Lalmohan at the Kali temple a few years back. He was also from Sandwip and came to Chittagong to study biology in a college before going to Calcutta and take admission in a medical college. He used to talk about the country and her miserable condition under the British. This country became so impoverished under their rule that it would take more than a hundred years to restore its old prosperity. Sisir was overwhelmed by his words.

Their friendship deepened because they could meet each other in Sandwip and Chittagong. The country had already gone through the non-violent movement led by the charismatic Mohandas Karamchand Gandhi. But young blood was pining for revolution. Savarkar had written that the Sepoy Rebellion of 1857 was the first war of Independence. Lalmohan told Sisir that he met a person who believed that independence would come through a war. The war of 1857 was the right model. We must inspire the native soldiers through our sacrifice to come out together for the liberation of the country. Gandhi had suspended his movement because of a violent incident at Chauri Chaura in 1922. To him, the means to achieve a pure goal like freedom must also be pure and non-violent.

"Our teacher says that such people should be saints and not be in politics. They will betray the people's movement at a critical juncture. Their ideas of non-violence will never be reciprocated by the imperialist forces. You have seen what happened at Jallianwala Bag. The British Army fired on the unarmed, non-violent crowd gathered in a largely enclosed arena. Contrast it with the absence of retaliation by the National Congress and the silence observed by its undisputed leader. People of this country will be disenchanted with such leaders at the end, maybe after the nation has paid a heavy price," said Lalmohan.

"Who is this man? What is his name?" asked Sisir.

"He never tells his name. We call him Master da."

One day Sisir heard that Lalmohan had left his house after breaking into his uncle's cash safe. The police came to Sisir's house to enquire from him about the hideout of the fugitive and kept him in the police lock-up for interrogation. Sisir was tortured, but he had no secret to reveal.

After his release, Sisir remained in the village under the surveillance of the local police. Fortunately, his degree examination was already over. When his result was declared, he joined Kargil High English School as a maths teacher. Shakticharan did not lose any time in fixing the marriage of his younger son with Madhuri. Sagar was two years old at the time.

Within a few months of his marriage, Sisir read in a newspaper that an armed uprising had happened in Chittagong Town, and the armoury was attacked by the revolutionaries. In a few days, Lalmohan Sen of Sandwip was captured with several others. This news came as a surprise to Sisir as he could never have guessed that his friend was a core committee member of the Indian Republican Army, led by the mysterious revolutionary Surya Sen. Lalmohan was sentenced to life imprisonment and transportation. He was sent to the dreaded Cellular Jail in the Andaman Islands. In 1932, the European club at Pahartali was attacked. A girl named Preetilata, who led this action, committed suicide to avoid capture after she was injured. In 1934, Surya Sen and Tarakeswar Dastidar were hanged after inhuman torture. The Bengali Hindus were proud of their children who could think of confronting the mighty British, not by individual killing, but by declaring independence and trying to defend it with arms.

Sagar heard the name of Lalmohan Sen in her childhood from her uncle. When she came from Chittagong on vacation, three of them would go to the seaside and hear the stories of the sacrifice of the freedom fighters.

When Opu was in the exclusive company of her sister, she would listen to the story of the fearsome Hostel Super, her naughty hostel friends, and their escapades. Sagar narrated how they used to circulate hand-made copies of Pather Dabi, a proscribed book written by the popular novelist Sarat Chandra Chatterjee. Sagar and her friends would go through the pages in candlelight after the hostel's lights were put out. Opu listened intently, as if with her eyes.

After Opu appeared in the annual examination of class five, her senior uncle Suresh took her to Rauzan with him to get her admitted to a non-residential girls' high school. Kanak also came along to look after her. Coming from a village, and that too from an island, Opu felt like a fish out of water in the populous city of Chittagong. When she heard that her senior uncle had received the appointment letter for the post of headmaster at Banaripara High English School in the Barishal district, Opu agreed to accompany her aunt and uncle to Banaripara, as it was a small town surrounded by greenery, like their Sandwip. If there were a girls' high school, she would prefer to study there. Within a week, Suresh left for Barishal with Kanak and Opu.

1.4 Opu comes to Banaripara

Suresh had sent a letter to the Assistant headmaster, informing him of his date of arrival. It took one day and night to reach the new place. Apart from the long journey by boat through Noakhali, they had to cross the mighty rivers — Meghna and Kirtankhola — by steamer after a night's halt at Kawakhali. When they reached Banaripara at noon, they found the assistant headmaster waiting at the ferry ghat with his son. The peon of the school was also there to help the new headmaster reach his earmarked quarter with his luggage. The Assistant headmaster introduced himself as Birendranath Guhathakurta. His house was in the vicinity of the school. In the meantime, his son Rabi touched the feet of Suresh babu and his wife, Kanak.

"My eldest son Rabi," said Biren. He continued after a pause, "He has just appeared in the Intermediate exam."

Rabi requested the new uncle and aunty to visit their house. His mother had invited them for lunch.

When they reached Biren's house, Soudamini opened the door and welcomed the guests. After exchanging namaskar with folded hands, they all entered the house. Kanak asked Opu to touch the feet of all the seniors. As Opu began to do so, one by one, Rabi left the room to check if Haru had cleaned the quarter of the head sir.

"Haru da, please take a spare cot from our house. You may ask us if anything is immediately required," said Rabi.

"Rabi bhai, don't worry. I'll not leave before my sir finds himself comfortable."

Suresh told them that Opu was his niece, and he had brought her along to put her in a good school. "Is there any good high school for girls here?"

"Sorry, uncle. At Banaripara, the only girls' school is up to class six. This is a private school run by an Anglo-Indian couple. Year after year, the local people are giving deputation to the District Magistrate to upgrade the school to class ten, but no decision has been taken till now. They may give permission to upgrade it to class eight from the next year. My sister Chhabi stays in our uncle's house in Barishal Town to go to a school," said Rabi.

"Rabi, will you get me the admission form for class six? Opu cannot afford to lose one year. After a year, if the school is not upgraded, I shall decide if she will stay in Barishal Town or go back to Chittagong."

"Don't worry uncle. We can go together in the morning and meet Mr Smith," said Rabi exuding confidence.

Soudamini had meanwhile laid the *aasan* (seats) for all and asked everybody to wash their hands and sit for lunch.

Opu was admitted to the St. Mary's Girls' School in class six. The school was nearly two miles away from their quarter through meandering lanes, by-lanes, open grounds, and ponds. As it was a morning school, Suresh used to take his niece to school in the morning at five-thirty a.m. But how would she return? Being the headmaster, Suresh had to reach his school before ten. It was decided that Rabi would bring her back when the school broke. This arrangement would continue for three months till Rabi's I.A. results were declared, admission for the degree course was over, and the new classes began.

On the first encounter, Rabi had hardly taken any notice of this shy girl, just eleven-year and a half old. He was past seventeen and considered himself much older and wiser than this girl in a frock with two braidings of hair dangling on the shoulder. Funny girl! She would have touched his feet if he had not moved out in the nick of time to talk to Haru da. He was, however, not unhappy with his new responsibility. He used to get up early, work out for an hour and read for some time. After his breakfast, he reached the girls' school just in time. Suresh had introduced him to the teachers as a member of his family.

In the beginning, Opu was somewhat unsure about her interaction with Rabi as she did not have a brother in their family. Aunty told her to treat him as her elder brother, respect him, and address him as Rabi dada.

"Aunty calls you Opu. What is your full name?"

"Kumari Aparajita Nandy."

"My goodness! A heavyweight name for a lightweight girl!"

Opu felt offended and did not say a word on the way. Rabi understood that it would be a hellish experience if he had to walk with a girl, howsoever little, without any word.

"You don't need to come from tomorrow. I can return on my own."

Rabi was totally unprepared for the summary dismissal. What would he tell the seniors? He said, "Then who will protect you from wicked people?"

The next day, he offered a truce.

"Opu, do you like this place? Is it not beautiful?"

"Sandwip is much more beautiful," Opu answered in a grave tone.

The answer hurt Rabi. He used to think that Barishal was the best place under the sun. But this stubborn girl said that the beauty of Sandwip could not be surpassed!

"Then why did you leave Sandwip?"

"Because our primary school is only up to class six. There is no high school for girls. The senior uncle took me to Rauzan to put me in a girls' high school. He thought that my standard of English needed improvement so that I could qualify for admission to Khastagir School. But Rauzan is so crowded and dusty! I couldn't breathe properly. I wanted to go back to my *desh*[2]. Then suddenly, senior uncle got this offer, and I did not get a chance to go back."

"Going back to your *desh*? Is this not your *desh*?"

"No, this is not. Sandwip is my *desh*, where my parents, my grandparents live in our house."

"Do you think that you are now in a foreign land?" Rabi delivered a googly.

Opu felt perplexed. She uttered some words which did not carry any meaning. She had to divert to another topic. "Why is this place called Barishal? What does it mean?"

It was the turn of Rabi to be foxed. "I don't know. But I shall find out."

---

[2] Homeland. It means a district or a country, depending on the context.

"I know. In fact, everybody knows. *Aite shal jaite shal, taare koy Barishal.*[3]" Opu burst into loud laughter.

They came to terms with each other in a few days. The walk from the school to their house, which took thirty minutes on the first day, gradually began to take forty-five minutes. Opu shed her initial prevarications and began to talk freely with Rabi. Sometimes she would ask him to catch a butterfly for her and sometimes pick a flower from the wayside Palash tree. When they came by the side of a pool, she would like to see his skill in throwing a flat piece of tile on the surface of the water, pitching it three or four times. The more the number of bounces, the broader was her smile. Sometimes Rabi had to account for the delay to Kanak aunty, although she had full trust in Rabi because of his good demeanour and family background.

One day, they took a detour by the road around the Boys' High School when they heard the prayer song sung by the boys in chorus. '*Hao dharamete dheer, hao karomete beer, hao unnato shir, naahi bhoy.*'[4]

Opu tried to follow the words of the prayer song, but being unable to do so, she asked, "Rabi dada, what is the meaning of this song?"

As Rabi explained the meaning of the song, her face brightened up. Rabi concluded by translating the last couplet with the words, "*This land Bharat is inhabited by people of many languages, of many beliefs, of different attires, but has a unique oneness in her diversity. Soon, the whole world will be amazed to see the rise of a great nation in Bharat.*"

Rabi continued further, "*Bharat is our country, our desh...*"

Opu interrupted, "You mean our desh is Bharat and not the Barishal district or the island of Sandwip. Is that what you mean?"

"Exactly. Conceptually Bharat is the country of all men living in this land. It extends from Hindukush and Indus Valley to the borders of Burma, from Kashmir to Kanyakumari. This land was described as Bharat Barsha in our ancient Puranas. Foreigners knew this land tract or its northern part by the names Sindhu, Hindush, Hindustan, or India. The country was divided into many independent kingdoms and ruled by several kings. When the foreign invaders came from Greece,

---

[3] 'It gives you a pain, when you come in or move out of Barishal.' – A popular satirical saying.

[4] A Bengali patriotic song composed by Atul Prasad Sen (1871- 1934).

Persia, Afghanistan, and Central Asia, they were defeated many times by the Indian kings before they conquered large parts of land from the Hindu kings. The Pathans and the Mughals settled in this country and ruled over the subjects, following their own norms.

At the time of emperors Asoka, Samudragupta, and Aurangzeb, the Buddhist, the Hindu, and the Muslim empires were the biggest, but some kingdoms like Kashmir, Kamrup, Manipur, Travancore, parts of Bengal, Rajputana, and Vijaynagar remained independent. Politically, the inhabitants were the subjects of different kingdoms or sultanates, but in a wider sense, everybody was a Bhartiya or Hindustani. Presently, we live in British India and are known as Indians. Although the princely states are under the British suzerainty, the subjects owe allegiance to their native Kings; and they too are Indians. Daman & Diu are ruled by the Portuguese. These are also parts of India. Now, Afghanistan, Burma, and Ceylon are also ruled by the British, but their inhabitants are not Indians."

Opu was apparently overwhelmed by the lecture and exclaimed, "My God, you know so much! Earlier I thought you to be just one of the unemployed boys in a roadside teashop!"

"Thank you, madam, for changing your opinion. Now, hurry up. We are quite late."

"But tell me why we don't sing such songs in our school."

"Because yours is an English medium missionary school, you have to sing in praise of Jesus and Mary. Students of Govt run schools are bound to sing in praise of the Crown, whether they like it or not. Only private Hindu schools choose such patriotic lyrics as this for their prayer song."

When they stepped in, Kanak aunty was visibly annoyed, and she turned her face away. So, for the next few days, they reached home before it was ten-thirty.

"What do you do in the afternoon?" asked Opu one day. "I see you go out on a bicycle, and you come back when it is dark. What do you do all this time?"

"Am I answerable to you for where I go or what I do?" said Rabi, sitting on the bricked staircases of the pond. "You mind your own business."

"Okay. I'll tell aunty that you've joined an opera party."

"What? How can you tell a lie like this?"

"Why don't you tell me what the truth is?"

Rabi realised that discretion was the better part of valour and disclosed that he went to a Kali temple at the outskirt of Barishal town, where there was a gymnasium attached to the temple, and he was doing physical exercise with many other young men. They had a trainer for boxing, knifing, and fencing. However, he did not mention that there was a secret group of men working for the freedom of the country by armed insurrection.

"We must be physically strong if we want to drive them out." Rabi punched in the air against an unseen enemy.

"Will you punch the Britishers out of India?" Opu giggled.

"Yes, we may. A strong body will give us physical strength and confidence. Arms will only be supplementary."

Rabi folded the sleeve of his shirt and formed an acute angle between his hand and the arm. His biceps muscle showed up like a cricket ball, drawing an exclamation from Opu. "Ugh!"

"See how strong the muscle is. Touch it," invited Rabi. Opu overcame her hesitation and pressed her fingers into the muscle.

"My god! It's so hard!" As she tried to feel the strength of the muscle with her palm, she felt a tremor within herself and shuddered in a jerk.

"Are you now satisfied? I can bend any iron rod of one and a half feet with my two hands."

She felt abashed for the unknown excitement in her. She took her hand away and said, "Hum. I find that my bodyguard is truly strong, and I don't have to fear anybody. Will you be my bodyguard for all time?"

"Your bodyguard? Ha! Ha!" laughed Rabi. "I need not do my graduation and further studies but work as your bodyguard!"

"Then who will save me from wicked people in future?' Opu was visibly upset.

"Worry not. Like Lord Krishna, I shall always be there beside you," Rabi said to console her.

"Really?"

Rabi smiled affirmatively. "Well, let us go now. Tomorrow I may not come as my Intermediate results will be declared."

"Best of luck, Rabi dada!"

1.5 Revolution at doorstep

Next Tuesday, when Biren was coming to the school, he met Haran Mukherjee near the school ground. Haran was the Town Congress President and an influential person in the locality. He greeted Biren sir and expressed his wish to know if he was still officiating as the headmaster. Biren told him about the new headmaster. Haran informed him that the Town Congress Committee would hold a meeting on the school ground on the ninth day of August, which was a Sunday, and he wanted to have approval for it. Biren asked him to take police permission first and then come to the headmaster.

The political situation of the country was rather hot. The world was going through the second global war in its history. Many countries of different continents were fighting each other in two groups — the Axis and the Allies. Germany and Britain were the main protagonists in these two camps. Britain involved India in the war without asking for the consent of the elected leaders in the Central Legislative Assembly. The bitter experience of extending unqualified support to the British in the First World War was not forgotten by the Indians.

Subhas Bose was already forced to leave the Congress party because of his strong anti-British stand. The Congress sought to bargain for the declaration of granting independence as a pre-condition for supporting the Allies. The Muslim League suddenly became a forceful political entity after the adoption of the Lahore Resolution in 1940. The British government began to listen to their demand for a separate state of Pakistan, and the Muslim League asked the Indian Muslims to extend whole-hearted support to the British. Although Subhas Bose had moved to Germany and Japan, agreeing to lead the Azad Hind Fauj and reached Singapore in 1942 to launch an attack on the British, the Hindus were indecisive about supporting the Axis powers and ambivalent about supporting the Allies. The Communist Party had initially decided to follow the Congress line but completely changed its stand as soon as Germany attacked Russia. They extended support to the Allies, treating the war as a people's war. Besides that, Savarkar led the Hindu rightists to the side of the British, having secured his release from Andaman and other jails by giving written undertakings to support the government.

Haran faced a tough time in the Police station to convince the sub-inspector that the meeting would be peaceful. He gave an undertaking that no slogan would be raised, and no speech would be delivered against the Crown.

"The S.I. told me that any attempt to foment trouble would be firmly dealt with. That is the instruction from the headquarters," Haran told Suresh and Biren, sitting in the headmaster's office. Suresh was a follower of Gandhi ji.

"What will Mahatma ji do now? Will he call for a bigger movement?" asked Suresh.

"Don't know exactly. We have been asked to call public meetings on the ninth of this month. Maybe some announcement will be made after the AICC meeting at Bombay next week," replied Haran.

"It seems that the Congress is in a tight corner. To take up an agitational programme at this moment is likely to annoy the government. But if the party does not follow up its stand, people will hover around Subhas Bose," Biren babu, an ardent supporter of Bose, commented.

Haran reacted sharply, "He will allow the Japanese to enter. We shall be enslaved afresh by them. Will the situation be better under the Japanese?" Disgusted, he got up after pocketing the letter of permission from the headmaster.

Outside, he came across Rabi on the road. Rabi was an active Congress Sevadal worker. Haran asked him to come to the party office in the afternoon as he was to allocate duties to the workers for the upcoming public meeting.

Rabi had already taken admission for the degree course in his own Braja Mohan college. The session was to begin after a fortnight. All these months, he continued to escort Opu on her way back home, although Kanak aunty told him to let Opu return independently. Now he would have to take leave from his duty. But this meeting had been called suddenly. Gandhi ji would be sending his message outlining the scope of the movement. Now for the next one week, he would have to work through day and night campaigning for the meeting. Of course, he was not alone, and there were many workers, some from his Vivekananda Gymnasium, some from his college, and some others from the locality. But no one had his energy and popularity. Rabi worked for the Congress in the daytime but met some people in the temple after the devotees had left. This group of people would avail of any opportunity that might come as a fall-out of the meeting. They were mostly the younger disciples of Troilokya Chakrabarty, the jail-bird revolutionary.

On the night of the eighth of August, the All India Radio broadcasted the decision of the AICC to launch a movement seeking the declaration of independence of the country. This was to be a fight unto death. Sensing the trouble brewing up on the horizon, Rabi went to meet Opu in her house. He gave her a copy of *Ananda math, written by Bankim Chandra Chattopadhyay.* "Read it. It is our inspiration. This book contains the hymn-like composition called *Vande Mataram*[5]. This slogan binds all patriotic Indians together, be they Congressmen or the revolutionaries. The book is written from a historical perspective, welcoming British rule against the misrule of the Muslims in the last days of the Mughal empire. You need to read between the lines and understand the true meaning in the present context. Hindus and Muslims must fight together against the British. Today we shall draw our strength from this incantation. See you after the meeting." Rabi left in a hurry.

By noon, the whole township congregated in the school maidan. People were brimming with excitement. Kanak did not allow Opu to go to the meeting place. However, she did agree to take her to the terrace of Guhathakurta House to get a better view from a distance. Soudamini also joined them with her daughter and younger son.

Suddenly, sitting in a rickshaw, two policemen started announcing that the District Magistrate had imposed prohibitory orders under section 144 of the CrPC in Barishal Town and adjacent urban centres and assembly of more than five persons would be held illegal and punishable. Haran babu became furious at this development. With

---

[5] We worship our mother.

such a huge gathering of people, how could he call off the meeting? Sarat Ghosh, the main speaker, had already arrived. Seeing the attitude of the police, he started his address without losing any time. He asked the crowd to be peaceful and restrained. He communicated to the assembly in a few words the background of the decision of the Congress and the outline of the Quit India Movement, where the administration would be paralysed, and the fight would continue till the British agreed to leave. Then he asked the assembly to shout the slogans given by Gandhi ji. *Angrezo Bharat Chhoro*, meaning Englishmen, Quit India. Azharuddin, the S.I., could not digest this. He jumped on the dais and pushed down the speakers. The policemen started wielding lathi severely on the crowd. Many fell to the ground, many were bleeding from their heads and noses, and many had their legs and ribs broken.

Azharuddin was exulting at his achievement when suddenly a group of youth started resisting the police. They were shouting, *Karenge ya marenge*, meaning do or die. The Sub Inspector fired a shot in the air. The boys came up with the sticks to which the party flags were tied. *Engrez Bharat Chharo*, the new slogan rent the sky. Some of them gheraoed the S.I. Haran babu was seen arguing with him, flaunting the letter of permission for the meeting.

Azharuddin charged at him like a wild boar, "Who are you to question me? You get lost otherwise..."

The boys started shouting around him. The S.I. raised his hand to hit Haran babu with the pistol butt. But before he could hit his target, a massive punch, an uppercut, hit his solar plexus, and the huge body of Azharuddin fell like a sliced plantain tree, gasping for breath. The young men thought that they had taken adequate reprisal for his high-handedness. They shouted *Vande Mataram* and quickly dispersed. The police arrested Haran Mukherjee, Sarat Ghosh, and fifty others. As the trouble was anticipated, reinforcement from District Headquarters arrived promptly under the command of the S.P., a British officer. Till then, Inspector Azharuddin did not regain his sense. He could not stand up and salute his boss.

The district force launched a house-to-house search for the assailants. The supporters of the Muslim League in the neighbourhood came out to help the police trace the Hindu boys from their homes. They spread the word that Azharuddin was dead, and removed the body The police caned and thrashed the inmates of all nearby houses; even the aged members were not spared. As they began to violate the modesty of housewives, the fugitive youths came out from their hideouts and courted arrest. The inmates of the surrounding houses witnessed the barbarity of the British police as they began to lynch Rabi and four other boys on the road in full public view.

The women and children on the rooftop were lying flat to hide from the police. As all the policemen gathered at the lynching arena, they raised their heads. To their consternation, Soudamini, Kanak and Opu saw Rabi taking the baton and kicks as the prime target of the police. One by one, the boys fell to the ground, and Rabi continued to take the beating with his head high and shouting Vande Mataram at intervals. His face was besmeared with blood. Unable to bear the sight, Soudamini fainted. Kanak held her tightly and asked her children to bring water. But where was Opu?

Opu ran out of the house to reach the spot. By then, the four boys were picked up in stretchers, and Rabi was being dragged by his hair to a police van-rickshaw. Some policemen continued to kick him under the belly and in his back.

Opu cried out, "Rabi dada, my Rabi dada. Don't beat him, listen to me, don't beat him, he will die." The policemen had already pushed him into the van. "Don't take him away. He is innocent. Don't take him away. He is my only friend. Leave him, please! Leave him, I say," she cried out as the van sped away. She ran behind the van for a distance and then returned slowly to the ground, weeping uncontrollably.

The ground presented a dismal look, as flags, festoons, white caps, and chappals were strewn all over. Aparajita picked up a flag from the grass and held it over her head. Overcoming her personal distress, she shouted, "Vande Mataram! Bharatmata Ki Jai[6]!!" People of the neighbouring houses opened their windows first and then the doors. Seeing the young girl who braved the police and was shouting slogans, they came out on the street and joined their voice, "Engrez, Bharat Chharo[7]!!"

---

[6] Victory to Mother India.

[7] Bengali version of the Hindi slogan – Angrezon, Bharat chhoro.

Chapter Two

2.1 Sagarika comes to Banaripara

Sagarika was preparing for the matric examination when the August Revolution was underway. Sisir came to Chittagong and took her back to Sandwip, as the school hostel was temporarily closed. The schools resumed after two months. Opu's school, however, did not reopen. Threatened during the peak of the movement, the Smith family left Banaripara, closing the school permanently. Waiting for a month, Suresh found no other option but to take Opu back to Chittagong via Sandwip and approach the school where Sagar had studied for four years. Opu was terribly upset to leave Barishal, and nobody knew why. Meanwhile, Rabi was incarcerated as an under-trial prisoner in Barishal District jail. The police had brought a criminal case against him on the charge of murdering a public servant on duty. Unlike others, Rabi's bail application was summarily rejected.

Later, three months after the incident, it transpired that Azharuddin was alive and was recuperating in his village. As the government was preparing the gallows for Rabi with fanfare, it became a source of embarrassment for the police administration, and nobody was ready to touch his file with a barge pole. Rabi was dumped in the jail without any trial or a chargesheet.

Based on the results of her half-yearly examination, Aparajita was allowed as a special case to appear in the annual examination of class six at Dr. Khastagir's Girls' High School. As she cleared the examination creditably, she became a regular student and was allotted a seat in the hostel. The Hostel Super greeted her as 'Sagarika's sister'. Opu did not find her face frightening.

The two sisters met each other after ten months. Both were exuberant to share their experiences of the intervening period. Earlier, Opu used to listen to what Sagar said about her school and hostel life, which was almost a one-way traffic. But now, she had lots to share, walking side by side with her elder sister on the familiar beach of Sandwip. The waves rolled over one another as they used to do earlier; the roaring sound haunted their ears for hours like the resonant yet booming sound from a conch shell horn. Now, however, Opu was chattering more than ever, surprising Sagar. Her stories ranged from Mr and Mrs Smith to Sodu aunty and their family and from Kirtankhola River to police atrocities in the maidan near their house. But Opu did not know why she could not come out with the tale of Rabi dada, why her voice choked whenever she attempted to mention his name. Only when she stood alone before the blue waves, she would utter the name as if the name came floating on the waves and found expression on her lips. Sagar noticed the change in Opu but could not make anything out of it. Within her closed hostel gate, Sagar never had an opportunity to interact with any boy. The bud of her mind remained semi-blossomed, as it were, although she was older than her sister by more than four years.

Sagar came to Sandwip once again after her Matriculation examination. As Opu was in the hostel, she spent time with her gracefully-growing-old grandparents. Sagar used to go out with grandpa to their farmland, where different vegetables were being grown with the help of some sharecroppers. She was interested in learning about farming and the different techniques followed for different produce. Apart from her grandpa, she used to ask questions to the *Kisans*. Though they were from Muslim or Scheduled Caste Hindu communities, she used to talk to them as if they were also family members and listen to their answers with regard. After passing the matriculation level, Sagar went to Dacca to study at the Eden College for Women.

After two years, when she returned from Dacca with her uncle, having appeared in the Intermediate exam, she was a young, attractive lady in a saree. Sisir had picked up Opu from the school so that the two sisters could meet each other after a long time. He also told them that Lalmohan had been sent back from Andaman to the Dacca jail, and someday, he would take them to his friend when he was finally released. Shakticharan and Nayantara, too, had grown older. They felt happy seeing that Sagarika had received a good education. The two sisters went to the beach to take the clean air in their lungs. They walked on the beach hand in hand and talked and talked endlessly. Sagarika told Opu about her plan to study B.Sc. in Dacca and then relocate to Calcutta to study Astronomy at Calcutta University. Opu listened to her in awe and made up her mind to follow the path charted by her elder sister. After a week, Suresh came to Sandwip to take Sagar to her mother at Banaripara. As they went via Chittagong, Suresh dropped Opu at her school. Sagarika would return to Dacca once the results were declared. Then she would complete her graduation.

At Banaripara, Sagar was beside herself in joy to see her mother Kanak after a few years. She found the place too small, placid, and boring. It neither had the natural beauty of Sandwip nor the attractions of big cities like Chittagong and Dacca. But unlike the general population of Sandwip, people here were more educated, and unlike the urbanites of Dacca, neighbours here were more friendly, outspoken, and helpful. Suresh was popular among the local residents, young or old, by the name headmaster moshai[8]. Sagar came to be known as the 'daughter of mastermoshai'. Her beauty and scholarship became the talk of the town.

Within a few days of her arrival, the approval of the Education department was received by the S.D.O. to open a morning girls' school in the building of the existing boys' school by staggering the school timing suitably. Co-education of boys and girls at the middle and high school level was still not acceptable to the conservative middle-class society. After the closure of the upper primary school of Mr and Mrs Smith in 1942, the girls of the locality were deprived of education for two and half years. The Muslim parents were not interested in exposing their daughters to western-style education. As a result, getting adequate students was also a problem. But the problem that immediately faced the educated people of the locality was to find out lady teachers for the school. There were very few housewives who had passed matric.

---

[8] The venerable headmaster

The school committee requested Suresh Nandy to double up as the headmaster of the girls' school and engage his daughter, Sagarika, as the teacher-in-charge for primary and middle levels. Suresh was in a dilemma. He had a dream to educate his daughter up to the postgraduate level, but this sudden development upset his plans for the future of Sagar. The local womenfolk thronged their house and met Kanak and Sagar to convince them.

"When so many people are sacrificing their lives for the sake of the country, will she not make some sacrifice for the younger generation? The son of Soudamini aunty is in jail for the last three years for taking part in the August movement," said the neighbours to Sagarika.

"She would also prove her patriotism in her own way," thought Sagarika.

She remembered the sacrifice of Lalmohan Sen, who wanted to be a doctor but went to the dreadful Andaman Jail as a prisoner. She gave her consent to join the school. She was appointed as the teacher-in-charge for classes up to eight and was confirmed as soon as the Intermediate results were published. The school started within a month after the admission of students. She had to manage the work with the help of eight teachers; some were the laid-off teachers after the closure of St. Mary's, while some more were recruited from outside through advertisement. Suresh babu did not agree to be the headmaster since his daughter was appointed the teacher-in-charge. On his suggestion, Biren babu was given the charge of working headmaster.

Sagarika began a new life as a teacher like her father and uncle.

2.2 Rabi given a public reception

Haru was doubling up as a peon for the girls' school in exchange for a nominal honorarium. His father had joined as a peon when the boys' school was established in 1889 by Shri Basanta Kumar Guhathakurta. After his retirement, the school committee agreed to appoint his son Haru Mondal as the peon as a reward for his father's long dedicated service. Haru had a strong attachment with the school as if he was an inseparable, integral part of the school. He used to live with his family in a single room quarter on the terrace. The caretaker and the *durwan* were also provided such accommodation.

Haru told his wife ruefully, "See the way of the world! That little niece of head sir was praying so much for studying in a high school here. But the sanction did not reach, and she had to leave this place with tears in her eyes. I still remember the girl."

"Yes, that little girl was very brave too. She ran after the police alone on that day of disturbance," commented Kamala.

"Yes," Haru continued, "but look at the playfulness of Lord Jagannath. When Didimani came here, everything started happening like magic. Sagar didi did not come to stay here for more than a month, but she got so tied up in the chain of events that she could not go back to her college in Dacca. She has now become the head Didimani of the new school. How differently fate worked for the two sisters! Interesting!"

Haru was quite close to teachers as well as students. He used to visit the houses of Head Sir and assistant Head Sir almost daily, carrying official papers, a cash box, or even a typewriter machine from the school to their house and back. This gave him the opportunity to be thick with other members of their families. Kanak used to offer him moa, made of delicately blended puffed rice and jaggery, whenever he came. He, too, considered himself a part of these families.

Rabi was known to him both as an ex-student and as the eldest son of Biren sir. Haru never believed that Rabi could kill the Daroga babu[9]. Although other boys got bail after a month or two, Rabi was accused by name in the F.I.R. lodged by the A.S.I., temporarily in charge of Banaripara police station, and therefore, he was sent to jail in the name of investigation. According to his school certificate, Rabi was less than eighteen at the time of the incident, but the judge did not show any leniency on that account.

Haru used to go to Barishal town to attend the court on the days of hearing on the bail application. Such days were, however, few. When it came to light that Azharuddin had reported for duty at Bhanga P.S. of Faridpur District, the file of Rabi was sent to the cold storage. There was a rumour that Azharuddin had declined to admit that a young boy had knocked him out by a single punch.

Three years passed like that.

One afternoon, Sagar was discussing the steps to be followed in conducting the first half-yearly examination with Biren sir in his house. Soudamini aunty was frequently opening the door as if somebody had just knocked at it and then, being disappointed to see nobody standing out, closed the door without making any sound. Sagarika looked up to Biren kaka and said, "Is aunty waiting for somebody?"

Biren heaved a deep sigh and said, "It is just another day of the hearing. She is waiting for Haru."

Hardly had he finished the sentence when the voice of Haru could be heard from a distance.

"Kaki ma, kaki ma, Rabi bhai has been granted bail. Rejoice! He will come back tomorrow!" Biren got up in excitement. Soudamini started weeping in joy.

Haru entered inside and began to describe, "Sir, today our case was heard by a new judge. He heard both the lawyers, asked them a few questions, and said the prisoner had already undergone a term of more than three years but the chargesheet was not yet framed. The case was a blot for the British judicial system. The gora[10] judge granted

---

[9] The officer in-charge of a police station.

[10] White-skinned person.

bail immediately and directed the police to file the charge sheet in three months. The cases of four others should also be clubbed."

Sagar saw that Biren sir was also weeping. Sagar had not seen or met Rabi earlier, but she had an image of revolutionary freedom fighters in her mind. A freedom fighter was going to be released from jail. She found herself empathetic to the situation, and her eyes became moist, holding the tearful Soudamini in an embrace.

Haru ran out from the Guhathakurta House and spread the good news in the locality, starting with Head Sir. Suresh and Kanak came rushing to Biren's house, followed by several other teachers and neighbours. Everybody felt so happy as if their lost son was to return home after three long years.

Within an hour, Congress party workers came to the house with a proposal to accord a welcome to Rabi to celebrate his release. Rabi's heroic fight, stoic fortitude, and self-sacrifice had already created a myth about him and many people, young and old, were eager to see him and congratulate him. The sentiment of the people needed to find an expression.

It was decided that Biren babu would be accompanied by one hundred men to the jail gate by 11 o'clock. Only Biren babu and the lawyer would go in and receive Rabi after completing the formalities. A procession of cycle rickshaws would go round the city streets of Barishal Town and end the first part of the program at Mukundadas Kalibari. After taking the 'bhog'[11] there, Rabi and his hundred companions would cross the canals and streams on their way in country boats. The procession would start from the border of the Banaripara urban area with about one thousand people. In this stretch, Rabi would be carried on a chair by his friends. Rabi would be given a floral welcome by local children when he reached the ground in front of the school. He would be received at the same ground where the police had lynched him. His four friends, who were released on bail after the movement fizzled out, would also join the programme there. The Town Congress leaders would deliver speeches in praise of them. It was decided that Sagarika Didimani would act as the compere of the proceeding on the stage.

[11] Food offered to deity, is later partaken by devotees with reverence.

Sagar had never seen the overwhelming spontaneity with which the crowd brought the bailed freedom fighter to the school ground, seated on a sedan chair. People were shouting *Vande Mataram* as well as *Rabi Guhathaurta zindabad* (victory to Rabi Guha'). Sagar had taken her position at the foot of the ramp to the dais. Haran Mukherjee of the Congress and Md. Akhtar of the Muslim League were on the dais. They asked the headmaster moshai also to come on the dais. Sagar's heartbeat accelerated when the familiar sedan chair of her father's office, carried by four boys, stopped where she was waiting with a bouquet. Down came a lanky, tall figure looking like Biren sir in his youth, glancing left and right and finally meeting her eyes with hesitation. She uttered 'suswagatam' in correct Sanskrit pronunciation and handed over the flower bouquet to the man standing before her. She struck the pose of 'namaskar' gracefully and said, "Please come on the dais, Mr Guha."

"Who are you, madam? I never saw you before," whispered Rabi, climbing the ramp slowly.

Sagar smiled and said, "I am Sagarika, the teacher-in-charge of the new girls' school."

Haran babu came forward and embraced Rabi and said, "I knew they would not keep you in prison for life."

Others also embraced him one by one. Sagar began to conduct the function with a prepared welcome speech. She invited young boys and girls on the stage to garland the chief guest, Mr Rabindra Guhathakurta.

In his impromptu speech, Rabi thanked everybody and hoped freedom would be achieved soon. The Azad Hind Fauj might have surrendered, but the sacrifice they had made shook the government. He ended by reciting the lines from their prayer song, *"A new nation will emerge, the sun is rising on the horizon."* In the end, five thousand voices roared, *'Vande Mataram! Jai Hind!'*

Sagarika was resting in her bed as the big event was over, feeling her body like the chords of a sitar being played by a maestro.

2.3 Sagar proposes, Rabi promises

The war came to an end with two big bangs. Two big cities of Japan were destroyed completely, with few survivors to recount the horror. Italy and Germany had already been defeated, and the surrender of Japan was only a matter of days, not weeks away. The two bombs exceeded the total damage caused by the war to the civilians the world over. This unnecessary destruction exposed the helplessness of humanity in the face of its own weapons. The victors lost their moral high. In the end, there was no winner.

The British government found itself unequal to the task of holding the empire together. If the British government declared granting the independence of India in 1942 with dominion status so long as the elected Indian government wanted it, it would have saved the Britishers their face and earned a lot of goodwill. They lost the iron grip over the military and were answerable for the man-made famine of Bengal in 1943 caused by siphoning and hoarding of food grain. They released Gandhi in 1944 for his ill health. After his recovery, Gandhi began to hold discussions with Jinnah at his residence in Bombay. The other leaders were released from jail in 1945 when the war ended. Churchill won the war but was defeated at the hustings. The release of Rabi on bail almost coincided.

Meanwhile, Opu came to know from a letter written by Sagar that she had joined a girls' school as a teacher-in-charge at Banaripara. Sagar wrote in detail how she had to stay back at Banaripara with her parents and why she gave up further studies. She insisted that Opu must be a postgraduate and would take up a job to be truly independent in her personal life. Both the sisters, however, discreetly avoided any reference to Rabi in their letters. Sagar considered herself much senior, while Opu considered herself too young to talk to her Didi about a boy. Opu inquired about the well-being of Soudamini aunty, Chhabidi and Kabi; Sagar replied that they were all doing fine.

She also mentioned that at the request of local people, she had to take part in a political meeting. The two sisters, so close to each other since their childhood, could not share the name of Rabi with one another; they kept him in their hearts as a closely guarded secret. One hid her bleeding heart, and the other would not disclose her so-far-unknown trepidations.

As Sagar was a frequent visitor to the house of the Guhathakurtas, Rabi could easily pick up a conversation with her. After all, she was the daughter of Kanak aunty! Yes, Opu had once mentioned her cousin sister living in a hostel in Chittagong.

"Namaskar, Didimani. I am Rabi. I find that one good thing has happened to Banaripara during my absence. I mean opening a girls' middle school and having you as the teacher in charge. Even before I was released, Haru da told me about you." Sagar blushed. *What was there in her that a freedom fighter like him came forward to talk to her?*

"I heard you were brutally tortured by the police."

"The police of a foreign ruler is not expected to do something different. Maybe when the country is free, the police of the independent country will be more humane and civilised."

"The country will not forget your sufferings. You will be gratefully remembered by the posterity, I am sure," said Sagar with throat-choking emotion.

"We shall see. But for the time being, will you entrust me with some work of your school, as I have no regular work on hand. I cannot get a job in a different city as I am required to report to the police station once a week till the case is decided by the court."

Rabi began to assist Sagar in her work. There was no clerk posted for the girls' school. After performing her teaching duty, Sagarika had to do a lot of clerical work under the guidance of Biren uncle. Rabi wanted to help her by sharing the drudgery. As his movements were restricted, he could not attend political programmes. As Rabi was known to be connected to the revolutionaries, the Congress Party leaders like Haranda began to keep a safe distance from him. They attended his reception programme only to keep the public sympathy with the party, but they regarded him as a hot potato. Rabi was then under the surveillance of the police as a suspected terrorist. He stopped visiting his old associates of the Vivekananda gymnasium lest they were exposed. But in the evenings, he would sneak out in the darkness and meet some boys who kept their faces covered. Sagar was aware of these escapades, but she never asked him questions. After all, Rabi da was a freedom fighter, and it would not be proper to show curiosity about his secret work.

Rabi used to visit their house very often and gossip with her mother, Kanak. Sagar knew that Rabi da became familiar with her parents when they came to this place. He was then a loveable teenager. Presently, he was a full-fledged young man with a halo. As he was facing a criminal charge, he was not given the status of a political prisoner that was accorded to people like Haran babu. Most of the common people arrested on that day were bailed after a few days. He was booked as an offender with criminal charges under the IPC.

The experience of life in jail was crushing him when the Indian jailor came to his rescue. On his suggestion, Rabi applied to appear in the B.A. examination of the University. He was then allotted a separate cell and was allowed to study. Rabi passed his B.A. Exam by appearing from jail.

One year passed, and the friendship between a handsome, tall, muscular young man and a beautiful, sober young woman thickened. Banaripara was a beautiful place, endowed with immense natural bounty. Its paddy fields, water bodies, trees, birds, and worms were so local, ethnic, and regenerative that love was a part of its ambience. Nature had provided all these with so much creative energy that human beings could not but be deeply influenced.

One evening, when the sky was overcast with early monsoon clouds and the moist air was laden with the smell of freshly wet soil, Sagarika said, "Some revolutionaries choose to remain unmarried forever. What is your plan, Rabi da?"

Rabi was somewhat taken aback. A less educated girl would not have posed the question on her own. But Sagarika was an educated, modern lady, having been trained in one famous school and college of East Bengal and presently working as a teacher-in-charge. She had a lot of confidence in herself and could ask a straight question without mincing words.

"I have taken a vow to remain celibate until the country becomes free, like most revolutionaries in our secret society. Till that time, our body, mind, and soul are all dedicated to the country, more specifically to achieve her freedom. We cannot sacrifice ourselves for the country if we get married and bind ourselves to the welfare of a small family."

"But there is no such binding in the Congress Party, as far as I know."

"You are right. It is not the dictum of the Congress Party. Some Congressmen do not marry to devote more time to party work on their own. All revolutionaries do not also remain celibate either. But the members of our secret society of revolutionaries take the oath before goddess Kaali at the time of induction."

"I see. When the country gets freedom, will you be free from your vow?"

"Right. There will be no bar for marriage at that time."

"Whom will you marry, Rabi da? Do you have anybody in your mind?"

Rabi could feel that Sagar was waiting for his reply in bated breath. "If I marry at all, I shall marry you," Rabi said in a clear tone.

"Really?"

"O, yes."

"Can you take a vow?"

"Certainly. I am taking the vow in your name, Sagar, that once the country is free, I shall marry you and no one else," Rabi pronounced it in baritone, touching her hand.

Sagar blushed. Then she gently pressed her hand on his.

Kanak was stitching an aasan[12] sitting on an ethnic mat laid on the veranda. It was getting dark sooner than on the other days as it was cloudy. Rabi came out from the sitting room and stood for a while, watching the handiwork.

"Aunty, how beautifully you are designing the aasan! For whom are you making it?" asked Rabi.

"I shall give it to your wife," Kanak said jokingly.

---

[12] Aasan is a seat on which people sit on the floor to worship or meditate, or for marriage-like ceremonies, and dining. Made of the hide of a tiger or a deer, or hand-woven cloths of jute and cotton in colourful yarns.

"He will not marry. I mean, not till the country becomes independent," intervened Sagar. "Better, you give it to me."

"No. This one will be for Rabi's wife whenever he marries. Soduboudi is looking for a *Kulin* girl."

Rabi left the premises quickly without looking back. Had he turned his face, he could have noticed that the face of Sagar had become white like the aspen leaf. They were not Kulins in the then existing intricate caste structure.

2.4 Calcutta holocaust and Banaripara

Suresh and Biren returned from the school after attending a meeting of teachers. They kept the wet umbrellas on the veranda. Suresh had a copy of a newspaper in his hand. It was the paper of a day before as it took one day in transportation to reach their town. Kanak and Sagar got the hurricane lamps ready after cleaning the glass domes, trimming the wicks, and filling their in-built tanks with adequate kerosene oil. Kanak kept one lamp in front of the two teachers who had a passion for going through the mufassil edition of the Amrita Bazar Patrika, line by line, including the advertisements. Today, they became excited to read the news that Jinnah had given a call to the Muslims for direct action to force the government to accept their demand for Pakistan.

"It is only a ploy to cow the Congress leaders to their demand for Pakistan," said Suresh. "He did not make it clear what he meant by 'direct action'. But they are running the government in Bengal. They must maintain law and order in the province."

"Janab Suhrawardy will address a meeting at the Ochterlony monument tomorrow… I mean today. My goodness, what is happening today in Calcutta by now?"

Rabi had gone to the police station to give his weekly attendance. There, he found the station officer busy taking telegraph messages with a grim face. After the transfer of Azharuddin to Faridpur district, a Hindu officer was posted in Banaripara, and he was murmuring, "*What is going on there? What is the meaning of these queer instructions from Anderson House?*"

Rabi went out. He went to the post office to make a telephone call to the Patrika office for information. What he heard stunned him. After the Prime Minister of Bengal delivered his speech, exhorting the Muslim audience to go ahead with the plan for direct action without any fear, the Muslim crowd launched a killing pogrom against the Hindus without any provocation from their side. The Hindus were entirely unprepared, and the Muslim hooligans killed Hindus in thousands till evening. The news was so shocking that Rabi ran to the Congress Office to alert the party workers of the impending trouble in their locality. When he came back to his neighbourhood, he met his father and Suresh uncle and apprised them of the riot situation in Calcutta.

No newspapers were delivered for the next five days. The filtered news from the government radio suppressed the riot news more than disseminated it. The information sneaked through the returnees from Calcutta spread communal tension in different districts, including Barishal and Noakhali. The failure of the British Viceroy to sack the partisan Muslim League-led government on the sixteenth of August showed clearly what the Britishers were up to. Both the government and the Muslim League played this nefarious game to drag the Congress into communal riots and prove that the Congress did not represent the Muslim cause. The Hindus in East Bengal experienced a cold shiver through their spine.

Chapter Three

3.1 Sandwip, October 1946

Opu wanted to go to Sandwip during the ten-day long Puja holidays. To take her to Sandwip, Sisir crossed the Sandwip channel by boat and sea-vessel from Guptachhara ghat and reached the Kumira Ghat of Chittagong at 9 a.m.

The life of the islanders was hard, and the tales of their woe never reached the higher Administration. There was a Police station at Sandwip, and a junior revenue officer represented the government. The offices of the District Magistrate and Superintendent of Police were at Noakhali, as was the District Court. So, for every interface with the government, the people had to go to Noakhali. Chittagong was the seat of the Divisional Commissioner, and the people of Sandwip had to go there as it was an important business hub and centre of education in East Bengal. It was, however, a big adventure to cross the channel. From the interior village of Sandwip, one would come to the ferry ghat by bullock-cart or bicycle or in an improvised van-rickshaw. One had to walk through muddy water to get into a boat during low tide or walk tiptoe over a piece of timber to board it in high tide. During the rainy season, the boatman would carry children in his arms one by one. The boat would carry the passengers to the ship waiting in the open sea. The transfer from the boat to the bigger vessel was an arduous and risky affair. The sailors would lift the passengers by their hands from the boat when the deck of the ship was at a higher level.

In her childhood, when Opu crossed the sea for the first time with Suresh uncle and Kanak aunty, she enjoyed the thrill of the multi-modal transhipment, but presently, she was a grown-up girl of class ten. She felt uncomfortable to be touched by the sailors and preferred to be lifted by her father. She performed acrobatics in a saree while boarding the country boat or getting down from it. Despite all these hardships, she was not able to resist the call of Sandwip for long. After the annual examination or during the long summer vacation, she must go to her mother and to the lap of her native place, or her *desh*!

She loved the simple people of the island, be they Hindu or Muslim. The birds and animals, different creatures, and plants and trees that abounded in the island used to attract her. The people used to communicate with each other in the Noakhalian dialect, which, though nearly unintelligible to many people, sounded like music to her ears. More than anything else, the rustic simplicity used to touch the heart directly. She had studied in the mixed primary school up to class five and gradually overcame her loneliness. The classmates used to live within walking distance, and one of them, named Amina, would frequently visit her in the afternoon to play together. Rahim bhai would join her in chasing squirrels in the garden. She knew that Amina or Rahim did not belong to their religion, just as she was aware of their inferiority in caste compared to that of Raju Chakrabarty, the son of their family priest. There were many restrictions on social mixing, but as Opu grew up within the complex matrix of the caste system from birth, she learnt the line that should not be transgressed. But the friendly relationships, neighbourly relationships continued with boys and girls of other caste and faith, unabated like the water of Karnaphuli River finding its course through the hilly terrains of Arakans.

When Sisir and Opu reached Sadarghat from her hostel, they had just two hours to catch the last ferry for Sandwip. Sisir took Opu to Sadarghat Kalibari to offer puja for a safe voyage. As they were about to come out, a bearded person touched the shoulder of Sisir from behind. Sisir turned his head, looked at the person and exclaimed, "Mohan! You're Mohan!" The stranger nodded. Sisir became overwhelmed with emotion. They embraced each other. "At last, you are free!"

"Yes, Sisir. I am free. But the country is not."

The man was scrutinising the marks of time in the face of Sisir, although he himself seemed to be ten years older than him. As he noticed Opu standing a little away, Sisir beckoned her to come closer and said, "She is my daughter, Aparajita. Opu, touch his feet. He is your Mohan uncle."

Mohan was also going to Sandwip after sixteen years. They hired a tonga and reached Kumiraghat after an hour. They entered a roadside hotel by the jetty to have a quick meal.

While eating, the two old friends talked in lowered voices.

"I heard that police had questioned you after I ran away from our house."

"Yes, but I could not tell them anything as I did not know of your mission and your whereabouts."

"Yes, that is what Master da had taught us, not to leave a trail. I could not follow his teaching immaculately and was arrested within a month of the uprising, but he could manage to avoid arrest for more than three years. Did they beat you up?"

"Yes, they did. My movements were also restricted to Sandwip for several years."

"Yes, the government has an easy way to deal with the people of the island. Just don't allow them to come to the mainland."

"Yes, even the troublesome people of the mainland can be kept confined in Sandwip on parole."

"I heard that Arun da and Burman da were confined in Sandwip as political prisoners."

"That's right. They are now worried about their kins in Calcutta."

"Quite natural. In Dacca, we got the information from some people who returned from Calcutta. The Hindus were surprised on the day of direct action and were massacred in one-sided hooliganism. Suhrawardy had kept his word and the police remained confined to their police stations. But the table was turned on the second day of the riot when Hindus organised themselves and retaliated. The Muslims then faced the heat and were killed almost in equal number. Suhrawardy's police did not know what to do. On the third day, when more areas came under the rioters, the situation was totally out of hand. The government finally called the Army on the fourth day when the rioters were totally routed. Many Muslims left Calcutta for districts where Muslims were in an overwhelming majority."

The passenger vessel sounded its horn. Sisir, Lalmohan, and Opu quickly finished their meal and rushed to the ship.

When they disembarked from the sea vessel and were transhipped to the waiting country boats, the sun had just set. The boats reached the ferry ghat in half an hour, and Opu got down from it, holding her father's hand. As they came up the ghat's slope, Opu saw a few Muslim youths looking at her like an eagle looks at its prey.

"These people do not belong to this place. Why are they standing here?" Opu asked her father.

"I can't say. May have come as guests to some house."

"Hello guys, what are you waiting here for? This vessel will not return today. Better, go home," said Mohan.

"Halah, who are you to tell us to go home? Is this ghat your father's property?" one of the young people replied in abusive language.

Mohan was as shocked as Sisir. He would have challenged them to a fight if Sisir had not pulled him away.

"You should not get involved in a scuffle right now. They are not local boys, or they would have recognised their maths teacher. Besides, they may be armed."

As they moved ahead towards the waiting cart for Harishpur, Opu saw two boats coming from Noakhali direction, loaded with men, drums, jerricans and box containers. As the boats closed in, the group of young men shouted in jubilation.

Three vessel-passengers boarded the last bullock cart waiting for them.

Mohan was still fuming in rage. "This island is ours. We are born here. We are natives of this place. I have come back to my motherland after sixteen years. How can some rowdies insult me on her soil? I shall find them out and settle the score. My name is Lalmohan."

Rahamat, the cartman, turned his head to see him. Even he was familiar with the name.

3.2 Riot in Sandwip

Rahamat lived in the nearby village. If anybody had to go to the ferry ghat to avail a particular voyage, Rahamat was a dependable first leg service provider. Especially in the rainy season, when cycles became unusable in the muddy, uneven village path, Rahamat used to provide connectivity with the civilised world with the help of his two bullocks. He had named them Ramu and Rahim and cared for them more than he did for his two ever quarrelling *biwis*. The bullocks and their owner were mutually dependent on each other for their livelihood and well-being. One would not survive without the other as if they were 'bound each to each by natural piety'.

The tenth of October was the date for Kojagari Lakshmi puja. Opu was preparing to go back to her hostel in Chittagong on the following day. She had enjoyed the Durga puja at Harishpur town hall, attending all important puja rituals. She would be appearing in the matriculation examination in March next year, and she needed the blessings of the goddess Durga and her daughter, goddess Saraswati. Kojagari Lakshmi Puja was a household celebration with an exclusive domestic fervour. For three days, Opu's mother and grandma were busy preparing Naru, Sandesh, and other sweetmeats, mostly made of coconut kernel or dried, condensed milk. Opu had designed the *alpana* (abstract folk designs) in the puja area beautifully. Puja was being held at night by the family priest to seek the bounties of Shri Shri Lakshmi, the goddess of family prosperity. This night the men and women would remain awake, waiting for the goddess to come to their home.

Sisir had asked Rahamat to come at seven-thirty in the morning so that they could avail the nine o'clock voyage. He was surprised to see Rahamat coming stealthily to their house at night after the puja was over.

"What happened, Rahamat?" asked Sisir. "Any problem?"

"Mastermoshai, I have come to tell you that we should leave by three-thirty a.m. so that you can take the first voyage at five."

"Why Rahamat? That is the trip meant for fishermen. No gentleman usually travels by that trip with his family."

"I am telling this for your safety."

"Why, Rahamat, why are you saying so?" Shakticharan asked in a worried voice.

"What should I say, Kartababu? Bad days are fast approaching. No one knows what is going to happen tomorrow. The people of Kasem Ali are landing here from Noakhali and camping in madrasas. They have held secret meetings in the mosque. Noakhali is already on fire. I suggest you all leave this place immediately for a few months. It will be wiser to leave in the darkness of night. I shall come with the cart at three if you agree."

"Yes, we agree. Opu must go back to her school immediately. This is her final year."

Rahamat came back at the appointed time and brought two burkhas with him. He urged the mastermoshai to take his wife with him to safety. The two ladies should board his cart in burkha, and mastermoshai should follow on foot in lungi.

Rahamat's apprehension proved to be correct. When the cart was passing through a Muslim village on the way, somebody shouted out of darkness, "Who is going?"

"I am Rahamat, the cartman."

"Who is travelling by your cart?"

"Sir, they are my wives. You know, sir, I have only two wives."

"Where are they going so early?"

"Sir, I am taking them out on a *sair* of Chattagram. These daughters of my fathers-in-law are feeling bored here."

"Okay, okay. Go quickly, or you will miss the boat."

Sisir had crossed the area silently, walking ahead of the bullock cart. Rahamat had anticipated correctly, and he steered them clear of any chance of detection. The three members of the Nandy family boarded the vessel for Chittagong safely.

Sisir, Madhuri and Opu escaping from the island, just before the riot broke out.

But in the wee hours, when the Hindus felt tired and sleepy, their localities were surrounded by unknown faces, with burning torches in one hand and swords or daggers in the other. The darkness before the dawn was suddenly pierced by flames of fire, followed by ferocious cries of aggression in the name of God and the prayer of the attacked, fearing for their lives. Lalmohan got up from his bed and saw the flames billowing up in the sky from the direction of Nandipara. He rushed out towards his friend's house, but before he could reach the place, he was challenged by the unknown faces and stabbed to death.

"Halah fought against the British. He thought he could fight against us. His desire to fight has now been fully quenched." The army of Kasem would not brook any nonsense.

Shakticharan had smelt petrol in the air, a foreign smell for the old islander who had never seen an automobile in Sandwip. Sensing danger, he dragged Nayantara to the courtyard. The marauders were looking for the young female members. They looted all valuables and then torched the house. The two aged persons could barely run out to the kitchen garden before their house was engulfed in fire and was completely gutted. The hoodlums left before daylight exposed the extent of their savagery to their Hindu neighbours. Some of their relatives were murdered, and some women were abducted. This carnage continued in different parts of the island for the next ten days. Killings, rape, abduction, and conversion were perpetrated freely. The army of Ghulam Sarwar joined with Kasem's to complete the job. The local peasants joined in looting the property of the well-to-do Hindu families.

The political prisoners were quickly rounded up by the police the previous evening, lest they get killed in the mayhem, and the police became answerable for their death. Since Lalmohan Sen was set free after sixteen years in jail, the police did not have any responsibility to save his life.

The homeless Hindus were kept in Kargil School, and the unaffected areas were cordoned by local Muslims to provide safety to the Hindus. In effect, the riot survivors could not contact anybody on the mainland for their rescue. Sisir came to know of the tragedy from some Muslim traders of their locality. One of them said that his parents were not traceable in the neighbourhood. In Chittagong, the husband and wife had taken shelter with one of his old college friends after they had dropped Opu in her hostel. Sisir came to know of the tragedy from some Muslim traders of their locality. One of them said that his parents were not traceable in the neighbourhood. Sisir wrote a letter to his elder brother narrating the reported incidents of the riot in Sandwip and not getting any information about their parents. The news came to Suresh like a bolt from the blue.

The people of Sandwip waited eagerly for Gandhi ji, who camped in Noakhali and Srirampur for a few months but did not have time to visit Sandwip even for a day. The frustrated Hindus were shocked when they came to know of the experiment in self-control the saint had kept himself busy with at Srirampur.

Suresh and Sisir visited Sandwip in the winter. After the outsiders left the island, the local Muslims agreed to allow the Hindus to return to their ravaged homes. The two brothers searched all houses in Nandipara and finally traced the old parents in the cowshed of Rahamat Ali in the adjoining village. He had picked up the old persons on his return journey from the ferry ghat when they were running helter-skelter around their burning house, dazed in shock and grief. Although Hindus began to leave the island for Hindu majority districts, this Nandy family could not go anywhere, leaving behind their old, infirm members. After another month, when peace was restored officially. Sisir brought his wife back to the island to look after the parents. Suressent money through M.O. to repair the house. Sisir could not leave Sandwip in the prevailing uncertainties, and on the request of the saner section of Muslim neighbours, he continued to hold his job at Kargil School.

3.3 Post War politics, Sagarika threatened

Sagar was terribly upset when she heard from her father about the ordeal faced by her grandparents. She began to cry when she heard how her childhood icon had met his end. The island of her dream had turned into a cauldron for the Hindus. She remained worried for the safety of her dear uncle and her dear grandparents and wrote a letter to Opu, forbidding her from moving out of the school and hostel premises.

The political drama had reached its final act, and the country was going through the phase of catastrophe. Lord Mountbatten was sent as the Viceroy by the newly elected Labour Govt to preside over the birth of the independent India. Rabi and Sagar discussed the day-to-day changes, analysing critically the moves played by the Congress and the Muslim League on the political chessboard. Suresh and Biren used to discuss the arguments of Jawaharlal Nehru during the trial of the soldiers of the Azad Hind Fauj in the Red Fort. After the naval uprising in Bombay, the British officers also became a stakeholder as they wanted to get rid of their Indian empire without losing a drop of British blood. Mountbatten declared that the British would either hand over the charge to the successor govt or relinquish it unilaterally by the thirtieth of June 1948. After a lot of dilly-dallying, the Congress and the Akali party realised that they had no way but to agree to the demand of the Muslim League for Pakistan. The proposal of the Cabinet Mission for a confederation with a permanently crippled centre was rejected by Nehru. The British had started the game of divide and rule in 1907 when they created a separate electorate for the Muslims. The Muslim League. Hindu Mahasabha and the Scheduled Caste Hindus under B.R. Ambedkar favoured the creation of Pakistan for Muslims. Congress leaders had dug their own grave by conceding to the demands of the Muslim League at every juncture without calling their bluff from 1940. The country faced two choices– partition of the country or a civil war. After discussing with all major political parties, Lord Mountbatten came up with his famous Mountbatten Plan and sent his recommendation to the Secretary of State on the third of June of 1947 for the partition of British India and the creation of a separate state for Muslims. He also proposed to advance the date of transfer of power to the fifteenth of August, 1947, finally to divide and quit.

"The Congress lacks the revolutionary spirit. They have always surrendered under pressure," remarked Rabi. "They have conveniently forgotten the example of the American Civil War where the progressive forces won the war and achieved the unity of the country."

"The unity and integrity of India must be maintained by our leaders at all costs. Any compromise with her boundary will be a betrayal," commented Sagar with firmness. The elderly people, however, thought otherwise.

Suresh said, "I hope this arrangement will be made peacefully and amicably. Jinnah is getting what he wanted. This air of communal hatred is suffocating and must be cleared."

"But Suresh da, Gandhi ji is not seen anywhere. He says he does not agree to the partition proposal. But he is not doing anything to prevent it. Now at long last, he has realised that he is surrounded by power-hungry people. He is repenting that if only Subhash had been there, things would have been different."

When the British Govt gave its consent to the fifteenth of August 1947 as the date for transfer of power, and not the thirty of June 1948, it exposed the hurry they were in. It was yet to be decided if the Muslim majority provinces like the Punjab and Bengal would entirely form part of Pakistan. The mechanism of Partition was still in the domain of conjecture. But the British officers were getting ready to hand over the charges to some yet-to-be-appointed successor. The District Judges were also in a hurry to clear old pending cases. The Judge of Barishal fixed, inter alia, the date for the final hearing of the case of Rabi Guha and four others. As the hearing might continue for a week, and the accused must remain present, Biren camped in his brother's house in Barishal Town with his son.

On Monday morning, Sagar was in a classroom, teaching her students, when entered suddenly a group of men, all Muslims from neighbouring areas, surprising her.

"Who are you? What do you want?" asked Sagar firmly, though a tremor in her voice betrayed her nervousness.

"Don't be afraid, Didimani. My name is Shah Jahan Molla. Everybody knows me here. I have come to give you a proposal, a marriage proposal," he answered her questions.

Sagarika felt so insulted to be proposed in front of a classful of girls that she burst out, "Get out of the school, I say!! How dare you enter the school and that too in a classroom? Durwan, durwan!! Haru da!!"

"Didimani, you are mistaken. Today we have not come to insult you. You know, this district is going to be a part of Pakistan, the country for the Muslims. All land, houses as well as women will belong to the Muslims. I like you for your beauty. Although I have two wives, they are not as beautiful as you are. You should know that if you don't marry me, fifty-year-old Sadiq Ali will marry you forcibly."

"No. I shall neither marry you nor Sadiq Ali. I am a Hindu, and I shall marry a Hindu boy. Now get lost."

"Didimani, please try to understand. This will be a land for the Muslims. We shall not allow the Hindus to stay here. Either they accept Islam as their religion, or they must quit. The third choice is the Noakhali medicine. We are preparing to celebrate the anniversary of the 'Direct Action' day."

At this point, the associates of Shah Jahan intervened, "Mian, why are you talking to her so sweetly? Give her three days' time. If she does not agree within that time, we know what to do with her."

"Okay, Didimani, you have understood everything. Now it is your choice. One word more. We know that Rabi likes you, but let me make it clear that no Guhathaurta will stay here after the fifteenth of August. Remember, my men will see you on the fourth day. And for your information, the Hindu S.I. has already taken transfer to Burdwan, handing over charge to a Muslim officer. Bye."

After the gang had left, Sagarika realised that her fifth standard students were looking at her in fear. Now other teachers, Haru da and durwan, all rushed in. The period was already over. Sagar could not attend her remaining classes. She came back home to tell her father all that had happened.

Suresh babu was not a man of strong nerves. So far, he used to be worried for his parents, his brother, and his wife living in Sandwip in hostile surroundings. Now the storm took him over all of a sudden. What would he do in three days? He went to school absent-mindedly. Some teachers came to know of the incident from Haru. The Hindu teachers were fuming in rage, but within their hearts, they realised that the count-down had begun. The Muslim teachers, however, opined that Shah Jahan had only given a marriage proposal. Sagarika might accept it, considering that Shah Jahan belonged to a rich family. If the proposal was turned down, he might express his disappointment for a day or two, but he would not behave criminally. Even after the transfer of power, the new state would continue to be governed under the same penal code. The head sir should not worry unnecessarily. Some Hindus were merely spreading rumours.

Haru thought he should inform Biren sir and Rabi, as they belonged to the place for generations, having relatives in about fifty neighbouring houses. They had a lot of say in all local matters. Suresh sir had come from outside, and he would not be able to stand up to face the challenge. Sagar also sent for Haru da the next morning to carry a letter to Rabi da. Haru took permission to meet Biren sir in court. He briefed Biren sir of all that had happened and handed over the letter to Rabi, saying, "Rabi bhai, here your hearing is going on. There Didimani is in deep trouble."

"Ask her to pull on somehow till the weekend," Rabi whispered to Haru.

Suresh spent the day waiting for Biren babu. He expected him to come back to Banaripara to give him correct advice.

On the third day, Suresh thought he should leave this place with his family without wasting any time. Before, going to school, he immediately sent a telegram to his brother-in-law, Kulapradip Das, a junior revenue officer in Nabadwip. Nabadwip was a famous pilgrim place for Vaishnavite Hindus and was a part of the Nadia district where Hindus were in majority. Some more relatives had reached that place from Sandwip after the riot of October 1946. Suresh asked them to fix up a rented accommodation for him immediately. While returning from the post office, Suresh went to the house of the secretary of the school committee and expressed his intention to resign.

The secretary advised him to wait till Biren babu returned. Suresh began to complete his administrative work and got the school cash deposited in the bank. He could not wait for a tragedy to happen. His ancestral house was burnt to ashes. His parents had to hide for two months in the cowshed of a cartman. He would not take any chance. He asked Kanak to get ready without any fuss. In the evening, the secretary accompanied him to the police station. The S.I. told them that he would ensure that the headmaster and his family were able to leave his jurisdiction safely. But he could not give any guarantee for days close to the fifteenth of August. Riots might break out before and after the day on any pretext. Although he was a Muslim, he did not like the way Muslim League was trying to play the communal card even after their demand for Pakistan was conceded.

Sagar had written a small letter to Rabi, expecting him to be by her side in her crisis. Rabi could not make much out of it and asked his father about the situation at Banaripara. "Haru told me that some Muslim boys had come to the morning school and disturbed Sagarika in the class. Your hearing will be over tomorrow, and the judgment is expected on the day after. I don't think the Muslim boys will take any drastic step before that. I shall go back after the hearing is over and meet Suresh da." Rabi asked Haru to tell Didimani to take a few days' time from Shah Jahan to make up her mind.

... The Mollah did not agree to give extra time. He asked her to go to the mosque on Friday evening without fail. His men threatened the headmaster with a dagger. Sagarika resolved within herself to surrender on Friday to save the life of her father.

Seeing that the hearing was not complete on Thursday, Rabi wrote a letter to Sagar at night to send it through Haru da next morning, stating that he would soon be by her side without fail.

Three days passed without any event except the visit of the Mollah and his associates to convey threats. Sagar did not go to school lest she would be abducted.

On the fourth day, Haru was feeling tense from the morning, *'What would happen to Didimani today?'* He met didimani before going to the Town.

He came back from the Town at midday before twelve after meeting Rabi. Suresh called Haru to fix a boatman to take them on a pilgrimage. Nobody should know who the passengers were and where they would go. Haru went out searching for a Hindu boatman. He could not ask the boatmen at the ghat because all Muslim boatmen would know about the program. Instead, he went to the cottage of Badal Majhi, who was known to him for years. He took him into confidence and made him agree to row his boat after dusk, but he did not agree to sail beyond Khulna as he did not know the route through River Matla.

Biren came to school at four p.m. and met the headmaster. Without uttering a word, Suresh signed his resignation letter and gave him a copy. Biren was totally nonplussed. "What is this, Suresh da? I have taken a week's leave to attend my son's final hearing. Tomorrow the judgment will be delivered, and you are resigning today! You don't want to celebrate his release, Suresh da?"

Suresh began to speak slowly, "Brother, please don't misunderstand me. I sent Haru to you for the last three days, but you were busy in the court. I understand your situation, but meanwhile, three days are over."

"Dada, please wait for one more day. Rabi and his friends will stand guard to her. Nothing untoward will happen."

Suresh shook his head and said, "The S.I. told me indirectly not to remain here, to avoid sparking a riot." Birendra received the charge-handing-over-note and said, "The biggest migration of human civilisation begins with you, Suresh da."

As they reached the quarter, Kanak rushed towards them and began to say something in an excited and jumbled up voice. "They came here half an hour ago. He said that his name was Shah Jahan. As we refused to open the door, he began shouting 'Didimani' from outside. We did not answer. He said if she did not reach the mosque by eight p.m., he would not take responsibility for what would happen thereafter. What will happen now? They will forcibly take her away!" she said, looking towards Sagar.

Biren understood that the situation could not be doused in the prevailing political climate. This may be the pretext for them to start the riot. He looked at Suresh da and said, "So, when are you leaving?"

"As soon as possible. It has already become dark."

Biren called Haru to get the boat ready at the ghat and take the luggage a piece at a time. He also asked his youngest son Kabi to go around the place in a cycle to find out if the Muslim boys were keeping surveillance over these quarters. On receiving a green signal from Kabi and Haru, Biren asked Sagar to come out, drawing a *ghomta* (veil) over her head like a married Hindu woman. Kabi went ahead as if they were all going to Barishal Town to be present at court to hear the judgment the next day. After fifteen minutes, Suresh and Kanak left together while Haru remained in the quarters, lighting up some hurricanes in different rooms. Then he put fresh coal in the oven of the kitchen so that black smoke kept coming out through the chimney for some time. He played these tricks to convince the watchers of Shah Jahan that the inmates of the house were inside as usual.

In the darkness of dusk, Suresh embraced Biren at the same river ghat where Biren had received him five years ago. Sagar touched his feet, and the boatmen pushed the boat to deeper water, uttering, '*Durga, Durga*'. He would reach Khulna in two nights sailing by an unfrequented route.

Sagarika escapes with her parents by waterway from Barishal under the cover of darkness.

At midnight, the sky of Banaripara turned crimson red when balls of fire, made of jute soaked in kerosene, were lobbed at the quarters of the headmaster. The sound of bursting bamboos awakened the neighbours. Some people rushed to save the lives of the endangered family. But Soudamini and Biren stood at their veranda, shuddering at what could have happened to the Nandys and invoking the mercy of mother Jagaddhatri for them.

Chapter Four

4.1 Satyabrata's marriage

Satyabrata married a girl when he was twenty-five. He had studied in Krishnagar Govt College and passed B.Sc. with distinction. He achieved a high position in the All Bengal Assistants' Grade Examination held in 1942 and was posted next year in the agriculture department at Writers' Building. A job in the government during the time of war, especially when the entire province was going through the harrowing days of famine, was considered a prize job by all middle-class families.

Satya used to live in a mess near the Bowbazar crossing on Nirmal Chander Street. As Saturday was a half-holiday in government offices, he used to leave for Krishnagar by the 16-00 Lalgola Fast Passenger. Although the family hailed from the district of Chittagong, his parents used to live there in a rented house opposite the Patra Market. His father was in a government job at Krishnagar, and his elder brother was then posted as a junior engineer in the municipality of Pabna. The elder brother was already married. Satya used to enjoy the company of his family members on Sundays. After spending the weekly holiday, Satya used to return to Calcutta on Monday morning and go straight to the office directly from the Sealdah station.

On the seventeenth, eighteenth, and nineteenth of August 1946, Satyabrata and his fellow mess members guarded the households of the locality opposite the Wellington Square. The boys of a famous physical training centre of the square were at the vanguard. The women of the locality sought protection from the young boarders of the mess, and the strong-bodied young men took upon themselves the responsibility of protecting their lives and honour when the police of the Suhrawardy

Government abdicated their duty in favour of the rioting goondas. Satyabrata actively participated in mobilising resistance to the rioters after their uncontested mayhem on the previous day. Being a government servant, however, he carefully avoided involvement in incidents on the street. On the nineteenth, when the army was patrolling the road, a large group of goondas appeared from the Moulali side and confronted the army personnel with firearms. The residents of the entire area remained inside their houses with doors and windows bolted. Satya was watching the proceeding from a partially opened window. He was tense in excitement. If the army personnel make a temporary retreat, the goondas would immediately force their entry into the houses protected by the local Hindu boys collectively for the past three days. But the resistance group members had withdrawn themselves after the army personnel enforced the curfew order. The Muslim boys took this as an opportunity to make the tally even.

Sh-sh-u-u-i Something whizzed past Satya through the small opening in the window. It kissed the left hand of Satya, and the sashes of the window were broken. Satya could not understand if he was hit by a bullet or shrapnel or by a piece of the broken glass. But he was bleeding profusely. The members of the house, who had kept Satya as their protector, were at their wit's end when injured Satya became a liability. The Medical College was only a furlong away. But if he were taken to the hospital, he would be arrested by the police for rioting. In that case, he would lose his job. The boarders of the mess got hold of a dresser of a private clinic, who stitched and bandaged the wound. After two/three days, when train services resumed, Satya sent an application for leave to his office and left for Krishnagar. The roads and lanes to Sealdah station were still strewn with undisposed dead bodies, and the air was laden with a foul smell. Vultures were having a feast on the streets of Calcutta, the second biggest city of the empire.

By the beginning of June of the following year, it became clear that India would soon become free. After a few days, the government employees were asked to give their options if they wanted to join the Indian Govt or the Govt of Pakistan. Satya went to Krishnagar to ascertain the views of their family members. The elder brother came from Pabna. Their father was still in his service in the Medical

Superintendent's office. The family members discussed and decided to settle in India, snapping their ties with Chittagong.

When the Ghosh family was busy planning their resettlement in new India after the partition, one *Ghatak* (professional matchmaker) approached the mother of Satya and narrated the qualifications of a few suitable brides and their pedigree. The mother was proud of his younger son for his bright complexion, academic excellence, and government service in the State Secretariat. She was not a woman to be easily convinced. If the proposed bride were beautiful, she would reject her on the plea of her lack of education; or if the girl were a graduate, she would fall short of the mark on account of her pedigree. At last, the Ghatak came up with an ace proposal and presented it as a trump card.

"All that you wanted, boudi[13], are embodied in this girl. You cannot reject her on any count," he said confidently. "The parents have come to Nabadwip with their twenty-one-year-old girl, fearing for her safety in the land of Muslims. They want the marriage to be held in a month before they go back to Sandwip, dispose of their property, and quit their desh for good. But it seems you are not in a hurry. Consider, the girl is extremely beautiful and I.A. pass."

When Satya came home the next Saturday, his mother revealed to him the short-listed proposals that were on hold for his initial approval. On Sunday, he went to Nabadwip, barely five miles away from Krishnagar, accompanied by his parents and boudi. The girl was extremely good-looking yet sober and well-educated. Her father was an experienced headmaster. Satya found all the qualities of a suitable bride in her and gave his consent to his parents before leaving for Calcutta on Monday morning.

Next few days, both sides kept on negotiating. Customarily, in the then Bengali Hindu society, the bride was sent to her *sasurbari*[14] with a lot of jewellery and sarees for herself and all the ladies of the in-laws' house, dress for the bridegroom, furniture, nuptial bed, utensils, etc. The system of paying dowry was still prevalent, although the educated

---

[13] Wife of the elder brother. Also used to address a non-related married woman in the same age-group.

[14] House of father-in-law.

section of the society was fighting against this evil practice. The parents of Satya were in a fix. Both the sons were earning, apart from the head of the family. They could easily afford their day-to-day household expenditure. But at that time, the Ghoshes were in the process of resettlement in a district that would remain in India. They were to forgo their ancestral house-property in Chittagong and needed to buy land in Indian Bengal. Why should not the bride's side contribute towards the purchase of land? After all, the bride and her children would live there and enjoy the property. Satya was not consulted in these parleys lest he raised objection to take dowry from his would-be father-in-law. The ladies of the groom's family tied up the negotiations amid high confidentiality.

The marriage was fixed for a date deemed to be auspicious according to the Hindu almanac. The bride's side had hired an ashram[15] premise for the marriage by donating to the ashram. Five rooms of the ashram were given to them, and the marriage was to take place in the Natmandir. A pandal was to be raised in the open ground for the feast. The ashram authorities imposed only one restriction. As the ashram was a temple of the Vaishnav sect, non-vegetarian food was totally prohibited. To agree to this condition was a big concern for the piscivorous Bengalis. The parents of Satya, however, did not raise any objection. To decide the menu of the dinner was the prerogative of the bride's side.

Satya and his family members camped at the same place in Nabadwip a day in advance to avoid the river ferry on the day of marriage. The ceremony was held without much pomp. Relatives could not come from distant places because of sporadic breaking out of riots here and there. On the eve of partition, many of the upper caste educated Hindus were busy quitting the districts that would be transferred to Pakistan.

The mother of Satya had an apprehension that the relatives of the bride would make a cut on the promised jewellery to meet the demand for dowry. She sent out a message from Krishnagar that the jewellery must conform to the promised weight of gold. This stand of the groom's mother placed the bride's maternal uncle in a scurry

[15] The premises for spiritual practices under the guidance of a Teacher.

as his game-plan was coolly checkmated by a lady of little education. To save his face, the father of the bride decided to buy a readymade necklace of gold. He borrowed money from his brother-in-law and called a smart young man in his camp to go to Calcutta by the morning train, buy the item from Bowbazar Street, and return by afternoon. The young man did not have any idea about the jewellery shops in Calcutta, so he introduced himself to Satya as a nephew of the bride's maternal aunt and took tips about the reliable jewellery shops in the Bowbazar area without divulging his errand. He left by the passenger train at nine a.m. At one o'clock afternoon, the local news of A.I.R. Calcutta mentioned some case of murder on Harrison Road. Although Harrison Road was some distance away from Bowbazar, Suresh and Kanak began to worry for the safety of their young hero out on a trip to Calcutta. The sweat on the forehead of the bride's father and uncle disappeared only after the young man reached the venue of marriage in the afternoon with a necklace. Then, the marriage ceremony began without any acrimony from either side.

The Shuva-Lagna[16] was at the moment of sunset. The bridegroom and the bride were led to the Natmandir[17], which was specially decorated with flowers. Four young plantain trees were positioned at four corners, limiting the holy arena of marriage. The ceremony began with Shuva-Drishti[18] and the exchange of garlands. The bride was to be lifted on a flat wooden seat and carried in a circle around the bridegroom. As the bride was a grown-up lady, strong arms were needed to lift her seat from two sides.

Satya heard somebody calling, "Rabi? Where is Rabi?"

No one responded. After waiting a minute or two for the person, other people came forward and completed seven cyclic movements around the groom. All this while the bride kept her face covered with two betel leaves. Then at the right moment, she removed the leaves, and her face became visible to the bridegroom. After many entreaties from friends, Sagarika and Satyabrata finally looked at each other amid applause from friends.

---

[16] The auspicious moment based on the position of stars and planets.

[17] A part of the temple complex, where dance, music are performed.

[18] Exchange of glances by the boy and the girl before marriage.

The bridegroom put his garland around the neck of the bride, and the bride reciprocated. This went on three times, after which the seat of the bride was lowered to the ground at the place of worship. The priest began to utter Sanskrit hymns. The father of the bride came forward, and he was asked by the priest to give away his daughter to the bridegroom forever, uttering some hymns. Then, one by one, the hands of the bride were placed on the hands of the groom, and they were asked to take the oath of loyalty to each other. One would remain true to the other in body, heart, and words. *'Let your heart be where my heart is. May my heart be where your heart is.'*

Finally, the priest performed a Yagna by lighting a small fire. The couple moved around the fire seven times together. The marriage became complete when Satyabrata put vermilion powder on the forehead of Sagarika. As husband and wife, they took the blessings from the priest and their parents.

When the bride sat on a bridal throne at the end of the ceremony, with the groom by her side, invitees were going to see the bride, and they blessed her when she bowed. They also gave her some gifts according to their relationship, status, and financial capacity. The parent of the bride appeared to be a highly cultured person. Satya saw him requesting the invitees not to present any gift and only give their blessings to the newly-wed. But his appeal fell on deaf ears as the invitees took the appeal as an affront to their financial standing.

At this hour, one guest turned up late, apparently coming from a long distance. Everybody noticed that he was well-known to the family of the bride. The mother of the bride told her brother that he was Haru, the peon of Banaripara school. He should be brought to her to relate the developments after their escape. Haru touched the feet of Suresh babu and Kanak debi and narrated how their quarters were burnt by the goons and how after a few days of his return, Badal Majhi was decapitated in broad daylight. They shuddered at the news. Kanak felt like throwing up, visualizing the gruesome murder of their benefactor. Relatives took her inside. Suresh told Haru not to discuss these with others, especially Sagarika.

Satya was watching that there was some tension in the bride's camp. The marriage was already complete. Then what did worry his mother-in-law? Satya moved inside the bride's camp. As Haru was coming out, he saw the groom and said with a broad smile, "Jamaibabu, pranam. I am Haru. Didimani must have told you about me. Anyway, I am not going back before attending your Boubhat[19] party. I hope you will not forget to invite me." Before Satya overcame his puzzled look, Haru moved forward.

Haru came forward to meet his Didimani as the guests had moved to the dining area. He expressed his happiness at seeing Sagarika married to a suitable boy of her caste and religion. "The groom is handsome and well-built," he commented.

He gave her the present sent by his wife and an encomium written by her students. Haru also handed over a letter that he had failed to deliver earlier. Sagarika kept the envelop in her vanity bag. Haru apologised for the late delivery, saying, "That Friday, he gave me the reply to your letter. But I was so busy tying up the escape arrangements, you know, that I forgot about it. Coming back home, when I put off my shirt, I could feel that there was something in the pocket. It was your letter from Rabi bhai. But I couldn't tell him about this and brought the letter to you..."

"Who gave you the letter?" Sagarika became furious in anger. "Don't take his name before me, Haru da!"

She started saying various things against the hero of Banaripara, calling him the most cowardly person living on earth, one who could not come forward to rescue his friend in a crisis, but came to Nabadwip to watch the wedding of his betrothed girl. "Haru da, you take him to the dining area and see that the foody eats to his heart's content."

Haru quickly retreated lest some relatives overhear her outpourings. Some of it did reach the ears of Satya, who felt the situation was emotionally charged but could not make out who the target of her invectives was.

Haru went out of the marriage premises to find out Rabi. Half an hour ago, when he was approaching the location, he met Rabi in front of a tea stall, talking to himself absent-mindedly, '*How did all this happen? Why did she change her mind? Why didn't she give me*

---

[19] The groom's family holds the function of boubhat at their house, when the new bohu cooks and serves meal to household members, followed by a party for all guests.

a chance?' Haru called him and briefed Rabi about the incidents at Banaripara after he had left the place. He did not hide that he had converted to Islam so that the lives of his family members were not in jeopardy. Rabi heard him without showing any interest and asked him to go to his Didimani.

After meeting Sagarika didimani, Haru came back to the same place, but Rabi was not there. The tea-stall boy said the tall man was enquiring about the last train for Howrah. Haru called a rickshaw and left for the railway station. Upon reaching the station, he traced Rabi on the platform.

When Haru reported to him the reaction of Didimani after receiving his letter, Rabi exclaimed, "Haru da, what have you done? Have you delivered my letter only today! Oh, ho, ho! I reiterated my promise to marry her on the day of independence, wherever she was. But she did not read my letter. In fact, she did not get the letter before her marriage! O, ho! What did she think of me? That is why she is so upset with me!"

Haru wanted to understand what big mistake he had committed. Despite his request to give her a reply, Rabi did not reply for three days. Only when Haru told him that Didimani considered surrendering herself to save the life of her father, that Rabi wrote a reply to her letter. But mastermoshai had already decided to leave the place.

"I was so occupied organising their escape that I completely forgot to deliver the letter. You can punish me if you want, but I never wanted to do you any harm."

The two men understood that the train of life of Rabi had taken a different route.

Rabi told Haru, "I came here to know from her why she did not wait for me. But she did not allow me to talk to her. Now I suppose I have got the answer. Okay, Haru da, you go back and have your dinner, and let me go my way. I made a cardinal mistake by falling in love before my vow to free the country was fulfilled. I must do penance for this."

After some time, when Haru came back to the venue of marriage, Suresh was seen asking Sisir, and Kulapradip if they had seen Rabi. The boy had performed such an important task on the day, but nobody cared to see if he had dined. He could not be seen anywhere, including the guest room. Haru could not say that Rabi had left Nabadwip. Satya felt bad for the young man who skipped the special dinner after daylong toil. "What is wrong with him?" he asked Sagarika innocently, sitting for dinner together.

Haru broke down during dinner and left his meal halfway. He was seized by a feeling of terrible remorse. "It happened only for me!" Tears rolled down from his eyes. People wondered, 'why did this odd man from Banaripara have such surge of emotion, when his Didimani was so happily married?'

H left Nabadwip at dawn, unnoticed by anybody.

The newly married couple was given a tearful farewell. The brother of Satya escorted them to their house in Krishnagar. Satya's mother and boudi performed the *'baran'* function (ritual of welcome) for the new couple, especially for the bride, who was taken into the house as a new member of the family. After the couple was seated in a room specially decorated for the occasion, the senior members of the Ghosh family blessed Satya and Sagar with paddy seeds and new grass leaves to have a long and happy married life, with many offsprings and earthly prosperity.

4.2 Migration of a Muslim family

Noor's grandfather was in search of safety after his house on Amherst Street in Calcutta was attacked, ransacked, and looted by Hindu goondas in the riot of 1946. He sent his eldest son, Anisur, to Dacca to find out if Dacca would be a safer place for them to settle. For the time being, Safiur Rahaman, the cashier at *Wachel Mollah*, hired the ground floor of a house on rent in Park Circus. Safiur was one of those up-country Muslims who considered Urdu their mother-tongue. These Muslim families were trained in *khandani* manners. They established shopping centres of European standard, having high-quality clothing and tailoring outlets and gourmet restaurants. Many of these could compete with the European houses in the Sahib Para of Chowringhee and Park Street. They considered themselves superior to the indigenous Muslims of Bengal, even to the descendants of Muslim aristocrats who adorned the courts of the Nawabs of Murshidabad and Dhaka. Till the time of Safiul Rahaman, the inter-marriage of up-country Muslims with the local ones was a rare event in the early twentieth century Calcutta. They were the *Ashrafs* (or *Kulin)* in the Muslim society of Calcutta.

Anisur spent his boyhood and youth in Amherst Street, a predominantly Hindu area. People in his surroundings generally spoke Bengali, and he had picked up the language from the neighbours. He studied in the Hindu school, a Bengali medium government school with Persian or Sanskrit as the third language. Those days, most secular schools offered the choice to the students of studying either Sanskrit or Arabic/Persian as classical language. In Islamia College, Anis studied Bengali as the first language and Persian as an optional subject. English, the King's language of the day, was the compulsory second language.

Anisur found that Dacca was so much dominated by ethnic Muslims that it would be culturally difficult for his parents to adapt.

He went farther ahead to Chittagong. This place had contact with the Arabs by sea and was culturally more influenced by Arabic preachers. Meanwhile, the partition of British India became a reality. A new nation-state, called Pakistan, was carved out by the British parliament as a condition for India's independence. The Rahaman family vacillated for long if they should move out of Calcutta and go to the East Bengal province of Pakistan or stay in West Bengal of India. Gandhiji's stay in a Beliaghata Muslim *bustee* had assuaged the communal fire in Calcutta post-independence.

By the end of 1949, the Constituent Assembly had adopted the Constitution of India and equality of all citizens was guaranteed, as also the right to practise any religion, faith, or belief. Belying all propaganda of the Muslim League and the British conservatives, the Congress rose above communalism and India was not declared a Hindu state nor a state where only a Hindu had the right to be the President, Prime Minister, or a Chief Minister. Safiul changed his mind and remained in India with his other children. They bought the house from the Muslim owner, who had left for Karachi voluntarily. Many Urdu knowing Muslims from U.P. and Bihar chose to move to Karachi in western Pakistan, where Urdu would be the state language and give them an edge over the Sindhis and Baluch people.

Anisur convinced his father that a second home in East Pakistan would be useful if, at any stage, his parents found it difficult to stay in India. He had seen that many Hindu families had left some members in East Bengal before migrating to India. As he was a refugee from India, he got a job for himself in the Municipality of Cox's Bazar, vice a vacancy created by the migration of a Hindu supervisor. He got the house of a Hindu family in Patiya from the Refugee Rehabilitation Department, as many houses were lying abandoned, being burnt in the riot, and forsaken by the Hindu owners. After three years, he managed to be transferred to the Patiya Union Board office and got the house renovated.

Politically, a conflict between the two wings of Pakistan was fast brewing up due to a false sense of superiority of the political leaders of West Pakistan. The original idea of a Pakistan had included Punjab, Afghanistan, Kashmir, Sindh, and Baluchistan. Initially, Bengal was nowhere in that idea germinated by Choudhry Rahmat Ali (in a pamphlet Now or Never-1933) and promoted by Iqbal, the poet. The idea was executed by Muhammad Ali Jinnah in a span of seven years after the Muslim League's Lahore Resolution. Muslim League was just one of the many political outfits before 1940 but emerged as the most outspoken mouthpiece of the Muslims in British India under the astute leadership of Jinnah. After the partition of Bengal, Jinnah did not know what to do with this bonus. The population of East Bengal was more than all the western provinces put together, and in a democratic polity, it was but natural that the leaders from East Bengal might someday ask for a fair share of the power cake. The agitation over the recognition of Bengali as one of the three state languages between 1948 and 1952 helped forge the unity of the liberal Muslim majority and Hindu minority.

In 1947, Anis joined the *Muhajirs* (refugee Muslims from Bihar) in torching the Hindu houses in his neighbourhood in Patiya out of anger for what the Hindus had done to their old house in Calcutta. But very soon, he realised that the riots in East Bengal were a one-sided affair, triggered by spreading some baseless rumour about the persecution of Muslims in India. He checked up from his parent that Fazlul Haq was safe in Calcutta, although the fake news of his killing rendered hundreds of Hindus homeless in Chittagong. A feigned injury of a woman paraded in the Dacca secretariat provoked the riot in Dacca and Barishal in 1950. A village-level incident over the fishing rights claimed by Hindu scheduled caste people brought a horrific reprisal in which hundreds of *Namahshudras*[20] were either beheaded or maimed. Jogendra Nath Mondal, the undisputed leader of the scheduled caste communities, resigned from the central cabinet of Pakistan when his demand for a high-level enquiry was turned down perfunctorily. Thousands of Hindus became refugees once again without a fresh influx from India. Anis understood how the game of communal politics was going on and the way Muslim refugees in East Bengal were incited against the Hindus. He dissociated himself from the Mojaher outfits. Instead, he joined the pro-left National Awami Party led by Maulana Bhasani.

---

[20] Namahshudra: is a dominant group of Scheduled Caste community from southern and central Bengal.

One day, when Anisur was returning from his office, he found a lady in a bookstall, buying a Bengali periodical. Anis used to speak in Bengali as it was commonly spoken in Calcutta. This language was closer to the language written in books or newspapers. His conversation with the vendor attracted the attention of the beautiful *mohtorma*—Jasmine. She could speak only in the local dialect but had a fascination for the language spoken by the elite in Calcutta. The Chittagong dialect was almost unintelligible to Anis in the initial years. But this hurdle was no match to shield them from the arrows of Cupid!

He married an educated Bengali Muslim girl to draw some strength from her family. In 1956, he had a son, named Noor by his father-in-law, Janab Noorul Chaudhuri, and thereby set up an extended family of the Rahamans of Park Circus in Chittagong.

4.3 Opu returns to Sandwip

During the 1946 riot in the Noakhali district against the Hindu minorities, Aparajita and her parents could barely save their life and honour due to the humanism of a Muslim cartman. At Chittagong, she stayed in her hostel with special permission till the final examination, although after two months, her parents went back to Sandwip to look for the missing old members of the family. After the examination, she stayed back in a friend's house until she moved to Dacca to study in a girls' college. Her heart pined to see her grandparents. They had witnessed the burning of their own house and spent two months hiding in a cattle shed. Such an outburst of mutual hatred was completely unthinkable a year ago. But presently, it was so real that she could not go back to Sandwip for fear of life. Her father came to see her only once for her admission to the college and travelled with her from Chittagong to Dacca. It was not possible for him to stay even one day extra leaving the family in Sandwip. She was in Eden College hostel and spent her days like a recluse. Sometimes, she used to brood over her days in Banaripara. It was such a lovely place; people were so large-hearted.

"How is Rabi dada? Is he still in jail? How are the senior uncle and aunty?"

She came to know from her letter that Sagar didi had started teaching in the new girls' school. She tried to keep herself busy in her studies, but the bruised and bleeding visage of Rabi dada haunted her mind during the idle time.

Suddenly, in early July 1947, she got a letter from her father. It stated that he was going to Nabadwip to attend the marriage of Sagar. His elder brother had already gone to Nabadwip, resigning from his school. Opu was left confused by the news as she could not understand how Sagar didi's marriage could take place outside Sandwip and without the presence of grandpa, grandma, her mother, and herself. Or it might be that the senior uncle did not want to draw the attention of the Muslim community by celebrating Sagardi's marriage in the house burnt by them less than a year ago. Moreover, no Hindu priests lived in Sandwip. Either they had run away, or they were killed.

'Who would've solemnised the marriage in Sandwip? My senior uncle is a sagacious person. He must have taken the correct decision,' she thought.

She wished she could be present at Nabadwip during the ceremony. It was possible that some people of Banaripara might go there. She could meet Rabi dada or know his whereabouts from Soudamini aunty.

Aparajita went back to Sandwip after clearing M.Sc. in Mathematics from Dacca University in 1953. Sisir, her father, came to Dacca to escort her. He was so happy that his daughter had fulfilled the aspiration of the family, and she was a postgraduate who could compete with any male for a good job. There was no lady in Sandwip with an M.Sc. degree before her. When they reached their home after a long train and steamship journey, Opu broke down entering the house. It had been seven years since she returned home after the fateful Lakshmi Purnima[21] night. Opu embraced her mother, grandma, and grandpa, and all began to wail together. The islanders were highly emotional people. Mostly they used to wail when the sea, a cyclone, or a flood took away some lives or demolished their houses and ruined their paddy fields. This time, the Nandys cried in joy. A girl from their family had become a post-graduate! Learning about the cause of this outburst, the neighbours brought coconut sandesh[22] from their houses for Opu. Some of them recounted how on the day she was born, they had gone back without taking sweets.

Opu began to look around to mark the changes. While she was in Dacca, she had watched the political changes in the country from within the closed gates of her college hostel. The partition of the country had brought joy to the minds of the Muslim majority. The tearful eyes of the minorities told a different story. The newspapers highlighted the cruelties in the Punjab and Sindh, where trainloads

---

[21] Full moon day

[22] sweetmeat

of refugees were butchered on either side of the border but did not publish any report of the ruthless killings in Dacca, Barishal, Noakhali, Sylhet, and many other districts. The riots of 1946 and 1947 were followed by the killings of 1950. Their house bore the tale-tell marks of arson, as the whole house could not be repaired for want of money. Opu could see that, barring two or three houses, the entire para was deserted by their Hindu neighbours. Their abandoned houses were occupied by the Muslims from other places.

"Opu!" Nayantara called her granddaughter by her bedside. She was shedding tears.

Opu came close to her and said, "Why are you weeping, thammi[23]?"

Nayantara replied after consolidating herself, "We never thought to see this day, Naatni[24]. An hour after you left with your parents that night, those goons came out of the darkness, shouting *'Allah ho Akbar'*. They quickly surrounded the whole para, sprinkled petrol, and kerosene on the bamboo structure and thatched roofs and torched them. As we were half awake after your departure, we smelled petrol and ran to the garden to hide. The goons rampaged around for two hours. Those who were caught in the fire were pushed back. They used swords, spears, and choppers to kill men and children. Then they raped the young women. Some of them were looking for you and your mother. We were trembling in fear behind the bush of banana trees and turmeric plants. They left the place with looted ornaments and precious goods and left behind empty petrol jerrycans."

"There is no motor car or petrol pump on this island. Where did the petrol jerricans come from?" Opu asked Shakticharan, but before he could guess any reasonable answer, she said, "I think I have seen those outsiders ferrying the jerricans and boxes from Noakhali. They were preparing for the carnage for many days. How is the situation now?"

"Quite bad. Any day one more onslaught may take place to wipe off the leftover Hindus." Shakticharan paused and said, "Naatni, you have come back after completing your studies. You are now a mathematician. We are proud of you. But you are also a fully grown

---

[23] grandmother

[24] granddaughter

woman now. There is no suitable boy here who can marry you. What would you like to do now?"

Within a few days, Opu realised how far the situation had deteriorated. Her childhood friend Amina came to see her one day with her husband, Nasir. Nasir sat on the veranda and talked to his once-upon-a-time teacher, Sisir. The two friends sat in the inner room and exchanged their untold stories. Amina congratulated her friend for passing all examinations, and Opu congratulated her for having been married to a pious madrasa teacher.

Amina told her that their school had since been closed as all Hindu lady teachers had left the island. Muslim girls were either sitting at home or going to some madrasa where they learned Urdu and Arabic more than English or Bengali. She hoped Opu would certainly do something for her *desh* and revive the old school. The word *desh* stung Opu like a shrapnel.

Her mind went on a detour as she was preparing *moa* (round sweetened balls of puffed rice mixed with a delicate proportion of jaggery). Madhuri was cutting a ripe papaya from their garden for the guests.

Opu began to recall the words of Rabi dada, *'Bengal is a part of Bharatbarsha, that comprises the entire land south of the Himalayas lying in the north of the Seas, surrounding her from three sides. That is our country, our desh, an integral, indivisible part of our being.'*

But what place is this? People are now calling this place Pakistan. The name had no history, no emotional bonding with this land. How can you change the name of your motherland? The Muslim invaders gave the name Hindustan to this geographical entity. It was a dream for them to become the Badshah of the whole of Hindustan. But they were not so childish as to change the identity of the people by renaming the country. They could never think that the very identity of the subjects could be changed so easily by driving a communal wedge. Just name one-third part of the land as Pakistan. That way, one-third of the population would lose their Bharatiya or Hindustani identity inherited by them for five thousand years.

But how come the majority community of people of this new *desh* burnt their house to frighten them away only because they were Hindus. The Muslims were in the majority in this province before the

British took over the political power. But they never tried to evict or eliminate the minorities. How could they be her brothers? How would she be willing to give her life for that country? No, she cannot accept Pakistan as her country.

When Amina got up to leave and sought permission from Madhuri aunty, Opu proceeded to the main door with Nasir to bid him farewell.

"I have a word for you. If you want to serve this country, you will get me by your side." Nasir continued without mincing words, "This country is for Muslims. You change your religion and stay here comfortably. You and Amina can stay together with me."

"How dare you say this!? Why do I have to change my religion if I want to serve this country!? No Muslim has been converted to Hinduism in India amid all riots," Opu protested.

Amina came to them quickly and said, "What happened?"

"Nothing. Come along." Nasir dragged her out and left angrily.

4.4 Preparations for emigration

The grandparents were suffering from many ailments, but during the last eight years, there could be no treatment after the evacuation of Dr. Nityagopal Das, their family physician. There were no other doctors, and they could not travel to the mainland as it was not possible for them to bear the stress. Sisir had to take leave from school and go to Chittagong to consult some reputed doctor.

The reason why they could survive in the hostile surrounding was that Sisir was the maths teacher in the only high school on the island. This school was on the verge of closure due to the exodus of Hindu students and teachers. This had brought the local inhabitants to their senses that keeping the school open would be impossible if Sisir master left the island. But the health of Shakti and Nayan had run down completely, and they left this world after a year at an interval of three months. Except for a few *Hakims,* there was no doctor even to issue the death certificates. Fortunately, the *doms*[25] and a priest were still available at the cremation point.

Sisir used to keep Suresh informed of all these developments through letters. Suresh had joined a school in Midnapore and had no intention of returning to Pakistan. After his mother's death, he advised Sisir to sell the land and house and migrate to India with his family as it was not safe for them, especially Opu, to continue there. That was already decided by Sisir, and he had applied for a passport immediately after the passport office was opened in Chittagong.

Selling the property was a big headache. Those who left for India in 1947 or '50 had to leave almost penniless as they had no time to sell their property. But the situation improved later. The Hindus were then leaving not because of a riot but because of the overall fearful uncongenial situation. They could transfer their property to another

---

[25] Persons engaged at cremation place to burn the dead bodies.

person under duress. As supply was was more than demand, the prices for land and houses were low. But still, the wily middlemen did not spare any effort to cheat the helpless emigrants of their dues under different pretexts.

Sisir could get a buyer in Chittagong, who was a professional property dealer, and he agreed to make part payment in cash and the balance through *hawala*[26] encashable at Agartala. The buyer gave them a month to vacate the property. Sisir tried his best to hide the information from his neighbours as they were no longer their well-wishers. He sent the letter of resignation by post to the secretary of the school after drawing the salary. They began to pack their luggage. Opu took her academic certificates in a waterproof bag and did not forget to take the book gifted by her Rabi dada.

They were to leave by noon voyage. In the early morning, Opu wanted to pay a visit to Amina and bid her goodbye. When she knocked at Amina's door, her husband opened it. He welcomed her and expressed surprise that she came for a visit so early in the day. Opu confided in him and said they were to leave by the midday voyage. Amina felt sad that the only friend she had from her childhood was leaving the island permanently. Nasir went out, leaving the two childhood friends to exchange their feelings. After an hour of reminiscing their innocent girlhood memories and exchanging some gifts with promises to remember each other, Opu got up to return home. When she was about to reach her house, she found Nasir with two unknown boys talking to each other near the door of their house. The boys looked at her as if they had got their prey just before it could fly to safety. Opu knocked at the door. The moment Madhuri opened the door to let Opu in, the group pushed them in and bolted the door from inside. They tied the hands and legs of the teacher and his wife, lifted Opu and carried her to the abandoned labour room.

Opu screamed and shouted, "Save me, papa, save me! Save me, Rabi dada!!"

---

[26] A traditional system of transferring money used in Arab countries and South Asia, whereby the money is paid to an agent who then instructs an associate in the relevant country or area to pay the final recipient.

In broad daylight, they outraged her modesty and forcibly subjected her to sexual intercourse. After more than an hour of the carnal fest, they left her naked body in a semi-conscious state.

"If you had agreed to marry me, you could have avoided this fate." Opu could recognise the voice; it was Nasir's.

Sisir and Madhuri could free themselves after painstaking effort for half an hour and rushed to their daughter. No neighbour had come forward to their help, although they had been shouting all the while. Madhuri helped her daughter regain full sense and held her in her bosom to console her. She brought a little milk from the kitchen and gave her to drink. The rice she was cooking before the onslaught for their last lunch on this island had, by the time, got burnt.

Sisir sprang up on his feet and ran to the police station. Soleman, the S.I., had passed out from Kargil High School twenty years ago and had a deep respect for his teacher. The S.I. took time to make out the complaint from Sisir's incoherent emotional outbursts. But how could he tell him that they had verbal instruction from the higher authorities not to record any such incidents? The publicity of it might lead to a violent fall-out in India and a massive chain reaction in East Pakistan.

He could only advise the teacher to desert the island as soon as possible. "Sir, if I record it as a case of rape, I must get her medically examined. There is no qualified doctor around, not to speak of a lady doctor. I need to keep her in safe custody, but there is no lady constable. How can she remain safe if she is guarded by male constables? If you take my advice, sir, leave this island as you have already planned. I am giving you two escorts to take you to the vessel. If the news of rape spreads, your lives will be in danger."

Sisir came back home utterly frustrated. Meanwhile, Madhuri had nursed her daughter up to stand on her feet. After a bath, she wore a fresh saree.

"Well, Ma, the story of Draupadi being saved by Krishna from being shamed in the court of Hastinapur was only a story, isn't it? In real life, no Krishna appears at that moment," said Opu.

"Did you call Him, as did Draupadi?"

"Ay, I did call my god, but he did not appear. We must fight ourselves for our own safety."

They would not stay in their house for one more night as the Muslims would not allow them to live now. Their lunch was already spoilt. The police constables came with a cycle van. They did not have any time to sentimentalise. With three side bags on their shoulders, the last of the Nandys left their ancestral home, never to return. The Muslim neighbours did not pose any problem as they had rushed to the house of Nasir to douse water on a burning woman. Ashamed to hear the violation of modesty of her friend by her own husband, Amina had consigned herself to flames.

4.5 Opu enters India – enters a new life

The boat moved upstream along the huge Meghna for a while and at Ashuganj entered a tributary named Titaas. At Akhaura, after completing the border immigration formalities, the passengers boarded the Indian boats to reach Agartala. Opu was not fully fit to undertake the strenuous journey. She felt happy to be finally on the Indian waters.

As their boat approached the vicinity of Agartala, Madhuri cursed the land they had to leave behind. "The people who conspired against us, set our house on fire, ruined our family, and finally criminally assaulted our daughter would one day get it back in their own coin. Yes, with interest from their own people. After what happened to us, God will desert Harishpur. The sea will swallow you up!" The tears from her eyes felt hot on her cheeks and salty on her tongue.

"The country was partitioned by power-hungry politicians after multiple rounds of mass killings. But why are the common people being ruined years after the partition became a settled fact? Will they not allow the minorities to live in the country?" Sisir asked the fellow travellers in despair.

Within his mind, however, he was tormented by some questions — What would happen to Opu? Will anybody marry her now? How would she lead her life in future?

At Agartala, the refugees reported their arrival to the officials of the Refugee Rehabilitation Department. Sisir thought he and her daughter were educated enough to eke out a living, and he decided not to go to a Govt camp. The stories of the poor conditions of Indian refugee camps were widely known. He searched out the address given by the *hawala* man. Disclosing his password and code number, he could retrieve seven thousand rupees from him after meeting his hefty commission charges. After a day, they proceeded to Silchar as some members of their clan had settled in Silchar. It took two days to trace one of them. Sisir got his assistance to buy a hut made of bamboo supports and *chatai* (*chanch*)[27] walls by the bank of the Surma river on the outskirt of the city. After spending three nights at public places like railway platforms or temples, the descendants of Shakticharan Nandy could keep their heads under a roof of tin on one cottah[28] land. At one corner of the plot, on the backside, there was a small kitchen, and at another, a basic toilet and a tube well. The change from their spacious house, sprawling kitchen garden and bighas of agricultural land to this 15*10 ft one-room tenement with a narrow front veranda brought tears to their eyes. But life must go on. Sisir and Opu went to the market and bought the essential utensils and the grocery required for cooking. Some neighbours, all migrants who came between 1947 and 54, were helpful.

The hutments had come up on government land unauthorizedly. The people who set up the colony initially had to fight for the cause of the uprooted people as the state government had little sympathy for the refugees.

Aparajita's struggle for survival began. For the last two years, she had lived the life of a third-grade citizen in East Bengal. The Constitution of Pakistan was in the making, but the newspapers were reporting important draft resolutions in the Constituent Assembly. It was known that Pakistan was going to be declared an Islamic Republic. Jinnah died within a year or so of independence, and his lieutenants were no match for him intellectually and dragged the process of drafting till 1955. It was clear to all that, unlike India, the new nation state would not ensure equality of opportunity between Muslims and people of other religions for the post of the President or the Prime Minister. The opportunity of declaring Pakistan a secular state in their constitution to checkmate India was given a pass casually.

Within two and a half year of independence, it became amply clear that the rights of the Hindu minorities to worship and follow their faith was merely ornamental. In case of a communal confrontation, the administration of the Islamic Republic would not be neutral and would not care for the protection of the minorities or their places of worship.

---

[27] Sliced bamboo fibre used for making temporary huts, fencing, etc.

[28] 720sft

"I think we had taken the correct decision to leave Sandwip. We had no future," Sisir told Madhuri and Opu. "At least we can now sleep peacefully at night."

"We should have left a few months earlier. My daughter could have escaped the trauma," complained Madhuri. "Now, who will marry her?"

"Sagar, I must say, was lucky to have escaped such a fate," said Sisir. "Dada told me at Nabadwip the circumstances in which he had to flee from Barishal. The safety of Sagar was at the top of his mind."

"Papa, you are a maths teacher. Why do you talk about fate? Can you say if we had lived on this side of the border, no such thing would have happened? Doesn't a Hindu woman ever get raped by a Hindu man? But I feel for didi as she had to marry in such haste. I hope she liked her groom and is happy."

"I saw the groom. A sober, good-looking person from a big joint family. She must be happy in her marriage."

"Papa, did anybody come from Banaripara to her marriage?"

"Nobody except one young man and a peon. After my brother had left the place in the evening, his quarter was put on fire by the goondas. The situation became so tense subsequently that Biren babu could not come to attend the marriage and left for Calcutta with other members of his family. His eldest son, I forgot his name, escorted them to Calcutta and then came to Nabadwip to attend the marriage."

"Rabi dada! He is Rabi dada!" Opu said with excitement.

Madhuri did not fail to notice the spark in her eyes. She faintly remembered that she had heard her uttering the name earlier but could not recall when.

"Yes, you are right. Rabi was his name. He stayed there till the beginning of the marriage ceremony and then vanished all of a sudden. He looked quite depressed, probably for leaving his desh, the home of his forefathers."

Soon, Sisir found that the then India was not the same India that existed before nineteen forty-seven. There has been a qualitative change in the attitude of the politicians and the government. Anything they would ask for, the politicians would reply in a patronising tone, '*The government is doing things out of compassion within limited resources. So, they should not grumble for delay or inadequacy.*'

While the refugees were mutually helpful to each other, the older residents of the place were suspicious of the incoming people as if they would eat away all the foodstuff like a swarm of locusts, grab all seats in schools and colleges, and secure all jobs on compassionate ground. Sisir could not anticipate that after facing so much pain in their homeland, he would experience such apathy and even resistance from the local people in India. Although they shared the same religion and spoke the same language commonly spoken in the valley, the refugees were frowned at by the old Bengali settlers and hated by the Assamese-speaking people as if these people came from outside Bharat Varsha. They could not raise a finger against the Punjabis, Marwaris, or Gujaratis doing business in Assam because such people belonged to some states of independent India. But Sisir Nandy and his family came from East Bengal, which was handed over to Pakistan. The people who left East Bengal seeking refuge in Assam were looked upon as foreigners.

Sisir was grumbling within himself, moving from school to school to get the job of a teacher. Finally, almost after a year, he got the job of an ad hoc teacher in Silchar on the recommendation of the M.P. from Karimganj.

Opu did not have any experience in teaching. On that pretext, her applications were rejected. She began to give private tuition at her home and in a coaching centre in the town. In her spare time, she began to work for the Udbaastu Sangram Samity/Association to fight for the Uprooted ones.

The woes of the Nandy family were not yet over.

In May 1956, they had completed one year of their life in the colony. During this period, they had experienced abject meanness from some of their neighbours. The colony people were a mixed lot. Many were uneducated and many were lazy. Having lost their agricultural land, many of them did not know how to eke out a living. They used to force their wives and daughters to earn money *the easy way*. Some well-dressed men were seen entering the colony in the evening, guided by one family member. Many residents used to object to such illicit trade in the colony, citing that if they could sell the honour of their women just to earn a day's meal, why did they leave Pakistan in the name of saving their religion and their women? Sisir was aghast to see the moral degradation of the people around them. Madhuri thanked her parents-in-law for encouraging their sons and granddaughters to be so educated, overcoming all odds, that her husband and daughter were able to earn money just enough for them without compromising their morality and conscience.

The colony had open drains to carry the effluent and the sewerage. These were dug when the colony was set up. By the time Sisir came to this colony, the inhabitants had lost their initiative, and the drains were choked by their own garbage.

One night when Opu was sleeping on her single cot at one end of the room and her parents were sleeping at another end separated by a foldable partition, water in the river suddenly swelled and rushed in.

At night, there was a heavy downpour in the upper reaches of the Barak Valley. The people of Silchar did not have any clue or prewarning of the cloudburst in the hills of Mizoram. Surma had a serpentine bend while flowing by Silchar Town. The huge mass of water flowing down the Barak Valley gathered momentum in Surma and charged against its bank, being obstructed at the bend. The roaring sound frightened the residents nearby. They ran for their life, and the river flooded the low regions of Silchar. Water entered the huts through the gaps in bamboo-chanch walls. They woke up when their wooden cots nearly began to float.

As the cot of Opu was low, she got up first and called out, "Baba! Ma! Wake up! It's a flood! Ma, we must get out. Get up, please."

Sisir and Madhuri got up and asked, "What's wrong!? What happened?" As it was midnight, it was pitch dark. Some people of the colony had gotten up already and began to loudly call every house-owner by name to come out of the hut. Sisir and Madhuri put their feet on the floor and realised the danger they were in. The water level was rising every moment. The structure of the hut might give way. They opened the door and came out to save their life. Inside or outside, there was water everywhere. All of them, including their neighbours, began to wade through knee-deep water to reach the safety of high land. The neighbours had some experience with floods in previous years, and they salvaged their valuables and carried those in an empty rice cooker on their heads. A cooking pot would not drown easily.

Opu had gone out with her parents in darkness. This flood caught them unawares, and they were unprepared to face it. Seeing their neighbours carrying some goods on their heads, Sisir suddenly remembered something and told Madhuri that he would go back to their hut and come back promptly. As the water level had risen further, Opu forbade him to go. Sisir passed his money bag to Opu and asked them to proceed to the nearby high school building, which was at a higher level, and that he would join them there in half an hour.

Sisir returned to his tenement. He was feeling very nervous as he had kept his residual cash, passports, and purchase deed in a new trunk. He had forgotten about it in his first impulse to save their own lives. Now he realised that he would become a pauper without the money and documents. He felt the key kept tied in a string around his waist. When he entered the hut, he saw that water was flowing above their cot. Everything was submerged. He knelt on the floor and tried to pull out the trunk underneath the cot. It had become much heavier than earlier.

"Water must have entered inside," Sisir murmured.

He continued his effort to pull it out. He felt that the trunk was tied at one end by an iron chain with the cot and was locked. He remembered that the key was kept by Madhuri in the ring tied to the end of her saree. Disappointed, Sisir got up from the floor. Then he picked up two dry sarees and one dhoti and left for the school building, searching for his wife and daughter. It was going to be dawn when he traced them out. When Opu inquired what he could retrieve, Sisir broke down, saying, "Opu, we are undone!"

The sky was still overcast with clouds, and the sunrays failed to shine. Rains started pouring in the area, and Nandys, with one hundred people of the colony, took shelter within the classrooms, by the courtesy of the headmaster. The downpour stopped after two hours, but it continued to drizzle.

The refugees in the school building opened a *langar* (community kitchen), and Opu donated some rupees from the purse of her father to buy the vegetables and spices. She also joined the team for cooking. They had khichuri lunch at noon, sitting with all refugees. The crisis was a leveller. It took eight hours for the flood water to go below the ankle level.

In the afternoon, when the flood receded, the residents of the refugee colony found that the earth at the base of their huts had shifted, developing cracks in the floor. Some of the supporting bamboo poles had capsized and the tin roofs were precariously hanging. The menfolk got down to repair the huts. More than fifty per cent people of the colony were Namahshudra Hindus who had fled from East Bengal after the Kalshira massacre. Having lived together in the same colony and going through the same travails, they had shed their ill-will towards the people from the upper castes. Moreover, Aparajita had already been known as Opudi to all because of her work in the Association. The *gharamis*[29] came forward to assist the people in distress. Sisir took their help to get his hut repaired. When the restoration work was partly completed, Opu and Madhuri entered their hut. She unchained the trunk with the key and dragged it out, and then Sisir and Opu lifted it upon the cot using their whole might. After opening the lock, she tilted the trunk and drained the water out. All the contents had become completely soaked in water. They were shocked to find that the currency notes and hut-purchase deed kept in a jute bag had become like wet paper pulps. The condition of their passports was also bad; almost nothing was legible in them.

"Opu, what will happen now? I have lost all the balance money I had after the purchase of this hut. We have lost all our deeds, passports, and certificates."

Hearing this, Madhuri became nervous and began to cry, "What will happen to us now? Now the Indian government will not allow us to remain here. There is no proof that we came here with a visa."

"Ma, control yourself. That visa would have expired after a few days. The problem is we cannot now surrender the passports to the office of the D.M. We cannot apply for Indian citizenship. Keep these in the sun. I shall go to the DM office tomorrow. Numbers of the passports are still somewhat legible."

"Halo, Mr, listen, please," Madhuri addressed her husband from the kitchen. "All the stock of rice and pulses kept in the *matka*[30] have have become unfit for cooking."

---

[29] People engaged in the profession of raising huts with bamboo, chanch, hay, or tin.

[30] An earthen vessel for storing water or food grain.

"But how shall we buy rice? All the notes have become unusable."

"Don't you have any money in your purse?"

"That is what I am saying. The few notes I had are spent on buying coir ropes and nails for house repair and payment of labour charges. Now we have no cash on hand. Oh God, what shall I do now!?"

"Let me see." Opu remembered in a flash that she kept her side bag hanging on a protrusion of the bamboo chanch of the interior partition. "Lo, it is there, and it is dry!"

Opu thanked God and found that her original certificates were there, among a few other things and ninety rupees in cash. She had earned the amount by giving tuition in the last two months. She handed the amount to her father. Sisir felt happy that his daughter was looking after her parents as good as a son.

Chapter Five

5.1 Opu finds her Rabi dada

"Who is Rabi?" Madhuri questioned Opu, pointing at the name signed in ink on the first page of a copy of Anandamath. She was surprised to see that Opu had carried a storybook in her side bag all along from Sandwip instead of packing her box of cosmetics.

"Why? Rabi is the name of Rabi Thakur. I mean Rabindranath Tagore."

"I know. We have read his poems in every class. Don't tell me that he has signed this book. He died when you were in class five. The classes of your school were suspended to mourn his death. But the date below this autograph is of 1942. You were then in Banaripara. Which Rabi Thakur gave you the book, Opu?"

"He is the son of Biren kaka," Opu gave in. "I met him in Barishal. He used to escort me from the school. His full name is Rabindra Guhathakurta. Are you satisfied now?"

"That was in 1942. But why are you carrying the book even now? Why?"

Opu remained silent. How could she say how much she loved this book gifted by Rabi dada! As she was growing older, she got more and more attached to his memory. The way he fought against the police was etched in her mind. In her dreams, she would see the lynching scene time and again and would break into tears. Sometimes, when her mind was free for a detour, she would enjoy recapitulating the time she spent with him by the side of the pond, below the Palash tree, and on the meandering village path, playing hide and seek with him. Her mother had no idea how happy she was at Banaripara!

"This book inspired our freedom fighters. It contains our national song. This copy is priceless to me as one freedom fighter gave me this book with his autograph on the day of his arrest." Opu said respectfully.

"I see. So, where is your freedom fighter now? Has he become a minister?' asked Madhuri in a shrill voice.

Opu remained silent again. Her mind had started travelling back in time. Kanak aunty and Sodu aunty used to exchange glances with each other whenever they saw Rabi and Opu together. Kanak aunty had also witnessed how Rabi had felled the huge daroga after he kicked the aged Congress leaders down from the dais. She used to refer to Rabi with an admiration for his valour. She used to tell Sodu aunty that she would prepare two asanas—one for Rabi and the other for his wife.

"Let him come out of jail, then you give them whatever you want," Soudamini said, glancing at Opu.

When her father went to Nabadwip to attend the marriage of Sagar didi, Kanak aunty had given him one aasan; its body fully embroidered with yarns of different colours retrieved from the borders of old cotton sarees, making it a beautiful work of art. She told Sisir that this was her gift for Opu whenever she got married. Sisir had carried the aasan in his bag to Silchar, sacrificing space for an additional dhoti.

One day Sisir showed it to Madhuri.

"Boudi stitched this aasan for Opu, working for three months. Her name is embroidered at the right corner.She should sit on it on the day of her *ashirbad*[31]."

"But will that day ever come in her life?" asked Madhuri.

"Shall I look for a groom for your daughter? We could not get a suitable boy in Sandwip after the massive exodus began from the island in 1947."

"Who will marry her now after she lost her honour?" Madhuri expressed her hopelessness.

"Three years have passed. If we do not tell others, nobody would know of it." Sisir spoke in a low voice.

"Don't you know that truth comes out at the most unexpected moment, from unsuspected quarters? Opu will never like to hide the truth from her would-be husband," Madhuri said.

---

[31] Blessing; a ritual before and after one's marriage when parents and senior members of a family bless the bride or bridegroom or both.

"Then what should we do?" asked Sisir. After a pause, he answered himself, "We can approach some liberal young man who will agree to marry her with full knowledge just as many youths came forward to marry young widows in the past." Sisir again began to argue with himself, "But if we reveal the secret to one, it will be known to everybody in the marketplace. Then not only her marriage will be in jeopardy, but her social reputation will also suffer a permanent dent. It will then be impossible for her to pursue an honourable profession and lead a decent life."

Madhuri intervened, "At Nabadwip, you had met a youth named Rabi. He was incarcerated for taking part in the movement of 1942."

"How do you know all that?" asked Sisir.

"Opu has told me." said Madhuri. "I think Opu loves this boy from her Banaripara days. She may not agree to marry any other man."

"How can she be so choosy when she suffers from such a big stigma?"

"Stigma or not, she would not agree to marry any other person. Check my word in future." Madhuri said emphatically.

"But where shall I find him? He has been untraceable since then." Sisir's voice betrayed uncertainty.

Opu was getting involved more and more in the work of the colony welfare association. Her educational background, free and rational mind, and selfless service were a source of strength to the residents of the colony. She could draft their petitions in English. The language continued to be used in all governmental work as the colonial legacy. She could talk to the S.D.O. or even the D.M. in a sophisticated way; they too liked to talk to her. She represented mostly for improvement of sanitation, supply of piped drinking water and provision of *pucca* drainage and roads in the colony. The colony was fast degenerating into an urban slum. The town's municipal administration was reluctant to provide the civic amenities as the government had not recognised the colony on the government land. Before the municipal election, the candidates became active in the colony to enrol the refugees on the electoral roll. Congress, being the party in power, opposed the move and sided with the people of Assamese origin. The refugees who had obtained a ration card applied for enrolment and got their names on the voter list with the help of Hindu Mahasabha and the Communists.

were enrolled in the electoral roll of the Lok Sabha and Vidhan Sabha elections of 1957. In subsequent municipal elections, all the refugees got their names included as they had already stayed for more than six years in the colony. The self-declaration of the applicants who did not possess a school leaving certificate was considered adequate in the prevailing situation. Most of the housewives, who were known by the identity of their husbands, never obtained any document in their own name. But the universal adult franchise demanded the inclusion of women on the voter's list. Opu pursued the officers to get the name of their entire family, included in the voter's list.

The influx of refugees had increased the population in Tripura, Assam, and West Bengal. The number of voters had swelled, and the voice of the refugees could not be ignored any longer. The permanent inhabitants, however, opposed the inclusion of new names on the voter list and stalled the process, wherever they were strong.

One day, when Sisir had gone to school, and Opu had also gone to town to take her coaching class, Madhuri was busy in the kitchen, preparing the masala paste on a slab of stone. She put her hand in an earthen vessel kept atop the kitchen shelf in search of some ginger pieces. Her hand touched the cold body of a living being. And before she could withdraw her hand out of the vessel *shshsh* she was bitten by a snake.

It was a venomous snake that came from the river during the flood and found the earthen vessel above the water level suitable for its cosy retreat. There was no doctor around to help her. The uneducated women in the neighbourhood wasted precious time calling a quack to perform some unscientific treatment. When Opu returned home from the coaching centre, Madhuri had already bid goodbye to this unfriendly world.

The event did not make any news even for the hand-written wall magazine of the colony. Every year, two-three people died of snakebite. What was so special or extraordinary about it? Even God does not give refuge to a person who is already a refugee. Only Sisir and Opu felt what big difference this bereavement would make to them.

Sisir had always received good support from Madhuri in sailing the boat of their married life. She was doing all household work without any fuss. She used to keep an eye on the needs of all family members, of her parents-in-law (when they were alive) and of Sisir and Opu. She possessed sound common sense and managed the domestic finance skilfully.

Opu began to double up as a homemaker as well as a bread-earner. Sisir was losing his stamina under the pressure of successive tragedies. If Opu could get the job of a teacher, she would have asked her father to retire and take rest. But the Student Union of Assam opposed the appointment of refugees against permanent vacancies in the Brahmaputra valley.

One day, when returning from her coaching centre, Opu slowed her pace at the turning of the road. A crowd of tea garden workers had gathered at the junction of the road, listening to a lecture. Opu heard a few sentences while wading through the crowd. Suddenly, a gut feeling seized her. She knew the voice. She could recognise its texture and quality anywhere in the world. Her feet dug into the road, and her eyes looked for the speaker.

Soon, the speech came to an end. The speaker got down from a stool. Before he melted into the crowd, Aparajita shouted out spontaneously in a full-throated voice, "Rabi dada!! I am here, Rabi dada!!"

Rabi was tall enough to spot the lady from a distance, but he was unable to recognise her. But the lady was confidently pacing up towards him, and her face was radiant with a smile. It flashed in his mind that a young girl used to address him as Rabi dada in his hometown Banaripara. She used to wear a frock and play hide and seek with him. What was her name? When the lady came almost within handshaking distance and looked up at her Rabi dada, it was not possible for him to make a mistake. "Opu! You are Opu!!"

It was pure joy when the two souls met each other. They did not know that they had so much love for each other, as they got separated before they could realize it. They began to walk together without saying any word. When the heart is full, words become superfluous. Our lips hesitate to shape the emotions into words as they would surely fail to be the true vehicle for the emotional content. As if floating in the air, Rabi and Opu went back for a while to the days of Banaripara when Rabi escorted Opu as her guardian via the meandering village path.

They did not know if they walked for an hour or ten minutes. They were only looking at each other and smiling when their eyes met. When the two reached the Tapoban colony, Sisir opened the door of the hut and was surprised to see them together. "Papa, can you recognise him? He is..."

"Rabi. I saw him at Nabadwip."

Rabi bowed and touched his feet and said, "Uncle, are you alright?"

"Young man! how can anyone of us be alright?" said Sisir. "But where have you been so long?"

"Uncle, I had been abroad for ten years. My parents were then in Calcutta. They had hired a house on Nalini Sarkar Street, together with other relatives. Some relatives were already living in a part of the house on rent since the beginning of the war. My father got a job in the Scottish Church Collegiate School."

"How is Sodu aunty? Biren Uncle? How are Kabi and Chhabidi?" asked Opu.

"Ma left us in 1957 after I returned. Father has just retired. Kabi has joined the Central Secretariat Service, and Chhabi is married to a businessman."

"They all have grown up!" commented Opu.

"So have you. You were only this much when you went to Banaripara." Rabi showed the measure by his hand. Opu smiled and did not object.

"What are you doing now? The country has become free long ago," said Opu.

"Yes, the country has become free only after people of the two faiths killed one another in lakhs. Lakhs of people of either faith became homeless refugees. But the leaders are still saying that India got her independence through non-violence. Coming back from London, I joined the Communist Party, and now I am a trade union worker here in the tea gardens. What about you?"

"I am doing fine. I did M.Sc. in mathematics from Dacca University and remained in Sandwip for three years, confined to the house. Having migrated to India, I am now applying for the job of a teacher for the last five years."

"She is fighting against her fate. Her mother died last year, and now she is also doing domestic work." Sisir continued, "You see, my brother could take the right decision at the right time. He could arrange the marriage of Sagar and settle in India just before independence. Sagar is also in Calcutta now. Her husband is now a gazetted officer of the West Bengal Govt."

Rabi remained silent for a few moments and said, "Is she happy?"

"Yes, she has become a seasoned housewife. She has two school-going children to look after. But our part of the family has faced endless disasters. By delaying our departure beyond 1946, we lost everything. Our house was burnt, our parents were humiliated, and our daughter...' Sisir left the sentence unfinished. He looked at Opu and resumed after a minute, "Those who left their home out of fear thought they would forget the past and build their life anew in India. We all came to this land thinking this to be our motherland, but we are made to feel at every step that after the partition, we are no longer the children of Bharat Mata. We are to apply for her grace to be taken as her foster child, and for the time being, the herd is attributed a common name - refugees." Sisir could not hide the bitterness in his heart. "My wife was born as an Indian subject of the British dependency and died as a refugee in Independent India, not as a citizen of the Republic of India. As a refugee, she lost her life by snakebite in this wretched colony without any medical care."

At this news, Rabi felt deeply sad and remained quiet for a few minutes.

"Uncle, you have correctly described our situation. Narrow-minded politicians had a law passed by the Parliament in 1950 to push back the refugees from East Bengal of Pakistan, terming them foreigners. The law[32] was recently repealed, as it was a bad law to segregate Pakistan from other countries. But their intent was clear from the beginning. The evicted and uprooted people, who came to the Indian Republic as refugees were to face the foreigner test and prove that they were forced to leave Pakistan because of civil disturbance. The refugees were, after all, Pakistanis. There was no law that a Hindu

[32] The Immigrants (Expulsion from Assam) Act, 1950: No. 10 of 1950. The proviso of Section 2 grants exemption to a person 'who on account of civil disturbances, or the fear of such disturbances in any area now forming part of Pakistan, has been displaced from...such area and who has been subsequently residing in Assam.'

Pakistani was not a foreigner. There was no law that a Bengali or Hindi speaking person couldn't be a foreigner. If anybody, be he a Hindu or a Buddhist, entered India from Pakistan, he must possess a Pakistani passport and Indian visa and must leave this country before the expiry of the visa. Otherwise, he would be held as an illegal migrant. Alternatively, he must surrender the passport and apply for citizenship. He must also substantiate that there was a civil disturbance in Pakistan. Ludicrous! Just think of it that a persecuted person would ask the Pakistan government to issue a certificate of riot, arson, and rape to the people who would emigrate! Then he would be allowed to live in a state of this country for ten years as a refugee. If all these conditions are not fulfilled, he would be treated as an alien. No state other than Assam raised these questions against the Bengali or Punjabi refugees and treated them as foreigners from the beginning. Most of the refugees came without a passport. What would they do now?"

Opu intervened at this stage and asked Rabi dada to dine with them. Having found the hero of her adolescence in such a dramatic manner, she wanted to spend more time with him. Sisir recalled the discussion he had with Madhuri a few days before her death and endorsed the proposal. Rabi was free in the evening, but he had not advised the comrade in charge of their party commune not to cook his meal. Other members would view it seriously if the food was wasted. After all, food was funded from the monthly levy deducted from the earnings of general members. He begged to be excused that evening and suggested that he would visit next Sunday and have lunch with them.

Sisir went out to buy biscuits for the guest.

"Promise that you will have lunch with us next Sunday without fail," insisted Opu.

"No promise. To me, a promise is a solemn affair. A lunch or a dinner does not merit a promise. Already some promises are weighing heavy on my life."

"Really? But you did not come forward to save me when they looted my virginity. You did not keep your promise. You must be habituated to that."

Rabi remembered that once, he had made that promise rather playfully. Did that girl take it so seriously that she called out for him at the most helpless moment of her life? How would he make amends for that breach of trust? He covered his face with his hands. That innocent girl had trusted him completely; she ran wildly after him when the police arrested him. But he had not come back to her after his jail term. He was fascinated by the beauty of young Sagarika and bound himself by a promise to her. Sagarika married an unknown person in his presence, whereas this girl spent the prime of her youth waiting for him. It was unlikely that she would marry anyone else for the rest of her life.

After taking tea, Rabi went back to his commune, brooding over these thoughts.

5.2 Will he or will he not?

Sisir had an interest in politics since his early life. Muzaffar Ahmad and Debajyoti Barman were his mentors, and Lalmohan Sen was his friend. Association with these people generated a love for reading books on the history of India. He made full use of his school library at Sandwip. At the age of fifty, he was still young to take interest in political and social upheavals. Whenever Rabi visited them, he took delight in discussing different problems of current times.

After exchanging initial curtsies one day, Rabi asked him, "Well, uncle, why are the Bengali refugees treated so unkindly by the Assamese people? A few years ago, were we not the subjects of the same king or queen? Did we not fight together for our freedom?"

"That is a good question," replied Sisir patronisingly. "We are to look for the answer in the history of last two centuries. Assam was an independent kingdom during the Muslim rule in India. But in 1786, if I remember correctly, an Ahom prince invited the British from Calcutta to save them from internal feuds.[33] After an intervention by the force of the Company, peace was temporarily restored. But when the land was occupied by the Myanmarese, taking advantage of the internal feud in the Royal family, the East India Company returned to save its interest. They fought the invaders away and entered into an agreement with the king of Myanmar.[34] As the Ahom princes could not still settle their differences, the British took over the reins of administration in 1836. The Ahoms surrendered their freedom without any battle."

"But I read in history that the ethnic Kings of Kamrup were very strong. They had thwarted Bakhtiar Khilji and stopped the Pathans from occupying the North-East."

---

[33] Encyclopedia Britannica – History of Assam.

[34] The treaty of Yandabo, 1826.

"True. But within twenty-five years of Bakhtiar's rout, Ahoms entered the Brahmaputra valley from outside and captured the Upper Assam. These Ahoms were neither Hindus nor Buddhists nor spoke Assamese language. They were few but strong in combat. They checked Mir Jumla, the General of Akbar. They expanded into the lower Assam after two hundred years by defeating the local kings. Over a few centuries, they gradually adopted the local language as well as the religion. They ruled for six hundred years, till handing over their kingdom to the British."

"Did the Ahoms go back to Myanmar after the political power was taken over by the British?" asked Rabi.

"The descendants of Ahoms did not go back. They had already mixed up with the original Assamese people, and they paraded themselves as Assamese, just as the descendants of Pathans and Mughals got mixed among the North Indians, Biharis, and Bengalis."

"If the Ahoms and the Koch-Kacheris could mix up," Rabi drew his conclusion, "the Bengali refugees would also get mixed up someday. After all, the population density in Assam is still much less than in the adjacent states. Like water flowing downhill, the population also flows from high to low density areas." After a moment he again came up with a question, "But why are they so hostile, particularly to the Bengali refugees?"

"Simple," replied Sisir, "The Bengali refugees have come as refugees, not as conquerors. Refugees cannot get equal treatment with permanent residents. Their resentment was not against the refugees of partition only. It is more deep-rooted. When the British took over Assam, many upper caste Bengalis entered the land, being the employees of the Company. They were already accomplished in English and naturally filled the second-tier administrative posts, making the Assamese unhappy. On the other hand, Bengali peasants were invited at the same time by the Assamese landlords to till their land. The Assamese people had resentment against the *Chhota sahibs* but not against the Bengali peasants. They are now known as Bengali speaking Assamese. The resentment of the ethnic Assamese was also on account of making the Bengali language the alternative official language for local administration and the medium of instruction. They did not get justice as the administration was controlled from Calcutta. This is the root cause of their hatred against the Bengalis."

"Uncle, it is most unfortunate that refugees from East Pakistan are today facing such resistance from the local people here."

Rabi said that many Bengali pilgrims visited Kamakhya temple in days of yore, but they never reported ill-treatment from the Assamese. The rural, agrarian people had never fought each other on the issue of language or religion. They were like two sisters. Then what went wrong recently?

Sisir tried to do some soul-searching.

"After a few years of British take-over, Assam was given the status of a province under a Chief Commissioner.

"From the beginning of the twentieth century, it all began with Lord Curzon. In 1905, when Bengal was divided on communal lines, Assam was appended to East Bengal to constitute one province. On the one hand, Bengalis were agitating against the Partition of Bengal, and on the other, the Assamese were unhappy to lose their separate identity.

In 1911, the Partition of Bengal was annulled, and Assam got back its status as a separate province. But the damage was already done. Bengali was introduced as an official language in Assam, and even when Assamese replaced Bengali after Independence, Bengali continued to be used in court and academic spheres."

"Now, I am getting a hang of the dialectics of the Assamese-Bengali relationship," said Rabi. "The subjects of the subcontinent began to look for political power. Morley-Minto reforms and Montagu-Chelmsford reforms introduced the Indians to democratic governance to a limited measure. People gradually realised that finally, the British would transfer power to the people of this country. The aspirations of the people rose to be self-governed, i.e., a homogenous group of people would be governed by the representatives from the same group."

"For one hundred years, the peasants of East Bengal went to Assam ceaselessly, irrespective of their religion, to till the fertile land left unused by the local inhabitants. They did not face any problems from the local people nor any threat to their lives. But from 1946, the Muslim League government of Bengal encouraged the Muslim peasants of East Bengal to move into Assam in bulk so that a part of it could be claimed for Pakistan. Migration became politicised since then. But I find that the Assamese people did not seriously object to these influxes even at that time."

"I understand that the induction of Bengali peasants and Bihari labourers was generating wealth for the Assamese. They were like a bank of cheap labour. As such, there was no clash of interest at the beginning," Rabi said like a communist leader. He continued, "But the influx of Bengali Hindus from East Bengal after 1946-47 unnerved the indigenous Assamese middle class. They became worried about maintaining their numerical superiority. To ensure this, they promptly allowed the Bengali dominated Sylhet District to join Pakistan[35]."

Opu was busy in cooking during the time, but she was also listening to the discussion from the kitchen. It was the first day she was cooking for Rabi dada. She had a feeling of excitement within herself. "Will he like her cooking? There are subtle differences in the recipe followed in Sandwip and Barishal."

So long as her mother was alive, Opu did not prepare lunch or dinner. For the last one year, she was cooking food but knew that her preparations fell far short of the standard of her mother. She left them so untimely.

When the two men were halfway through their lunch, Opu could not resist asking, "How is food? Is it good enough for eating?"

"Oh, superb! I have not eaten such food for years."

"But you didn't say anything till I asked."

"I thought Kaka babu should have the first say."

Everybody burst into laughter at his extra politeness.

"To speak the truth, I am eating such preparation for the first time after I left Calcutta. For the last two and a half years, every day, I eat in our commune rice and the same watery pulse, and either one egg or a small piece of fish in curry. There is hardly any spice or any variation."

"Rabi dada, hereafter, you will have lunch with us every Sunday. We do not eat many items, but I can serve you some items of shrimp or Ilish."

Rabi smiled in agreement.

---

[35] Encyclopedia Britannica: Assam since Indian Independence – 'With the partition and independence of India in 1947, the district of Sylhet ... was *ceded* to Pakistan.' Italics added by the author.

After the two had finished their meal, Opu removed the plates and went to the kitchen to take her own.

Sisir seized the opportunity to talk to Rabi outside the hearing range of Opu. He asked Rabi about his plans for entering a family life. Rabi was about thirty-seven years old. Though late, he could still marry.

"You are a handsome man having good health. You belong to an educated family. When I saw you for the first time in Nabadwip, I learnt from my elder brother that you had gone to jail for three years taking part in the August Revolution. My brother should have chosen you for Sagar. As that did not happen, may I select you for my daughter?"

Rabi knew that he liked Opu but didn't know if Opu loved him. He had loved Sagar and took a vow not to marry any other woman. What should he do now?

"What are you thinking? Make up your mind."

"I want to discuss the matter with her. Uncle, I cannot marry her, just because you have selected me for her."

"Before her death, Opu's mother told me that Opu might not marry anybody except a boy named Rabi. She had not seen you but must have heard of you from her," Sisir tried to convince him.

"Uncle, why are you insisting on marriage? We have been friends since our teenage days. Let us be friends for life. I shall stand by her all the time."

"Papa, are you over with your serious discussion?" Opu entered the room after finishing her meal. "Leave him now. He has to walk down to his dorm."

"He wants to talk to you."

"Okay, papa, we have grown up enough to talk to each other. Don't worry."

Rabi had already stood up. "Let me go with you up to the main road.," said Opu. "Papa, I shall be back in ten minutes."

Opu went out with Rabi. After a while, she wanted to know what Rabi dada would like to say. Rabi was in two minds. His heart was prodding him to go ahead and accept Aparajita as a life partner. But his conscience told him not to break his vow. A vow determines the strength of one's character. Sometimes vows are religious, sometimes temporal, or worldly. Whatever it may be, a vow must be kept at any cost. If a vow is broken, one becomes a liar to oneself. He loses self-respect in his own eyes. Rabi would not be able to cast himself in that hellish existence.

Opu understood that there was a dilemma in Rabi's mind. What was the dilemma in his mind? Was it regarding her chastity? Her maidenhood? God, that was the only thing she hated to hear from her idol. He must be above such petty, masculine ideas. He could not be a prude. She prayed to God silently. Let him not marry her for any reason other than this.

"Opu..."

Opu looked up. Their eyes met. They were calm like a deep sea.

"Yes, tell me."

"I realise that you have some emotion for me in your heart. Of course, you have not told me that through words. But I could feel it when you shouted for me at the crossing of the road, where I was addressing a crowd. Your high-pitched voice reached my ears and went through my heart as if somebody in search of me for many years had suddenly found me by the wayside. Your uninhibited call for me exposed in one moment how the skylark called for its mate from the high reaches of the sky.

I had met you about twenty years ago and took you as a playmate. But now, at this age, I cannot wish away the feeling as adolescence infatuation. I must say I am also feeling deep love for you."

Opu was listening intently, holding her breath.

"Uncle gave me the offer to marry you. But...'

"But...?" Opu turned her face and prepared to go back. "But you didn't accept it."

"Please listen to me. Opu, if you want something, I cannot refuse you. I love you very much. But..."

"But you will not marry me because once I was raped."

"No!" shouted Rabi. "I didn't say that."

"You are a freedom fighter. How will you say that? Please don't say anything. Please don't break the image you have in my mind. Let me go."

"No, you will not go without hearing me." Rabi took Opu's hand in his. "I never had any such thing in my mind."

"Then what?"

"Listen, Opu. We met each other long back, about twenty years ago. During this gap, many things happened in our lives. After being released from jail, I met a beautiful young lady who proposed to me. I gave her my word that I would marry her after the country became free and that I would not marry anyone else. Finally, the marriage did not take place. But I am still bound by the latter half of the vow."

"But you could have met her and settled the matter. Is she also not married?" Opu queried.

"She married even before the country became Independent. She was not bound by any vow," clarified Rabi.

"Then meet her and get yourself freed from your vow."

"I shall do that when I meet her. But I have no contact with her." Rabi exposed his helplessness.

"What will you do now?"

"Do you want me to break the vow?" asked Rabi.

"No, I don't. Then I shall not be able to respect you."

"Then what will happen to us?"

"We shall not marry till your vow is discharged." Opu asserted firmly.

"Can we remain as lovers, betrothed to each other, yet to be married?" proposed Rabi.

"Yes." Opu agreed. She would be happy with his companionship. Rabi pressed her hand in confirmation and joy. They bade goodbye to each other.

Opu could not ask him who that lady was. It would be unethical to pry into his privacy. He would tell her about the lady on his own, someday.

5.3 Opu moves to Tezpur

The Government of Assam passed a law in 1960, declaring Assamese as the sole official language, English being granted life for a temporary period. The agitation launched by the Assamese speaking people in the Brahmaputra valley could be quelled by the passage of the Act. Some Assamese people laid down their lives and became martyrs for the cause of their mother tongue. *'But why did it take eleven long years,'* Sisir thought, *'for the Assam government to pass the Act?'*

The Bengali people of the Barak Valley launched a counter Satyagraha to protest against the arbitrary derecognition of the Bengali language altogether. Aparajita joined the protest. Her forceful speeches in the street corner meetings drew large crowds. In Sandwip, she had heard the speeches of Muzaffar Ahmed with her father and learnt to use sarcasm as a formidable figure of speech in her lectures. The bitter experiences of her life and the deceptions practised by the politicians provided enough fodder for her. Of late, she could further improve her arsenal through her discussions with Rabi dada.

On the nineteenth of May, a dawn-to- dusk hartal call was given by the Cachar Gana Sangram Parishad. Opu went out early in the morning on a long protest walk with her comrades. Similarly, different squads of agitators started picketing before the government offices. The student unions had taken care that no school or college students attended the classes. The government had already announced the repressive measures on the line of the British government during the non-cooperation movement. Much more than that, when the Satyagrahis sat on the railway track at Silchar station, the government deployed its para-military force at the railway station. An agent provocateur was used to put fire to a govt truck in front of the station. On this plea, the armed force opened fire on the non-violent Satyagrahis inside the station and killed many of them. Many were beaten with the butt of rifles. The entire platform became filled with the screams and groans of the injured. Those who could escape by jumping the fence spread the news to the people outside. The mob then started pelting stones at the policemen and their vehicles on the road. The district magistrate did not lose time to impose curfew in the city.

Opu came back home before curfew but did not find Sisir there. She became worried for him as Army jawans were marching on the streets. She cooked rice and fish curry for their meal at noon. She kept waiting for her father for hours, but he did not return also during the night. At 6 a.m., when curfew was relaxed, a few boys carried him seated on a chair to the door of their hut. He had a bandage on his head, and his body was wrapped by a bedsheet. The boys found him near the railway colony in the evening, crawling in an injured condition. Two boys recognised him as their teacher. The teacher was taken to the nearby Railway health unit, but it was closed at the time. The boys went to the quarter of the dresser and persuaded him to give first aid to their injured teacher. Sisir had received multiple injuries. He was hit by the butt and fell from the platform on the track. The dresser was initially unwilling to treat a person injured by the police, but the students promptly changed their version. They said the teacher fell from a rickshaw, which lost its balance at a pothole on the station road. The dresser cleaned the wounds and bandaged them. He advised the patient party to go to the general hospital for an X-Ray. Since the city was under curfew, they kept him on a bench in the waiting space of the health unit and took care of his requirements. The boys left after telling Opu to get him treated by a doctor.

Opu nursed his father for two days. The injuries on the surface showed signs of recovery, but Sisir was becoming unconscious frequently. Opu went to a Bengali doctor known to them. The doctor examined the patient and advised immediate hospitalisation as there were chances of an internal haemorrhage. Opu feared that if Sisir were taken to the General Hospital, the police would bring a charge against him for rioting. But the police did not do so firstly because there was no bullet injury mark on his body and secondly because he was mostly unconscious, not in a position to give a statement. They were not in a hurry to step up the number of casualties.

"Opu, I am here." Opu found that Rabi was calling her from the reception. Rabi went to her colony in the morning, but a neighbour who knew him informed him that Opu didi had taken her father to the General Hospital. Rabi rushed to the hospital immediately.

"I was in Tezpur. The party did not allow us to participate in this movement. This is not a class struggle."

They reached the bed where Sisir was languishing. Opu touched her father's forehead, and Sisir opened his eyes. "Please take me home, Opu." Opu held his hand. Her voice was almost choked. The X-ray report confirmed their worst fears. For a few days, the condition of Sisir remained unchanged.

One day, when Sisir was in his senses, he saw Rabi standing behind Opu. He muttered, "Rabi, please marry Opu and look after her." Rabi came closer and said, "I will, uncle. Today or tomorrow. I shall always be there beside her. Don't worry about Opu. Please take rest now."

Sisir closed his eyes. He did not open them again. He was in a coma for five days and then left this world for his heavenly abode.

Opu wrote a brief letter to her senior uncle, informing him of the demise of her father. Sisir used to exchange letters with his elder brother, but he had stopped writing for the last one year. After ten days, Opu received two letters, one from Suresh and Kanak and the other one from her Sagar didi. Suresh and Kanak expressed their grief and asked Opu to leave Silchar and stay with them in Midnapore. Opu knew that they harboured genuine affection for her. As she became an orphan, they would gladly accept her in their small family. Sagar didi wrote a long letter, mourning the death of her uncle, who was very dear to her heart. She felt sorry for not keeping in contact with her uncle since her marriage. She requested Opu to come to Calcutta and spend a few days with them.

The two branches of the Nandy family had drifted apart from each other when Suresh decided to stay in India right from the time Sagarika got married and did not go back to Sandwip. Sisir was hurt when the elder brother abdicated his duty to their old parents. Sisir had to stay back in Pakistan till the demise of his parents and had to live the life of a refugee thereafter. Opu knew how much hurt his father was when the senior uncle passingly enquired about the amount received from the sale of the property.

Opu decided to remain in Assam and fight her own battle. She now began to look for a job outside Silchar. She lost her parents there, so she decided not to stay in Silchar any longer.

Finally, Rabi came to her rescue. He had worked in Tezpur for a few years and had contact with many people. In 1962, during the Chinese aggression, the schools, and colleges of Tezpur remained closed. Most of the people had evacuated the city, fearing Chinese occupation. When the Chinese finally withdrew, the schools were left with many vacancies. Rabi came to know that the post of Maths teacher of Bangali Balika Vidyalaya was lying vacant. He met the secretary of the school and checked up if they would appoint Ms Aparajita Nandy, M.Sc. The secretary asked him how soon she would be able to join. Opu reached Tezpur in three days with bag and baggage. She joined as a temporary teacher after a walk-in interview.

5.4 Noor grows up in India

Safiur and his wife were not happy with Anisur for marrying in a Bengali family. They ensured that their other sons married in some Ashraf family of Pathan or Turkic-Mongol origin. Once Anis came with his wife, Jasmine, to Calcutta to participate in his younger brother's marriage. He found that his father had prospered much more in the business of fresh fruits in independent India than he was earlier. He felt happy that their family could make such a turn-around after the incident of forty-six. But his wife felt neglected not being introduced as the 'Badi bahu' by her mother-in-law, and she decided not to come to Calcutta again. Anisur's visits to Calcutta became few and far between. After five years, he came to Calcutta once again with his child Noor to attend the marriage of his youngest brother. Noor enjoyed his stay in his grandpa's big house in Calcutta. Compared to their tin-roofed house at Patiya, this was like a palace.

The riot broke out in East Pakistan once again in 1964 on the fake report of the theft of the Holy Relic from Hazratbal mosque in Kashmir. The Hindus of East Pakistan were targeted once again. A few Hindus were killed, but many more were rendered homeless. Temples were desecrated, idols were broken to pieces, and priests were humiliated. Anisur led peace committee processions in different pockets, reciting the poems of Kaji Nazrul Islam. He used to take his nine-year-old son, Noor, to recite 'Kandari Hushiyar' before the crowds of people.

Jasmine Bibi's parents lived originally in a village named Uttarbhurshi, and the family members were supporters of the Awami League. The party was fostering Bengali nationalism. West Pakistani leaders used to suspect its leaders of hatching conspiracy against Pakistan.

Anisur continued his association with the National Awami Party of Maulana Bhasani till the middle of 1970. But when Bhasani withdrew his party from contesting the election of 1970, he joined the Awami

League led by Mujibur Rahaman. He got an opportunity to talk to him at a meeting and mentioned having studied at the Islamia College in Calcutta. The Shaikh smiled as he was an ex-student of the same college. Anis became marked as a muhajir supporting the cause of nationalist Bengali Muslims.

Trouble started as soon as the results of the election were declared. The Awami League won all the seats in East Pakistan except two and held a majority in the federal Legislative Assembly. Mujibur Rahaman was not sworn in as the Prime Minister by President Gen Yahya Khan. He was kept confined at an unknown destination by the army generals. The Muhajirs began to kill the Hindus in East Pakistan, presuming that all Hindus were supporters of the Awami League. Anisur realised that the political situation would go from bad to worse. He was already marked as a traitor by the Muhajirs. He left his wife in her father's ancestral house, picked up his fourteen-year-old son, Noor, and entered Burma through Cox's Bazar border. Overnight, they came by a motorboat to Sandeshkhali in India and reached Calcutta before the Muktijuddha broke out. Seeing them alive, Safiul was relieved of his tension for the safety of his eldest son and his eldest grandson in the middle of widespread trouble between the Bengalis and the non-Bengali refugees. The Jamaat-e-Islami was mostly constituted of the Muhajirs. The Razakars, too, began their offensive against Bengali Muslims. With the declaration of independence, the military offensive turned against all Bengalis — both Hindus and Mussalmans. The War of Liberation began with the war cry 'Jai Bangla', pronounced by Sheikh Mujib. A new country named Bangladesh was born out of the ashes of East Pakistan by the year-end. This proved to the world that a new nation could not be created just by enacting a law by a foreign ruler but by the struggle of people and is earned only through their sacrifice.

Noor stayed back in the household of his grandfather when his father went back to Chittagong suddenly. The war was already over, and the new government of Shaikh Mujibur Rahaman had taken over the governance of the new country. The rumours of genocide perpetrated by the Pakistani army and their lackeys were getting confirmed by the journalists of the world. One day, a man came from Patiya to the Rahaman House in Park Circus. He was looking for Anisur. They talked to each other privately for ten minutes. When the visitor left, Anis broke down before his father and sought his permission to leave for Bangladesh alone. His raped wife did not want to face her innocent son.

"It was all my fault. I thought she would be safe in her father's house. The Muhajirs targeted me for supporting Mujibur Rahaman. They would not spare my son too. But I could not foresee that the conflict would grow so big as to engulf the whole of East Pakistan. All the male members of her parent's family were killed, and women were physically tortured. If only I had brought her along with me, she would have escaped this fate. It was my fault. In shame, the mother does not want to meet her son. She would not be able to face his questions. This new country will be in turmoil for some more years. Abbajan, please take care of my son. I am leaving him in your charge."

Noor's grandpa and uncles assured Anisur that Noor was a member of the family and he would live in the house with all rights. Anisur hugged his son and left for Patiya to live with his ravaged wife forever.

Noor felt a stinging pain in his heart. How could he live without his father and mother? His mother loved him so much! How would she live without him? What did the soldiers do that she could not face his own son? To a fourteen-year-old boy brought up in conservative family settings, there was no clear answer. The taboo had left the facts of life indistinct, opaque, and mysterious. As a fourteen-year-old, Noor could only cry within himself for her mother, whose feeling of shame had overwhelmed her love for the son.

Noor's cousins, younger than him by three and five years, were studying at the Don Bosco's, but Noor could not get admission in that school because of his poor communication skills in English. But he was strong in mathematics, Bengali, and history. He got admission in a Bengali medium school near Sealdah. Although his uncles were kind to him and his cousins quite friendly, Noor could feel that the aunties were somewhat indifferent. They would not always remember to get his clothes washed by the maid or buy him new ones when they bought dresses for their children. Even for the stationery required in the school, Noor had to wait for their good mood to place his demand, lest his request would be met with chilling looks. Gradually he understood that his aunties used to look upon him as an undeserving shareholder of the family property in future.

Noor did well in his higher secondary examination and went to Maulana Azad College for graduation. In this college, Muslim students were in good number, and there was a namaz hall on the ground floor. Noor had studied in East Pakistan up to the eighth standard. He had seen the namaz facility in that school also, but he did not expect to see the facility in the government college of a secular state. He learnt that the college had the facility since its inception and the facility continued after independence without any problem.

Noor sought the blessing of his grandfather after he passed his M.A. in history from the University of Calcutta. Safiul asked his grandson if he would like to join the family business. Noor wanted to do research in history and be a doctorate. Safiul grinned as Noor talked like a middle-class Bengali intellectual and wanted to pursue an academic career.

"Do you want to be a professor like your maternal uncle?"

"Yes, if I can."

"But your standard of living will go down. Will you like that?"

"I shall be happy if I can pursue what I enjoy, grandpa."

"Okay. There is nothing wrong. But if you do not join the business, your uncles may not give you any partnership benefit. In that case, I need to think about how I can give you some share in lieu of your father. By the way, why don't you pay a visit to your father and take his blessings on your post-graduation? I may not live long. Tell him to come to India for once before I die."

Noor decided to go to Bangladesh to see his parents. They did not write any letters to him for the last eight years. If his mother was ashamed, why did his father not keep in contact with him? Noor had a few questions in his mind.

Noor did not have a passport so far. His grandfather had got his name included in the family ration card in 1971, although the family had hardly ever used the ration card. His uncles knew many people in influential positions, so getting a passport in a month was not a big deal for them. They presented the school leaving certificate as age proof and continuous stay in India for years in his grandfather's house in India as proof of residence. The passport was issued after police verification. Noor did not lose any time getting the visa for Bangladesh and booking a flight for Chittagong.

When Noor reached Patiya by taxi from Chittagong Airport, he was in for a big surprise. In place of a narrow rural road, a two-lane highway had come up within the last eight years from Chittagong to Cox's Bazar, and the look of Patiya had changed from a remote village to a semi-urban settlement. In place of bullock-carts, vans, rickshaws, sedan and hatchbac cars, and micros whizzed past either way every second. Noor appreciated the development that happened in Bangladesh after her independence.

Noor asked the cab driver to take a left turn after the police station, which he could recognise. After a minute's drive, he came in front of a two-storied house, where, he remembered, their single storey tin-roofed house existed. The Krishnachura tree planted by his father after his birth had grown huge, and its beautiful branches, with nicely down-stepped foliage, undulated in the wind. The tree had blossomed in red, tinged in yellow. Noor felt happy that the tree had accorded him such a lavish welcome.

Noor got down from the cab. At the sound of an automobile at the door, a woman peeped curiously from the first-floor balcony.

'Who is this woman?' Noor wondered. *'Hope my parents still live in this house!'* Hesitatingly, he walked inside the outer gate and called out, "Ammi! Abbu! Open the door."

He banged the iron rings against the wooden door. A woman with a veil drawn over her face asked, "Who? Noor?" and without waiting for his reply, she opened the door ajar.

"Ammi, this is your Noor."

"Noor, my son." The woman pulled him inside and embraced him.

The woman on the first floor hurriedly came down the stairs and exclaimed loudly, "Hey, old haggard! What are you doing with this man! Is he your boyfriend? How did you befriend such a handsome young man!"

"Shut up, Meher. He is my son, Noor. He is the eldest son in the family."

"Really! I never heard that you had a son. You are joking! Mian married me because you were sterile."

At this, Noor said, "Ammi, who is this woman?"

"Your father married once again. She is your stepmother."

"But father came back here to look after you."

"Yes, he has kept me in the household. He provides for my food and clothing, but after that horrible event, he could not sleep with me. I can't blame him." Jasmine said in muffled voice. Meher could not make out what Jasmine said. She raised her voice, "Don't tell me stories. Let him come back from the office. I'll see if he is his father, or he had told me a lie," said Noor's stepmother and went upstairs, fuming.

Noor sat on his mother's cot. He was reminiscing over his childhood when he was treated like a prince in this house. Presently, he was uncertain if he would be able to spend the night here. His mother had gone to the kitchen and returned with some *nadu* and *sandesh* for him.

"Amma, how could you totally forget me?"

"You are a fool, my son. You are my only son. How can I forget you? You left this country with your father before the beginning of the war. You had your grandparents in Calcutta. You could take shelter in your grandpa's house. Your father dropped me at my father's house. No member of the family is alive today except me. You remember your granddad and your uncle, don't you? All were killed. I was physically assaulted for days by the hungry army men. After the war was over, there was nobody to give me food. Had your father not come back promptly to save me with food and shelter, I would have died. In India, you were safer than in this country. Here, the Bangabandhu was killed within three and a half years in his house along with his family members. Your father said if you remained in India, at least one of his descendants would survive."

In the evening, his father returned from his office, riding a scooter. As he was parking the two-wheeler, a four-year-old boy ran towards him, saying, "Papa, papa, give me a ride." But Anis saw that a man as tall as him was sitting inside. As he raced to the door, Noor had already stood up. The two men saw each other, stood still for a moment, and then in a burst of emotion, hugged each other tightly. 'Abbu' and 'beta' were the two words that could be heard by the two women.

The young woman holding a one-year-old girl in her arms shouted at the peak of her voice, "Beta!? Mian, who is your beta? This man? You never told me that you had a son from that old witch."

"You never asked me the question, so I did not tell you a lie," Anis replied. "I knew one day you would come to know of him. But so long as he does not show up, you may not believe me." Anis turned his head to Noor, "Beta, why didn't you send me a letter before coming?"

"Papa, you didn't write to me in the last seven years. How could I guess in what mess you were? I thought I would give mom a surprise."

At dinner, Anis sat with his two sons and tried to put them at ease. The child was very suspicious of this sudden intruder from the vibes of his mother and would not agree to call him 'dada'. Noor told his father that he had passed M.A. and wanted to do research on the liberation struggle.

"Before the call was given for liberation, I was marked as an agent of India, and I had to flee with you. When I came back, the Awami League boys began to harass me for not joining the Mukti Bahini. But when they learnt that Nurul Chaudhuri was my father-in-law, they extolled the sacrifice of our family. By doing research on the liberation struggle, you can pay tribute to him."

"Papa, please come to see grandpa in Calcutta. He may not live long. He wants to see you."

"Can't say. When I came to Dacca in early 1947, I did not have an Indian passport. It was not necessary at the time as the country was not yet partitioned. Even up to 1954, nobody travelled with a passport. The border existed only in paper. Trains ran from Chittagong to Chandpur, where we changed to the river transport. We used to get down from the steamer at Goalando and again board a train for Darshana. A border slip was issued before one boarded the Indian broad-gauge train running between Darshana and Sealdah. People from either side travelled to the other side freely, and there was no ban. I visited my parents once in this manner after my marriage. Then I visited India once again in 1961 with you to attend the marriage of my youngest brother. That time I had approached some agents, who took the money and managed our passage to and fro smoothly.

In seventy-one, when I crossed the border twice, the situation was different. The second mass migration had begun. People entered India and went back through the border wherever there was a pore. Now we cannot travel without a passport from one country and a visa from the other. I was born in British India. I came to East Bengal before it became a part of the Dominion of Pakistan. I was charmed by this beautiful land and decided to settle here. Gradually the Pakistan govt gave me some facilities as a refugee from India. But I have no document with me of crossing the border and seeking refuge. If I apply for a passport now, somebody may raise a question. I have no dearth of enemies, and I tell you, all are Muslims. They may call me an Indian infiltrator and like to see me behind bars."

Noor left for India after three days, bidding goodbye to his Bangladeshi parents.

5.5 Noor falls in love

Noor was waiting in the lounge of the magazine section for his requisitions to materialise. A young lady was seen entering through the long entrance hall housing the card catalogues kept in six beautifully polished teakwood cabinets. Noor could see her from the sofa at the far end of the next room through the large opening in between. The gait of the young lady draped in a saree of khoir[36] colour, wearing a matching bindi, and two ethnic earrings were so stately that the elegance of the interior of the once-upon-a-time-residence of the governor of Bengal was not a bit compromised. Noor was spell-bound for a few moments. He lost his sense of etiquette that it was not gentlemanlike to stare at a woman. The lady sensed that she was perhaps under surveillance after she had entered the journals and periodicals lounge and quickly swiped her eyes around before turning right to the reading hall. And her eyes met Noor's.

Both became self-conscious and shifted their glances. The lady entered the majestic reading hall and turned to the issue counter on the left. Noor got up from the couch, leaving the magazine on the table. The books he had requisitioned ought to arrive by the time. He rushed to the counter. He could not afford to miss her from the range of his sight. The books reserved by her were quickly handed over to her by the counter clerk. She moved ahead through the aisle to the farthest end of the magnificent hall.

'How beautiful!' Noor exclaimed within himself. *'How can a girl have such a wonderfully long braiding!'* The black braid of hair had come down her slightly stooping back beyond her slender waist and lustfully flowing further down her bottoms to end its undulating journey at her calf. Left, right. Left, right. Wonderful!

---

[36] Khoir or khair is reddish-brown colour of the khoirwood kaath used to prepare a paan leaf for chewing.

"Sir, here are your books." Noor came back to this world in the harsh voice of the counter clerk, who stretched his hand for the reading room card.

Collecting his books, Noor proceeded hypnotically to the end of the hall, where a tall antic clock stood guard and alerted the absorbed readers, oblivious of the fleeting time with its sonorous chime. The long table at the centre ended two yards short of the wonder clock, and readers were sitting on either side with a shelf before them. Fluorescent lights were provided over the table with shade to focus light on the reading material. Season flowers spiked in decorative brass bowls were kept at an appropriate spacing to break the monotony of the long reading table in the centre. The hall was illuminated with beautiful chandeliers and other light shades bracketed on the side columns and inner walls.

The readers were busy with the books they borrowed; some were rummaging the pages to reach the portion useful for them, while some were going through a book line by line. Some were taking notes selectively in their diary, while others were copying out entire chapters in longhand in a copybook at speed enviable to a stenographer. The two flanks of the aisle had rows of four-seater tables at right angle to the central table. Beyond these rows, on either side, were spacious alcoves, partitioned by credenzas containing reference books and encyclopaedias, reserved exclusively for the research scholars.

Noor was not enjoying his surroundings like other days. His sole attention was claimed by the owner of the beautiful face, who had occupied a seat on a side table for four readers. Noor coolly went up the aisle till he found a seat vacant at the same table diagonally opposite to the young lady, the other two seats having been already occupied.

After a gap of fifteen or twenty minutes, Noor's eyes would move here and there and come back to the book only after taking a glance at the beautiful countenance across the low bookshelf on the table. Noor was an educated boy of high pedigree. He knew that it was not correct to stare at her directly, but despite his endeavour to avoid such a situation, his eyes met her several times before the girl closed her books, deposited them, and left the library. Noor felt guilty and could not concentrate on his work for over an hour and finally got up. The girl had reserved her books, and therefore, she might come the next day.

On the following day, Noor went a little early. No reader had occupied a seat at the table where they sat the previous day. Noor occupied the seat next to that special seat.

'Will she come and occupy the same seat today?' Noor said within himself. The ancient clock was counting the hours—eleven, twelve, one, two. *'No, she won't come today.'*

Noor got up and went to the canteen to quench his hunger. The canteen sold some à la carte foodstuff at a cheap rate. Although the canteen was meant for the staff of the library, the regular readers used to visit the canteen, as there was no eating joint nearby. Noor went back to the reading room with renewed energy. From some distance, he could see that his heartthrob had occupied her old seat and was casting a glance at the titles of the books on the neighbour's shelf. As Noor came from behind and drew his chair, the girl shifted her body weight to its centre of gravity and stole a smile red-facedly. It was not possible that Noor would miss the dolly opportunity to begin a dialogue.

"Hi, are you interested in any of these books?"

"No, no. I am only looking at that book... Gunnar Myrdal's Asian Drama. My professor has referred to this book many times in his lecture. I wanted to have a look at it, but my requisitions were returned with the remark, 'issued for the reading room'."

"I see. But if you want..."

Noor stopped abruptly as the library staff on watching duty came to them at an accelerated pace and said, "Silence, please." As Noor was a regular visitor, his face was well known to the staff. He whispered, "If you want to discuss any point, you can use the lobby near the entrance."

"Thank you." Noor opened a book he was reading earlier and tried to concentrate on its pages.

The young lady felt bad at the discomfiture of the tall, fair, courteous young man. After an hour, she looked at the fellow reader, suggesting if they could take a break for tea.

"My name is Noor Rahaman. I teach history in a college at Garden Reach and do research simultaneously," Noor introduced himself, climbing down the grand staircase facing the beautifully manicured lawn with beds of dahlia and chrysanthemum on its borders.

"I am Sahana. Student of M.A. Political science," the young lady said softly.

By the time they had taken a round of the library building, after taking tea, they had begun to exchange their views on the roles played by different parties in strengthening or weakening Indian democracy vis-à-vis the fate of democracy in Pakistan and Bangladesh. They began to take a second round as the discussion had enlivened, and both felt an urge to express their views on the subject. After they completed the seventh round, she noticed that sunlight suddenly began to dim, and it was going to be 5 p.m. They came back to their seats. The readers, sitting opposite them, were somewhat surprised by their sudden disappearance and equally sudden reappearance. Sahana picked up her books, deposited them, and went to the parking lot beside the lotus pond to avail her car. Noor bid her adieu from the top of the grand staircase and waited there till the green fiat car went out of his sight.

It was winter in Calcutta. But it bore similarities to the springtime in Europe. Flowers from Marigold to Roses, Dahlias and Chrysanthemums, Phlox, Cosmos, Petunia and Hollyhock etc., were blooming all around. The earth was celebrating its fecundity through the ripening of paddy and harvesting. Humans in Bengal held *nabanna* fest in their homes. Migratory birds were twittering in lakes and *jheels,* searching for breeding space. Located in a posh area of the city, the library provided an excellent space for young readers to take some time off the volumes of books. Noor and Sahana were often seen together moving in the sun amid flowers for one hour or so, and Nature conspired to fill their hearts with sweetness and love.

Sahana Chaudhary used to narrate the romantic developments in detail to her roommate Shefalika Sirkar. Sahana came from Guwahati to Calcutta to study at the Presidency College. Shefalika came from Ranchi to study medicine at the Medical College of Calcutta. She had a two-room flat on Central Avenue and shared it with an undergraduate tribal student. Her parents were owners of a well-known shop of surgical instruments below their flat. After the other girl finished her graduation, she went back to Ranchi. With her recommendations, Sahana met Shefali and became her flat partner. Although Shefali was much senior to Sahana, they became close friends because of their simple, straightforward nature. Shefali was a *Prabashi*[37] Bengali from Ranchi, and Sahana was an Assamese, originally belonging to the Khasi tribe of Shillong. She could speak fluently in Assamese, Bengali, Hindi, and English, apart from the Khasi language. Her father decided to remain in Guwahati permanently before Meghalaya became a separate state.

Shefali was listening to the story of Sahana with keen interest. "How could you go out with him for tea even before you were introduced to each other!"

"No problem. He had chosen his seat by my side, carefully leaving my seat and exposing his intention. But he appeared to be a gentleman of the first order and would have taken a month to invite me for tea."

"Hmmm, he must be very good-looking," said Shefali.

"Not bad. Then we started talking. He can talk only about history and politics. I asked him provocative questions, and he went on and on explaining the rationality of political situations. We went around the massive library building seven times, you know."

"Really! So you completed the saat-paak as well!"

"What is that?'

"You don't know saat-paak? What do you call it in Assamese when the bride and the groom go round the fire seven times? Saat fera? That is an essential part of Hindu marriage."

"But he is not a Hindu. He is a Muslim."

"Oh. Then why are you wasting my time? Let me sleep. I am to pick up morning duty."

Several days passed, but Shefali did not show any interest in listening to the story of the romance of Sahana. But she could feel that Sahana was floating in the air. When she used to come back from the library, her face glowed with delight, her eyes scintillated in ecstasy. And her heart might burst if she did not give vent to her emotion.

Being senior to her by three years, Shefali had a sisterly feeling for Sahana. One day she asked her, "Are you really in love with that professor?"

"I think, yes."

"What!? Do you not understand the consequences of such an affair?"

---

[37] One living away from one's home district, province, or country.

"What consequences? I think he, too, loves me. He is just taking time to propose. I cannot do anything unless he proposes."

"Yeah. But then it will be too late. I mean to say that you should come out of this relationship. Otherwise, there will be a huge social problem."

"Shefali di, what consequences you are talking about? Is this not a modern democratic country? What is the problem you are worried about? Why should society intervene in this? Two adult persons will marry of their own accord... what say can anybody have in this matter? Is there no law to protect the rights of individuals? After all, we have such a beautiful constitution in this country. Shefali di, you must go through Article 25 of the constitution."

"Sahana, my sweet sister, that is your forte. I feel that our constitution is too advanced for this society... much ahead in time as well. Don't you read in newspapers what atrocities take place in case of inter-caste marriages?"

"Oh, you are worried that I am from Assam, and he is from Bengal... is that the issue? I know there is a strong feeling against the Bengalis in Assam, but still, there are many cases of inter-state marriages. We'll manage."

"If you are so confident, I have nothing to say. But both of you must know the background of each other fully before you commit anything, okay?"

Shefalika closed the discussion for that night. "Good night."

The next day, when Sahana met Noor in the library, she wanted to know from him if her roommate wanted to marry a Muslim boy from Assam or Meghalaya, what kind of social objections might arise. Noor told her that it might vary in the relationship between the two societies. If the boy is an Assamese, the boy's family would not like a Bengali bride, but a Bengali boy may not face that problem.

"My mother was a Muslim from East Bengal, and she was not welcomed by my grandmother, who was a Muslim from U.P. But these problems remain mostly within the family. But in case the marriage is between a high caste and a low caste Hindu, it may flare up a conflagration in some states. West Bengal is more tolerant because of the political ideology prevailing now. But this government will not defend the marriage between a Hindu and a Muslim, lest it takes a communal turn and affects their vote bank. Hindu and Muslim organisations will oppose such marriage lest the strength of their community decreases on account of conversion. If your friend is a Hindu, she will face negativism from the religious as well as regional angles. These forces work against the spirit of the constitution. But Sahana, are you anxious about me being a Muslim?

"No, I am worried about me being a Khasi."

"We shall overcome the problem. Even if you are a Hindu, we can follow our religious practices independently. Akbar allowed his Hindu wife, Jodhabai, and King Ganesh of Gaud allowed his Muslim wife to follow their faiths. Ganesh's son, Jodu, was free to choose his own faith when he grew up."

"But when did I say that I am a Hindu?"

"What?"

"Yes, I am tribal. When Meghalaya state was formed, my father, a senior govt officer in Assam, did not go back. But you are correct in saying that children should have the freedom to choose their faith. Till they become a major, they should be treated as having no religion. Do you agree?"

"I do. Will you now marry me?"

"Yes, I will," she confirmed unhesitatingly.

PART TWO

ALIENS OR INDIANS?

Chapter Six

6.1 The purge begins

C. 2014. A few men gathered in a corner outside the Nagarik Sahayata Kendra[38] with a microphone; they pulled a bench from a teashop and connected the microphone with the switchboard of the shop without seeking any permission. *'Halo one, two, three, four microphone testing...'* The testing went on for some time, irritating the people around. The men were carrying flags and banners of a student union.

Like many other people, an old man of eighty-eight was coming towards the NSK office. Immediately some touts approached him for unsolicited assistance. Some offered to get the Gram Panchayat certificate, while some offered to produce a copy of the electoral roll of 1967, and some others offered a package rate. Scornfully ignoring them, the old man went inside the NSK office.

One of the Union members raised a slogan, and the others shouted the refrain in a chorus at the top of their voices.

Leader – Assam is for the Assamese!
Chorus – Yes, yes, only for the Assamese!
Leader – Drive out the infiltrators!
Chorus – Drive out! Drive out!!
Leader – Who is Hindu!? Who is Mussalman!?
Chorus – Non-Assamese dur hato!! Hindu ho ya Musssalman!!
Leader – Infiltrators and illegal migrants...!
Chorus – Get out, get out!!
Leader – Bengalis from Bangladesh!
Chorus – Go back to 'ur own desh.

---

[38] Citizen's Assistance Centre.

After two-three rounds of slogan shouting, the leader stood up on a chair to address the gathering at the end of the slogan-shouting session. One of his followers announced that their leader would now make an address to the public, and he asked the crowd to cheer him...

"Dear brothers and sisters!!

We have come to tell you a few words of grave importance. We are now in the climax of our final struggle. In the past, we remained united during our movement, and we achieved success. It is necessary that we remain united now to achieve our goal. Friends, our ultimate destination is a strict implementation of the Assam Accord. We want a foreigner-free Assam.

I shall not take much time of yours to recount the long history of our struggle. At the time of Independence, not only the Punjab and Bengal were partitioned, but Assam also had to sacrifice its Sylhet district. Streams of refugees from East Pakistan entered West Bengal, Tripura, and Assam. It was but natural that West Bengal would receive the maximum number of refugees. But the states of Assam and Tripura, having long borders with East Pakistan, were also subjected to this burden of refugees. From the time of the Partition, Assam raised her voice against the dumping of refugees in Assam. These refugees were mostly Bengali Hindus. The sudden increase in their number threatened our culture and, more than that, our employment opportunities. The central government did not make any sincere attempt to distribute and rehabilitate them in other Indian states proportionately. The population of Assam now comprises the Assamese speaking Assamese, the Bengali speaking Assamese, the Bengali speaking Bengalis, the tribal Assamese, and others like Marwaris, Nepalis, and Biharis... mostly Hindi speaking people.

Because of the surging population of non-Assamese groups, we, the Assamese people, have been cornered in all walks of life. The Hindu refugees did not have any land, so they started sending their children to schools and colleges. This new generation of boys and girls is capturing all the white-collar jobs. If our boys and girls do not get jobs through competitive exams, what will they do? If the business is monopolised by the Marwaris, how will our men prosper? If the Bangladeshi and the Bihari labourers occupy the labour market, what will our poor people do? We have launched a prolonged agitation for six years from

1979. We have also boycotted elections for the Parliament and the Assembly. All along, our motto was Detect, Detain, and Deport. The Central Government finally yielded in 1985 and agreed to detect and declare all Bangladeshi migrants as foreigners, delete their names from the electoral roll, and detain them.

We demand that these foreigners be deported from the shore of this country altogether. We made big concessions when we agreed to give citizenship to the people of Indian origin who came before January 1966. Those who entered after 1965 but before the twenty-fifth of March 1971 may get the refugee status if they prove their date of entry and their regular stay in Assam. The latter group of people will get back their right to vote after ten years. For this, they are to go through the process of trial in the Foreigners Tribunal. First, they are to be declared 'illegal migrants'. Then the tribunal will make their recommendation to the registration authorities if the person can be treated as a refugee under probation or not. They will also decide if the person is an infiltrator or an unwanted foreigner.

Friends, you see, we made enough concessions. It was for the Central Government to take quick action and implement the Assam Accord, incorporated in the Amendment Act of 1985. But the Central Govt failed to gather courage for twenty-five years to implement this Amendment.

Enough is enough.

Now that our Assam Public Works body has made a PIL petition before the Supreme Court, our revered Chief Justice of the Supreme Court has given a judgment together with another judge to implement the Act within a timeframe.

Now that the party which has come to power at the centre is committed to the removal of infiltrators from the Indian soil, we shall install the same party in the state to act hand in hand and complete this exercise to take the Assam Accord to its logical conclusion.

The post of State Coordinator has already been created and filled up by appointing a senior IAS officer. We appeal to all citizens of Assam to cooperate with us. We shall see to it that no true citizen is harassed unnecessarily. But we shall also ensure that no *ghuspetias*[39],

---

[39] infiltrators

whatever be their religion or caste, remain in this state. We urge the government employees and officers inducted into the NRC not to show any mercy to the people who have come across the international border. They should keep in mind that if they drive out one trans-border migrant, they will secure one job for an Assamese. We shall keep watch on their work.

Let us remain united till we achieve our goal. Friends, Unity is our strength. We shall not rest till our goal is achieved. Thank you, folks.

Jai Bharat. Jai Assam."

Slogan-shouting was resumed by the cadre. After collecting two sets of forms from the counter, the old man listened to the speech with a poker face and proceeded toward his cooperative housing complex.

Malati was busy mopping the floor of the one-bedroom flat. An old lady was sitting on a chair, chopping some vegetables to keep her hands active.

At that moment, some groups of people were seen conducting a search operation against foreigners in the residential area on the other side of the road. The people who escaped or migrated from East Pakistan or Bangladesh since the partition were the targets of their ire. Unlike other days, some policemen were accompanying the group.

Malati came back to her mistress, her visage reflecting the sudden increase in the pounding of her heart. "Madam, what will happen if they come in and attack us!"

"No, they will not. After all, this is the capital city of the state. The government would maintain law and order. They will not allow them to kill us. They have to prove that we are foreigners."

The lady had told her during conversation that she was a teacher in a girls' school at Tezpur, and after her retirement, she came to Guwahati to stay there permanently. Rabi babu came to know of this self-financing scheme project on govt-allotted land for cooperative housing. They applied for two small flats. As the demand for one-room flats was low, they could avail two flats in the same block. However, the retired school-mistress did not reveal the sufferings and the misery she had passed through in the refugee colony of Silchar. She was now conscious of her elevated social status and was careful to maintain it.

"Haan, you are an educated lady. You can speak and write in English. They will not have the courage to send you to the camp. We are not *bhadramahila*[40] like you. All these noises are meant only for poor people like us."

"Malati, I do not mean that the sword is hanging only over you. We all are probably in the same boat. Which way the wind will turn, nobody knows."

"Madam, they are saying that the Bengalis who came before the *muktiyuddh*[41] of Bangladesh would be accommodated in this country as refugees, but no relaxation would be given to people who came after the twenty-fifth of March 1971, when the liberation war was declared. You have come well before that date. You are, therefore, on the safe side. But I was not even born in seventy-one."

Malati was born in 1982 in a village of Jessore. Unlike her parents, she was born in the maternity ward of the district hospital. Her birth was also registered in the municipality. Her Bangladeshi origin was, therefore, a verifiable fact. She was worried that if she was caught by the police, her antecedents could be cross-checked easily, and she would be deported to Bangladesh.

"What made you come over to India? Unlike the riots of 1946-47, 1950, and 1964, no major riot had happened in Bangladesh except the genocide of 1971. You could have stayed in the sole independent country for the Bengalis on the earth."

"Madam, we did not leave Bangladesh because we did not regard her as our own country. No, we were brought up singing the anthem, '*O my golden Bengal, I love you.*' There, everybody speaks, reads, writes, and sings in Bengali. I had studied up to class eight, and my husband had cleared the tenth-class exam of the Board. I was married to Sukhen Das of Sylhet in circa 2000. Our forefathers were persecuted during the time they lived in East Pakistan, although we did not face a similar situation in our time. But we had no means of livelihood. Although we were basically farmers, we had to sell our land and work as labourers on the land that was once our own. There were very few industries. We did not have regular work. We left Bangladesh for India to get some work. We hoped that the granny would allow us to stay with her when we were in distress. After all, only sixty-five years ago, India was the motherland of our parents."

---

[40] Educated, sophisticated woman, a lady.

[41] War of Liberation,1971.

"Will you return to Bangladesh if jobs are available there?"

"Of course. Who wants to play hide and seek with the police without committing any crime?" Malati was doing her work one by one while talking to her mistress.

Rabi babu came to meet Aparajita Debi and gave her some blank forms. He asked her to go through the forms carefully, fill up the same and attach all relevant documents. The old man said he would submit both the applications together after they were ready.

When he saw Malati, Rabi babu asked her if they had applied for citizenship. "If you want to stay in Assam, you must get yourself registered. Assam Police will arrest anybody if he has not submitted an application to the Panjikaran office."

"But, uncle, as we are much younger than those born in 1971, will they accept our application? Or will they immediately put us behind bars?"

Rabi understood that the common man's understanding of a situation was always the most pragmatic one. They would promptly work out the maximum individual sacrifice they would be called upon to make vis-a-vis the minimum common benefit they would derive for their group or class of people. After a lifelong struggle for the suffering people, he had turned somewhat cynical. Aside he told Aparajita, "About 3.5 crore people of the state would go through this citizenship ordeal because of people like her." Rabi could not suppress his bitterness; he told her aloud, "Lakhs of people who came before 1971 and are applying for citizenship, will be crushed in this rat-trap because they will not be able to produce some pieces of old papers."

He also added that his grandson would come to Calcutta from the USA, and he would spend a few days with him in the bungalow of his nephew. He wanted to submit the forms before going to Kolkata.

As he left, Malati asked Aparajita, "Madam, who is Rabi babu to you? He also lives alone. You say he is unmarried. But now he says that he has a grandson. Extremely queer and puzzling!"

"You don't bother about him', Aparajita rebuked her like a teacher. "Oil your own machine. Have you finished your work?"

Malati understood that her madam was displeased at her show of undue curiosity in Rabi babu. She completed her work without uttering any word and left.

6.2 The Indian diaspora

The year 2014 was crucial in Indian politics. The Manmohan Singh government was beaten at the hustings by the Bharatiya Janata Party and its allies. This was a strident version of the party previously led by Shri Atal Bihari Vajpayee. The new team of leaders used new ideas and idioms and captured the imagination of a large section of the Indian people. The number of followers increased everyday by leaps and bounds.

Soon after his anointment, the new Prime Minister visited the USA and found time to address a huge gathering of the Indian Diaspora in America from the Madison Square Garden in New York. He extolled the virtues of the non-resident Indians, their contribution in changing the outlook of the world about India, and her trained workforce and educated scientific community. The Indian Diaspora immensely contributed to the growth of the economy of the country they had settled in. The Indians who had accepted the citizenship of the USA were granted the Overseas Citizenship of India card so that they could commute to their former motherland without any embargo. They would not face any restriction in their movement or the acquisition of property within India any more than those imposed on an Indian citizen by a statute. The Government of India would examine if the dual citizenship facility could be extended to these worthy people, by which they would enjoy the citizenship rights in both the countries, choosing to exercise their voting rights only in one of the two countries.

The excellent oratorical skill of the new Indian PM overwhelmed all the people in the assembly and the Indian viewers of the television the world over.

Among the audience were four Indian Bengali boys and girls- Shrilekha, Roop, Choity and Babul. Common heritage and language brought them together. When they had an opportunity to meet as an exclusive group, they would enjoy talking to each other in Bengali, but as soon as any Indian from another state or a person from another country joined them, they would immediately switch over to English. They knew the language reasonably well and had acquired the American accent to a fault.

Among the group, Shrilekha was an American by birth. Her father, a Bengali originally from Mymensingh, had married a Scandinavian-American lady, but five years after Shri was born, the woman forsook them. Shri was brought to Calcutta by his father, and she grew up in her aunt's house and was schooled in a reputed institution. Although she studied in an English medium school, Bengali was her second language, and she had acquired proficiency in speaking, reading, and writing in Bengali from her aunt. When she came back to the States for graduation and further studies, she used to make friends with Bengali students from the Indian subcontinent to get an opportunity to rehash her knowledge of Bengali. But she was not a great lover of Bengal and her culture. She considered Bangladesh a backward rustic place and Kolkata a sub-urban, stultified, and growthless town. She liked the candid approach of the Bengali boys but could not bear their company for long. She thought they were more engrossed in the bygone days of the early twentieth century than in the modernity of the early twenty-first century.

On the other hand, Roop, Choity, and Babul were all from Kolkata, and they were Bengali at the core. On any pretext, they would start singing Rabindra-sangeet, recite lines of the poems written by Rabindranath Tagore and Nazrul Islam, and discuss the cinematic art of Satyajit Ray and Rituparno Ghosh. Roop was doing post-doc research in Computer Science at Pennsylvania University under Prof. Swarat. Shrilekha was working as a Research Assistant under the same Professor. Choity and Babul were relatively young. Choity was working in a multi-national IT company and came to America only six months ago. Babul was doing his MBA from New York University. He had met Choity in a musical function organised by the Bengali NRIs, whereas Choity met Shri on her arrival in New York with a recommendation from Mrs. Pramila Chatterjee, the Calcutta-based aunt of Shrilekha. Shri had fixed up a YWCA hostel accommodation for Choity and used to guide her to come over the early blues.

Shri introduced Roop to Choity, and Choity introduced Babul to others. After the speech was over, they rushed to the nearby Starbucks coffee shop. The applause for the speaker and the chanting of *'Modi, Modi'* was still reverberating over the length and breadth of the sprawling Square.

The speech of the new prime minister made a huge impact on Roop. He was keen to become an American citizen but hesitated to give up his Indian passport. In his family, the senior-most living member was a freedom fighter. The *Taamra-Patra* presented by the President of the Republic of India to his senior grandpa as a veteran of the August Kranti movement of 1942 adorned their drawing-room. The Prime Minister depicted his vision for the new India and charted out the path for development. He urged the Indian Diaspora to come to India and join hands with him and revive the past glory of the motherland of their forefathers.

Moved by his speech, Roop declared emotionally, *'I am now clear in my mind. No one can now stop India from becoming a developed country, a super-power of the world. We must go back now and take part in this karma-yagna.'*

Choity and Babul concurred. "Sir, when I complete my MBA, I shall go back to India. Just one more year, and by that time, there will be a beeline of American, Korean, Japanese, and Chinese investors for India. I shall definitely get a good job in one of these industries," said Babul.

"Ay, but don't sir me, please. I am your friend, not a teacher at your college."

Babul smiled and asked, "Can I call you Roop da? Like Ghana da or Felu da?"

"Yes, yes, no problem," said Roop. "Only do not call me Teni da. My nose is no match for his."

Choity and Babul burst into laughter. "You have such a cute nose. You cannot be mistaken for Teni da. *'Roop da'* fits you superbly as you are so handsome."

Srilekha became angry as the joke went over her head. Roop became conscious of her discomfiture. He got up to get coffee from the counter. Babul followed him to assist.

In western countries, friends do not buy coffee for one another. If a friend buys any foodstuff for other friends, others immediately settle the debt. When three/four friends travel by bus, everybody buys his ticket. Nobody expects their friend to pay for him. If, by any chance, one does not have the required coin, a friend may offer to help one out, but it is the duty of the recipient of the favour to return the same at the next meeting unfailingly together with profuse thanks. But the Calcuttans do not care for these niceties of social behaviour. Some Bengali friends always buy tram tickets for their companions or offer cigarettes to their friends before lighting one for themselves. The taker never considers this favour a debt, not even a gratuity to be acknowledged by offering thanks. In Calcutta, if four friends are in a coffee house and one of them orders *pakora*, all the friends share the pieces without waiting for an invite to share. Since one cup of coffee cannot be shared, the order must be given for all, or no coffee will be ordered. He will be branded as selfish if he orders only one cup of coffee for himself.

"I hope you understand that we are in a relationship," Shri asked Choity.

"I was just guessing," replied Choi.

"Yeah. Here people honour the relationships. Nobody interferes. There is no story of a triangle. I know that things are just the opposite in Kolkata. A love story will not be successful unless it is triangular. Here people grant enough space to a pair. You must understand."

When Roop and Babul came back with two trays, each holding two cups of cappuccino, Shrilekha opened her purse and settled the account with Roop, whereas Choity, a new arrival from Kolkata, just smiled at Babul for his pains and picked up a frothy cup to her lips as her natural prerogative. After all, young bachelors are born to be chivalrous to young ladies.

Shrilekha poured cold water to the enthusiasm of the three Calcuttans. "When did he ask the NRIs to return to their native country? He only asked them to invest in India. He is tingling them emotionally to secure an advantage for foreign investment in India."

She was right when she said, "The country is worried about brain-drain, but no politician will call these people back and provide them suitable jobs, research facilities, and social security."

"I shall not go to live in India, a Third World country," Srilekha said emphatically.

The face of Roop suddenly lost its radiance. Choity consoled him, "Roop da, you can take your time. There are many options. Even if you accept American citizenship, you will get the OCI card and go to India at will. There is little difference between the normal citizen and the overseas citizen if one is not keen to have political rights."

"You see, my senior grandpa was a freedom fighter, a revolutionary. When I think of him, I cannot decide how I shall give up my Indian citizenship."

Srilekha was peeved at these words of Roop. She got up from her chair, said, "Good night, guys," and left in a huff.

Three and half years had passed. Roop was still in America and had been to Kolkata at least once a year, but he did not see any major change in industrial growth. The country was busy fighting terrorism through spectacular military actions like the surgical strike. A major political initiative was taken to bring Jammu & Kashmir at par with other parts of the country. But where is the beeline of investors? There seemed to be hardly any change in the economic situation. Roop continued to be in the USA, and Shrilekha thought that Roop had turned over the India page.

Babul, Choity, and Roop met each other for the second time in a musical programme. Babul was curious to know about Roop's senior grandfather, and Roop always loved to talk about him. "My grandfather was late Kabindra Guhathakurta. His elder brother, Shri Rabindra Guha- thakurta, my senior grandpa, is still alive. He is the hero of my childhood. As he remained unmarried, he treated us as his own progeny. Whenever he visits Kolkata, he stays with us."

Roop told them about the incidents that took place in Barishal in 1942 and the incarceration of his senior grandpa for three years. When he finished the heroic tale, Roop became sombre and said, "But can you believe that this gem of a man is now subjected to a test for his Indian citizenship?"

"Why?" asked Choity and Babul.

"Because he was born in Barishal. Because after independence, he lived mostly in Assam. He still lives in Guwahati. My father requests him to stay with us permanently, but he will not. He cannot live as dependant on somebody."

"Yes," said Choity. "The government has launched a drive for registration of citizens in the state of Assam. My father appeared in some PIL cases before the Gauhati High Court. Now the highest court is deciding the dispute, and it is also monitoring the execution of court decisions. However, the Bengalis in Assam are spending sleepless nights."

Choity suggested that Roop da could discuss the problem of his senior grandpa with her father in Kolkata. He was a well-known advocate. Roop told them that he had booked his ticket for Friday. He would stay in Kolkata and Guwahati for a fortnight to help him. Choity gave him his father's address and the landline number. When Roop bade goodbye to his new friends, Choity and Babul exchanged their mobile numbers with him and hoped to meet again. When they proceeded to the metro station, Choity asked Babul what his parents did in Kolkata. Babul said that his father was a professor at Ashutosh College and his mother was a senior journalist with the biggest media house in Kolkata. His father was to retire after six months.

Choity asked him again, "What is your mother's name?"

"Why?" questioned Babul.

"Simple curiosity. A friend of my mom is a journalist of repute. She is working for The Telegraph. Her name is Sahana Chaudhary Rahaman."

"O my goodness! You are the daughter of Shefali aunty!"

"Yes, my mother is Dr. Shefalika Ghosh. But how do you know her?"

"She did the caesarean operation of my mother in Matrimangal to bring me to this world. They were close friends. My mother wanted that the operation should be performed only by her. She did an excellent job. My mother is so much full of praise for her."

They boarded the Metro train for New Jersey but got separated in the crowd.3

6.3 The Nostalgic couple

Sagarika was sitting beside her husband on the balcony of their house in South Calcutta. Satyabrata Ghosh was only twenty-four when Sagar was married to him. Back then, he was a young, smart employee of the provincial government of Bengal. When the family lived in Krishnagar, their daughter was born in 1952 and a son in 1955. Satyabrata wanted to bring up his children in Calcutta. When Sagarika's father fell sick at Midnapore and was shifted to Jadavpore in South Calcutta, Sagarika asked Satya to shift to Calcutta where the children would get a better education, and she would be able to take care of her parents. Satya was also tired of living in a mess for over fifteen years. He, therefore, rented a two-room flat near the Charu market. Bratati studied at Gokhale Memorial and Debabrata in Mitra Institution.

Before retiring as a Deputy Secretary in 1981, Satyabrata purchased an old house near the Rabindra Sarobar.

Debabrata grew up in the city to be a lawyer and made a name as a rising star in the bars of Calcutta, Patna, and Gauhati High Courts by dint of hard work and perseverance. He renovated the house of his father, built an upper storey with a staircase from the drawing-room and added a chamber to the ground floor for his office use. He got married somewhat late in 1987 to a lady doctor named Shefalika.

The two old people were talking to each other about old times. They had lived long enough; the husband was aged ninety-four and the wife was about ninety. Not only most of the contemporaries but also many members of their successor generation had left this world. Long-life was not really a blessing; the memories of those who left early hung heavy in their mind. If death was the destination of human life, many reached the touchline overtaking the co-runners who once began the race together. Many brothers, sisters, and cousins who were younger in age had overtaken them. But the most painful were the deaths of children whose life could not blossom to the full. They had a daughter, Bratati, who died at the age of nineteen in a road accident.

The two oldies, however, were not ruminating over any untimely departure of a kin. They were fishing in deep waters and recovering some treasures from the seabed, as it were. That day, for the umpteenth time, they were rewinding the event of their marriage.

"Everything happened so suddenly! One Saturday evening, I had just reached home for my weekend visit when my mother told me that they had chosen a beautiful and educated girl for me and I was to go to Nabadwip to see her the next day. I asked my mother why they were in a hurry. She told me that the parents of the girl came to Nabadwip to see if they could settle here after the Partition. They already had some relatives there. Our ancestral home was in Chittagong, and the girl's family belonged to Sandwip, which was a part of the Chittagong division. Because of all these reasons, my parents had chosen you as my prospective bride."

"But did they not tell you that I was working as a teacher for three years?"

"This was not brought to the notice of my mother by the *ghatak*. Perhaps, he was afraid that it would be treated as a disqualification."

"That is no excuse. Two years after our marriage, we shifted from the rented house near Patra Market to the newly built house at Anandamayeetala. The parents-in-law did not allow me to join the local primary school just across the road, although the school was set up at the initiative of my father-in-law himself. Nor did you take any initiative for my admission in Krishnagar Govt College for further studies. My aspirations to become a teacher came to nought after my marriage." Sagarika was in a mood to fight.

"Those days, people were conservative, by the current standard. When I did my B.Sc. from the Krishnagar Govt College, some unmarried girls were also studying with us in the college, but the girl students moved in groups, entered the classroom with the professor, and went out with him to the staff room corridor after the class. The side benches were conventionally reserved for the girl students. The boy students almost died to talk to them, but more than a year, or maybe the whole session, passed without any verbal interaction. But no housewife studied with us."

"Yes, housewives must be confined within the boundary walls of the house. They are to put on *ghomta* (veil) over the head to avoid the glances from males. That was the first lesson I was given in your house, which is to never remove ghomta before the Sasur, Bhasur[42], or other senior male kins. The housewife must not come before an outsider or unknown person. If she is to serve before any guest, she must increase the length of the ghomta to make herself *asuryampashya*, not to be seen even by the sun. You see, I was born and brought up on an island, running on the seashore and bathing in the sea. How difficult it was to accept these shackles for a free bird like me!"

"That's true. But your parents should have enquired about the kind of family they were sending their daughter to as a housewife. Every family has its own norms and traditions. These disciplines are for the common good of the family. My mother and the wife of my elder brother were also subjected to the same rules. Those days sons were taught to be obedient to their parents and be submissive to the seniors. It was not possible to do something different or exceptional for one's wife lest people taunted him as a henpecked husband. You were more advanced than the other members of the family. You were like a square peg in a round hole."

At that point, Shefalika joined them, and Padma, the cook, brought tea for them. Shefali asked the older people if they were feeling alright. She kept watch on the fluctuation in their sugar level, blood pressure, uric acid, cholesterol, etc. Under her care, the senior-most members of the family were hopeful of remaining alive for three/four years more and participating in the marriage ceremony of their granddaughter.

"Ma, do you like this tea? Padma has opened a new container today."

"Yes. This is top quality, Makaibari... Excellent!'

"Your mother-in-law is a connoisseur of tea. She is going strong because of this addiction," remarked Satyabrata with mild sarcasm.

"Since when are you taking tea, Ma?" asked Shefali.

"I started taking tea when I began teaching in the Banaripara school. We had a peon named Haru. Haru da used to prepare tea and serve us after the morning assembly and also during the tiffin break.

[42] Elder brother-in-law.

I found it quite stimulating to fight the morning yawns. Whenever he changed the packet, he used to ask me if the leaf was good. That was how I started paying attention to the different tastes of leaves of different gardens."

"Is this Haru the same man who came to attend our marriage?" asked Satyabrata.

"Yes. He was the only representative from the school. Haru da told my parents all that had happened in Banaripara after our departure. How the house was set on fire one hour after we left, and a riot broke out with the killing of Badal Majhi."

"I see. He had a chat with me before I was taken to the dining place. He appeared to be quite jovial and happy. But the next morning, I could not find him. He had a plan to stay in Nadia for three days and attend the reception at our house. But no one knew why he left Nabadwip unceremoniously. Nor did I see the young hero after we were led to the marriage venue."

6.4 Rising of bigotry

Noor and Sahana were preparing to celebrate their thirtieth marriage anniversary in their flat at Golf Garden. After their marriage, Noor had lived for a few months with his wife in their house in Park Circus. Very soon, he found that his relatives were not prepared to accept Sahana in the family when they found that Sahana was originally from the Khasi Tribe and did not know the *khandani* Muslim culture. The wives of Noor's cousins used to taunt his wife just as his aunties taunted his Bengali mother many years ago.

After working for a few years as a reporter for some lesser-known newspapers, Sahana got a job with the Statesman and was appointed as the paper's Guwahati correspondent considering her knowledge of the place, language, and her connexions in the bureaucracy. Noor was working as a lecturer at Harimohan Ghosh college in Garden Reach. He, too, joined a college in Assam. After working for five years, he realised that the governing body of the college would not confirm him as a permanent lecturer, and he would not be given any promotion. The relationship between various communities had soured so much over the Assam Accord that it became difficult for him to breathe freely. If Sahana ever mentioned that she belonged originally to Meghalaya or if Noor said he was a Bengali, they were certain to meet cold looks from the Assamese speaking people as if they had committed a grave crime by coming to Assam for their livelihood. All such people were looked down upon as outsiders, although, to remain on the right side of the law, they would use the term only against those who once lived in East Pakistan or Bangladesh. Their son was born in a Calcutta hospital in 1987. Sahana had taken a break to take care of her son and then joined the Statesman. After some years. Noor joined the Ashutosh College of Kolkata as a senior lecturer. Since then, they began to live in the middle-class locality of Tollygunge in a rented flat. When Sahana got promoted to the editorial team and Noor became an Associate Professor, they bought a flat in a housing society and settled permanently in Calcutta.

To celebrate their thirtieth marriage anniversary, they invited Shefalika and her husband for dinner. Sahana always maintained contact with Shefalika, whether she was in Kolkata or Guwahati. The Ghosh family always liked their company.

Noor had cooked mutton biriyani himself in his kitchen, and the *haandi*[43] was still on a slow fire in the oven, spreading the aroma of ghee, clove, cinnamon, cardamom, bay leaf, mace, nutmeg, rose-water, keora-water, and saffron all over. When Deb and Shefali turned up in the evening, the smell gushed out of the door to the delight of their nostrils. The prospect of approaching pleasure to their taste buds brought a smile to their faces.

"Welcome, Debu da, welcome, Shefali di," exclaimed Noor and Sahana in rapturous warmth.

"Congratulations, Noor bhai," Shefali came up to Noor, handing over a beautiful bouquet of orchids and gerberas. Deb wished many happy returns of the day while giving a soft hug to Sahana and handing over a beautifully wrapped gift box. The guests were seated on a cosy sofa in the tastefully decorated drawing-room. Sahana brought them sherbet made of roasted green mango as a welcome drink.

"Aahh..." the guests were visibly satisfied by the reception.

"So, how do you feel after completing thirty years?" asked the doctor.

"Not bad. Had I been a Hindu, I would have said, 'May you be my wife in my next six rebirths'," said Noor.

"Orre baba! One lifespan is good enough to spend with you. It's good that Muslims are not born again and again. It would be so boring!" remarked Sahana.

"Maybe you have already spent six lives trying to know each other, understand each other, and in this life, you have reached the culmination of your love," Deb conjectured.

"Haan, it looks like that. Otherwise, how could a girl from Shillong Hill fall in love with a fugitive Pakistani boy in Kolkata, born in distant Chittagong? God has designed the path of your lives in a manner that you two would meet each other on a given day, at a predetermined time in the National Library of Kolkata and fall in love," commented Shefalika.

---

43 Round cooking pot with a wide middle and a narrow top.

"As if you were eagerly waiting for each other," added Deb.

Both Noor and Sahana blushed, being reminded of their romance in the Belvedere. Noor wanted to change the subject and said, "You reminded me of my Pakistani origin. I had almost forgotten that. In fact, my grandfather told me always to say that I was an Indian. Once I got admission in the school, nobody questioned my nationality ever after. I, too, believed that if my grandfather, father, and uncles were Indians by birth, I could legitimately call myself an Indian. It is not necessary to tell people that my Pakistani mother gave me birth in a village near Chittagong in East Pakistan. No one really knows one's place of birth. That is what others had told the child."

"Why are you raising these unpleasant topics?" Sahana murmured.

"I am forced by the circumstances. Debu da knows that the party in power has a dogmatic view on citizenship. They call all migrants from East Bengal *ghuspetias* until the individual proves with document his Indian citizenship. A test case is being made out in Assam, taking advantage of the animosity of the Assamese against the Bengalis. Sahana was born in7 Shillong in the sixties. Shillong was then the capital of Assam. Subsequently, Meghalaya was carved out as a separate state. The Assam government would not give her the status of a citizen of Assam. My son was born in Calcutta when we lived in Guwahati. He has a birth certificate issued in West Bengal. But his father is not sure if he would be treated as a citizen or an illegal migrant when the test is extended to West Bengal."

Sahana was feeling uncomfortable since Noor was harping on the subject, spoiling the party mood. Sahana wanted to draw a curtain over the discussion. Shefali realized her situation and came to her rescue. She proposed that Sahana and Noor should visit their house on Sunday morning and discuss the subject with Deb, and presently, Noor and Sahana should sing a song in a duet. The couple agreed. They were trying to fight their worries away.

"That day, we two went to the garden and swung together in a swing. The ropes were decorated with flowers[44]." When the song was over, the guests offered warm applause.

---

[44] A popular Bengali love song by Tagore.

"Well, Debu da and Shefali di, may I serve the dinner now? Please come to the dinner table. I am serving hot biryani with galauti kabab."

The guests used liquid soap to wash their hands and took their seats. While serving the most favourite dish of the present-day urban Bengalis, Sahana introduced Noor as 'today's chef', adding in a low voice, "Hope you have no objection to eating food cooked by him."

Deb was somewhat nonplussed by the question. Shefali replied promptly, "No, no, time has changed."

"Yes, we cannot carry the baggage of religious bigotry of the early nineteenth century to the twenty-first century," Debabrata confirmed gravely.

Deb and Shefali congratulated the chef even before they began to eat. When all the guests and hosts began to eat, praises were showered on Noor with every gulp. Deb wanted to know how Noor learnt such excellent cooking.

"My father's great grandfather came from Lucknow with Wajid Ali Shah. The exiled Nawab was a dilettante of many arts and a gourmet of Moghlai preparations. The technique was passed from generation to generation. I learnt it from my grandmother after my father had left me in Calcutta under her care. She loved me for my bright complexion and pointed nose and taught me *khandani* manners. I had also developed a taste for Bengali cuisine like sorshe-ilish, kochu-loti with shrimp, etc., from my Bengali mother of Chatgaon."

"Excellent! Very well-cooked! The mutton in the kabab is so soft that the pieces melt in the mouth."

"Let me give you another plate of kabab," Sahana insisted.

At that moment, the calling bell began to ring unduly long, and everybody stopped eating. Noor got up and opened the door. Outside the collapsible gate, there were six-seven men standing and furiously chanting the name of Lord Ram. They began to abuse Noor in filthy language, asking him to open the gate and let them in. Fortunately for the insiders, the gate was locked after the guests had entered.

"Open the door. You are eating beef in this housing! How dare you? Don't you know that we do Durgapuja in the basement of this building?" howled the angry neighbours.

"Yes, I know, and I give as much subscription as any other neighbour." Replied Noorfirmly.

"But that does not give you the licence to eat beef on the premises." A committee member shouted at Noor.

"Who says that we are eating beef? We are eating mutton," protested Noor.

"Don't try to bluff. We have secret information that you were cooking beef in your flat. You got the stuff from Metiaburuj yesterday. See, we know your movements. Now admit it."

"It's a lie. You cannot force me to admit."

"Come out, you Haraam Jada. We shall teach you a good lesson."

Debabrata, Shefali, and Sahana came to the door after washing their hands. Debabrata disclosed his full name and began to talk while Sahana switched on the video recording on her mobile.

"I am not only a Hindu, but I am also a senior advocate of Calcutta High court. I am saying that we are eating mutton biryani and mutton kabab. What more proof do you want?"

"You are telling a lie. We don't believe you."

"Then let me call the police." Deb took out his phone.

By then, Noor had washed his hands and returned with a tong from the kitchen.

"Let me go out and see these humbugs," Noor began to shout. Tension rose high.

When Deb finally called the police, the hooligans lowered their volume and retreated after making threats to Noor. The police came within half an hour.

Deb helped Noor to lodge a complaint. The police inspector said that nobody had the authority to check what a neighbour was eating. There were laws against cow slaughter in many states, but there was no law in West Bengal prohibiting the eating of beef. Therefore, the police would act against the rowdies for trying to violate individual liberty.

The party ended in chaos. Deb and Shefali felt bad that people of their community could behave in such an intransigent manner. They were ashamed of the incident. Noor and Sahana, on the other hand, felt humiliated. Their guests could not finish the meal peacefully.

"India had declared herself a secular country. The Muslims in India were reassured when the 42nd Amendment was passed. This gave us a constitutional guarantee. But the minorities are still brow-beaten by the majority here as in all other countries, wherever the country's population is divided by religion or language or skin colour. Unless the people trust each other and respect each other's rights, the Muslims in India or the Hindus in Bangladesh will continue to suffer. The poor and the middle-class people cannot afford to engage a lawyer in the Supreme Court to secure justice."

The video recording of Sahana was telecast by the electronic media. As usual, the media arranged debates on the subject with representatives of political parties, and quite expectedly, the public opinion got divided based on political lines.

6.5 Rabi comes to a lawyer in Kolkata

The next Sunday, after breakfast, Sahana and Noor went to the house of Debabrata. Noor wanted to discuss the fall-out of the untoward incident in their flat. Debu da had promised to write a letter to the Police Commissioner to highlight the dangerous trend brewing up in the city.

Shefali and Sahana were discussing the ugly incident of last week at Tollygunge. They were unhappy because the police did not make any arrests. They would not precipitate a crisis without consent from the political boss.

Noor said that as a member of the minority community, he often experienced neglect and slight in day-to-day life. He understood that in a dispute, it was inherent that the majority group sometimes adopted an overbearing stance, but to interfere in the privacy of an individual was something new, something unheard of. How could they decide what one should wear or eat? Bengal never had this culture earlier. Deb had written a letter to the Police Commissioner of Kolkata, depicting the incident in detail. But he knew from his long experience that the C.P. would have no time for a case that did not end in a blood spill.

As a liberal Bengali, brought up in the ethos created by Tagore and Nazrul, Deb was shocked at the behaviour of the group of men who were residents of the housing of Noor and Sahana. They were educated and well-dressed but exuded a different ethos. They were not lumpens, but lumpen-like; not uneducated, but lacking the humility of a truly educated person; they were Hindus but did not have the tolerance and catholicity of the religion. The aggression writ on their face bore a resemblance to the faces who once shouted blood-curdling slogans on the streets of Calcutta '*Bagalmein chhuri, muhmein paan, ladke lenge Pakistan.*' The ferocity of the slogan shouted by the new generation of Hindus was equally nauseating. The father of the nation used to sing, '*Raghupati Raghava Raja Ram... Ishwar O Allah Tero*

Naam, Sabko Sanmati De Bhagwan', meaning, 'May God endow everybody with good sense'.

'We have drifted a long way,' thought Debabrata.

The doorbell rang for the second time; Padma came out from the kitchen to open the door. Shefali suddenly remembered that Choi had told her last night about the visit of her friend. What was the name? Her memory betrayed her for a few moments. The figure of a young man appeared at the door.

"I am Roop from New York."

Padma stepped back as the visitor introduced himself in English. But Shefali could hear the name and remembered everything that her daughter had said.

She whispered to Deb, "He is a friend of Choi. His grandfather needs your legal assistance. Please talk to them. I had asked them to come over."

Suppressing his annoyance, Deb went forward and asked, "Yes?"

Roop introduced himself as a friend of Choity Ghosh, who had fixed up their appointment. He had also tried to make a call on the landline but could not get the line.

Shefali came forward and welcomed them. "I am the mother of Choity. She has told me about your visit. Please come in. You are most welcome."

An old man now came forward to say in Bengali, "Namaskar, Mr Ghosh, my name is Rabi Guhathakurta. Roop has made the appointment on my behalf. In fact, I could not get you through the landline number since yesterday."

The old man had tanned skin, a sharp nose, and a stout body. He appeared between eighty-five and ninety but still fit to move about and mentally alert. Impressed by his personality and baritone voice, Deb welcomed him warmly, "Please come in, Mr Guhathakurta. The landline service has gone to dogs."

They were offered seats in the drawing-room. Shefalika wanted to know about her daughter. It was more than a year since she visited them. Despite years of stay in the U.S., Roop did not forget Bengali culture. He touched the feet of Shefali and addressed her as Aunty. Shefali began to say that their daughter was all alone in New Jersey. True, she spoke at least once a day, but Shefali was unsure if

Choi was facing some problem there. "Where did you meet Choity? How is she?"

Roop apprised her that they met each other for the first time in Madison Square three years ago and were introduced through a common friend. "It appeared that she was doing fine. In fact, for any guidance she called up Shrilekha, our common friend. Recently we met again in a Bengali cultural programme. After the programme, we were discussing the problem of citizenship in the U.S. and India. I mentioned the problem being faced by my senior grandpa in India. Dadamoshai was a freedom fighter, and we have a Taamra-Patra from the President of India recognising his contribution in the August Revolution. He was in jail for three years. But now Assam Govt wants him to prove his citizenship."

"How strange! How is the Assam Govt concerned about his citizenship? Are you from Bangladesh?" questioned Noor, who had been sitting quietly at a corner since the arrival of the old man and his young companion.

As the faces turned to him, Debabrata introduced him by saying, "Mr Noor Rahman is a professor at Ashutosh College and is my close friend. His wife Sahana has been a close friend of Choi's mom since their student days. They are like a part of this family."

Roop smiled at Mr Rahman and started saying with enthusiasm, "Originally, we are from Barishal. You know Barishal, the land of..."

Mr Rabi Guha raised his hand to stop him and began to speak.

"Halo, Noor Saab, how do you do? Yes, we originally belonged to Barishal District. I had also taken part in the freedom struggle, as did lakhs of people. I do not claim any special credit for that. How will the present Assam govt know that I spent three years in jail for fighting the British police? I am now required to go through the process of Assam's NRC, as I have lived in that state for the last sixty years. I am now ninety-one plus. I do not care if they send me to the camp for the remaining years of my life."

Having answered the question of Noor, Mr Guha turned to Debabrata and said, "Mr Ghosh, I have come to you, not for myself, but for an old lady who stays in our building in Guwahati. She hails from East Bengal like me. She has submitted her application form, but she could not produce any certificate or document mentioned in the Rules.

The documents she had attached were not accepted by the Panjikaran office. The software did not permit such entry. The lady had worked as a schoolteacher at Tezpur for thirty years and retired in 1993. In the last twenty-three years, her service-related papers have all perished."

Debabrata heard him patiently and said, "Have you brought her papers with you? Can I have a look?"

As Mr Guha nodded positively, Deb asked him to follow him to the adjacent chamber. Roop protested at this moment, "Grandpa, this is not correct. I had sought the appointment with Ghosh sir for your problem, but you are only talking about your neighbour. What will happen to you if you are declared a foreigner?"

Amused at the grandson's concern for his grandpa, Deb turned his face to give a smile and asked Shefali to have a chat with Roop and treat him with lassi.

Noor got an opportunity to pick up a conversation with Roop. "So, Mr Roop, I am glad to meet you. I am also from East Bengal. We both are Bangaals."

"Yes, I am so happy to meet you! The people from East Bengal are so open-minded, especially those hailing from Barishal, that it takes no time to be friendly with them! Barishal is such a lovely place... full of rivers and canals!"

"Does he, by any chance, know Babul?" The question was hovering in the mind of Sahana. "What are you doing in the States? How long have you been there?"

"He is a brilliant scholar. He has done his doctorate and is now doing post-doc research. Choity told me all about him," Shefali gave the reply on his behalf.

"Which University?"

"Pennsylvania," replied Roop.

"Oh! I thought you were in New York. Actually, my son is doing MBA from New York."

"Aunty, will you forward me his name and number so that I can make friends with him when I go back. I am giving you a missed call."

"Definitely." confirmed Sahana.

Noor resumed by asking him what his relationship was with Rabindra babu. Roop explained in short that Boro dadamoshai was his senior grandfather, i.e., the elder brother of his direct grandfather.

Mr Kabindra Guha, his grandfather, used to have high regard for his elder brother because of his sacrifice for the country. His elder brother never asked for any return for his service to the country. Later, after independence, he became a full-time worker of the CPI and lived life like a sannyasi." Roop continued further, "My grandpa Kabindra Guha worked in Delhi as an officer in the central government. He made a move in the home ministry to accord appropriate honour to Rabindra Guhathakurta as a freedom fighter. After prolonged investigation and a lot of dithering, the Ministry honoured him with a Taamra-Patra. Sr. grandpa was not happy that his brother had spent so much time and energy to have the copper plaque in the family as its memento of pride instead of working for the upliftment of the poor and downtrodden. However, he used to love his brother and his family. My father and I both are his fans."

Lassi was not available at that hour.

Padma entered with samosas on a platter and began to serve tea to everybody present in the room. Shefali signalled her to serve tea and snacks in Vakilbabu's[45] chamber as well.

Shefali then asked Roop, "When will you go back to New York, Roop? Can I send one small packet for Choi with you?"

"No problem, aunty. I have not yet bought my return ticket. I shall pick up the packet later."

"After your research work is over, will you come back to India?" asked Noor.

Roop was hesitant to give a straight reply. He said, "Let me see. If I do not get a suitable job here, I may not come back. The PM sent out an invitation to the NRIs to return to India, but I don't see any change here."

"Your parents are here. Who will look after them in their old age?"

"That is a problem even for those who work outside their home state."

"This is the motherland of your grandparents. How can you forsake this country for good? One's own country is always the dearest to one's heart. See how your senior grandpa made so much sacrifice for this country! You have the same blood. You cannot leave this country and call America your motherland."

---

[45] Vakil is a legal expert, an Advocate.

"It does not depend only on what I want. My girlfriend also has a say in the matter. She does not want to stay here."

"I see. But this is *your* country."

"America is *her* country. We are to choose between India and America. It is not easy to become a U.S. citizen. The U.S. Govt has put a strong filtering mechanism in place."

"You can choose your life partner from this country."

"Uncle, you are living in the early twentieth century. Things are changing fast. The idea of patriotism has also undergone a change. Now, people are changing their citizenship at the drop of a hat."

"We always believed that one's mother and motherland were greater than heaven. '*Janani janmabhumishcha swargadapi gariyasi*'. We read the shloka in our school, and we believed in it. It pains us to see the long-cherished ideal lying by the dusty roadside."

Deb and Rabi came back to the drawing-room, having finished their conference. Deb looked at Roop and said, "My friend, you have reasons to be worried. They require at least one strong piece of evidence in their favour. Law, you know, is an ass. You cannot prove whether this is daytime or night unless somebody equally stupid swears an oath to say what it is. But they are so old! It is difficult for them to run about to collect evidence. They need your assistance. I shall tell my assisting lawyer in Guwahati to guide them when they appear before the NRC. Okay?"

"Thank you, Mr Ghosh. I remain grateful to you," said Rabi in a perfect British accent.

"Goodbye, Mr Guhathakurta. It has been a pleasure meeting a person like you. Goodbye, Roop. Please keep me informed of the developments."

Everybody in the room stood up to show courtesy to the old freedom fighter. Roop called a cab, and they went out.

"What happened, Noor bhai?" asked Deb, seeing Noor's thoughtful mood.

"You see, Debu da, Rabi babu is not only a Hindu, but he is also a freedom fighter. How can he be denied the citizenship of India?"

"The law does not discriminate between a Hindu and a Muslim. As no special dispensation is given in the law, a freedom fighter undergoes the same process as an infiltrator," clarified Deb with professional authority.

Shefali came closer to Noor to give him an extra piece of samosa and whispered to him to consult his Debu da on his problems. Noor seized the opportunity and narrated the history of his family—from their Turkic origin to their settlement in Calcutta, his father's search for a new home in East Bengal after the Calcutta riots, his birth in Chittagong and escape to India in seventy-one, his schooling and higher education in Calcutta. Noor had declared himself as Indian on the strength of their permanent residence in Park Circus.

Having heard the detailed account of Noor's cross-migration, Deb realised that as Noor was born in Pakistan to a Pakistani mother and a deserter Indian father he would lose his Indian citizenship. Bangladesh would not accept him as her citizen since he did not go back after the Liberation War. But it could also be argued that when his father was abroad, he was born in East Pakistan, and his father brought him back to his paternal house in India before twenty-fifth of March of the fateful year. He could get the status of a refugee and wait for some time to get the right to vote. But did he possess any documentary proof of his coming to India?

Noor began to think of the mess he was in.

The state of Assam began the process of NRC once in 1951 when Meghalaya was a part of it. But when the citizenship Act of 1955 was amended in 1985, Meghalaya was not a part of Assam, and the new state did not go for NRC in 2013. Should Sahana participate in the present NRC process of Assam? Or she should wait for the NRC of Meghalaya? Their son Babul was born in Calcutta. Should he apply for Indian citizenship as a permanent resident of West Bengal? Fortunately, he got his Indian passport two years ago from Delhi, where he studied for more than five years, and then went to America for further studies. But someday, he would also face the problem and his father's status as an 'illegal migrant' might become a critical issue for him at that time.

After a long discussion with Debabrata, Noor realised that he must get a proof of the date of his entry into India before the registration of citizens commences in West Bengal.

6.6 Malati's bid to escape

Aparajita Debi was busy sifting her small archive of old records and letters that somehow escaped the ravages of time. When they left Harishpur, they had only a side bag on one shoulder that contained one spare set of dresses, academic certificates, and a few letters. The letters were considered precious for sentimental reasons, and they had the address of the sender. Generally, people used to write letters in postcards, the cheapest form of written communication provided by the Governmental postal service. The space for writing was so small that people did not spare the space on the reverse side meant for writing the sender's address on it. Personal or confidential letters were written on 'Inland letter' stationery. One had enough space, three pages in all, to write and fold it in a way that ensured confidentiality of the content and to have a specified area to write the address of the sender and recipient on different sides. Aparajita sorted the Inland letters from other papers.

Malati was watching her mistress while doing her work. Normally, at this hour, she used to cantillate the name of her god, bead by bead, sitting at one corner. She had taken *diksha*[46] from the holy man, Ram Thakur, in his *ashram* at Rauzan in her childhood. But she was not a typical devotee or a religious person for the most part of her life. A few years back, she discovered among her precious possessions a small piece of paper containing the name of the god as given to her by the guru. *Jai Ram, Shri Ram, Jai Jai Ram.* She uttered the line to herself. It sounded quite soothing. She uttered it again, then again, and again. The lilting rhythm gave her a lot of peace, acting as a balm over the known and unknown pains she had been carrying for nearly seventy years. She got a photograph of the guru from a neighbour, framed it, hung it on the wall, and began the ritualistic practice of

---

[46] Initiation as a disciple.

muttering her god's name every morning, sitting quietly before the photo of her Gurudev.

Unlike her usual routine, Aparajita had not taken her bath till then. It seemed she did not have a good sleep. "What are you looking for, aunty? You appear quite disturbed," said Malati.

"Yes. I am looking for a letter written by my didi. I think this is the one. Yes."

"Didi? You have an elder sister? You never said so."

"Hum. This letter is from my Sagar didi. We were from one family. We called each other sister, not cousin. She wrote this letter after the death of my father. Here is her address."

"Is she still alive?"

"Is she not? I don't know. She was older than me by four years. Let me write a letter and see if I get a reply. You cook only *khichuri* for me today."

By the time Aparajita was through her letter-writing, somebody knocked at the door and called out, "Malati! Malati!"

Malati opened the door and allowed the man in.

Aparajita raised her eyes in a frown and signalled the man to wait till she completed writing the address. She could recognise the man. He was Sukhen, the husband of Malati.

After three minutes, Aparajita said. "What do you want, Sukhen? She would go back home in a few minutes."

Sukhen was feeling restless. There was fright in his eyes and tension in his voice. Malati was already out of the kitchen. "We have to run away, Malati, as early as possible."

The fear of an uncertain future oozed from his words.

"Why? What happened?" Malati questioned. She knew this day would come but did not know that it would come so soon.

"What is the problem, Sukhen?" queried Aparajita.

"Madam, the Verification Committee is going around the city to find out if people are residing here without applying for citizenship before the Panjikaran Adhikari[47]. They are issuing a notice to the suspected foreigners to meet the officer-in-charge of the police station in three days, with the acknowledgement slip issued by the NSK. Those not having the slip are directed to surrender to the police."

---

[47] Officer registering the names.

"I see."

"Madam, they visited our colony two hours back. Our children were inside so they could not seal the door, but they pasted the notice on it. My twelve-year-old son Vishal ran five km to my worksite and gave me the information. Our contractor advised me that instead of surrendering to the police, we should flee to other parts of India. He gave me two thousand rupees for our transit expenses and three thousand as my wage for this week."

"Do not panic. They have given you three days' time," said Aparajita.

"That is all sham. I know the police will raid tonight or in the early hours of dawn. If anybody resists, their agents will put the colony on fire," Sukhen said with conviction.

Aparajita shuddered, remembering how they once fled from their house before it was set on fire. Those were communal goondas; these are parochial xenophobics marauding with police support. "Once people were driven out from East Bengal, and now they would be driven back from India." Opu said to herself.

"Where shall we go with our children? What shall we eat?" Malati broke down in despair.

"We are labourers, not thieves. I have learnt different jobs over the years. So long as these hands are there, we can get work anywhere and earn our livelihood. We must remain free and not go behind bars."

Aparajita got up to pay Malati her salary. "You can at least try to run away. When my turn comes, I shall not have even this option. I shall pray for you so that you remain free. Without freedom, everything is meaningless."

Malati and Sukhen bowed to touch her feet. Opu handed over the letter to Malati to drop it in the post box on their way. Malati said, "Aunty, we are leaving. I don't know my destiny. You should go to Kolkata to your didi. These people are ruthless. They will not spare you for being old."

"Goodbye, madam," said Sukhen.

"Durga, Durga."

After they had left, Aparajita was in a trance for a few moments. She was brooding over the distress caused by human beings to the fellow humans. *Sometimes they wage war for annexation of territory, and sometimes they launch a racial purification campaign, some other times, they engage themselves in crusade or jehad or communal riots; this time, it is the panjikaran exercise to screen the so-called foreigners. Who knows what its final toll will be?*

A strong smell of half-burnt rice entered her nostril, and she became aware of the reality. Malati forgot to switch off the gas, and her meal of khichri started getting burnt at the bottom of the cooking pan. Aparajita rushed to the kitchen to turn off the gas. She opened the lid of the pan and retrieved her meal to the extent possible. She quickly took her bath and sat before the photo of her gurudev to do the *jop*[48]. Then she went to the kitchen to fetch her meal.

Hardly had she finished her lunch when a familiar call from a well-known voice entered through her hearing aid.

"Opu?"

'He has come back!' Aparajita responded, "Rabi dada, I am coming." She dropped her plate quickly in the sink, washed her hand, and wiped her lips before coming out of the kitchen.

The smell of partly burnt rice was still there in the air. Rabi asked, "Where is your helping hand? She has become very negligent, it seems."

"She has left the job. Tonight, they will make a bid to escape from Assam. The Committee has served them notice."

"I see. The exodus begins once again. How are you?'

"Well, you spent ten days in Kolkata, although you had said that you would be back in seven days!"

"What do I do? Roop came from the USA. He said he had fixed an appointment with a senior lawyer on Sunday. Therefore, I had to cancel my reservation. He took me to his friend's house. Choity's father is Debabrata Ghosh, a well-known advocate of Kolkata."

"I can understand that Roop has an interest in a girl named Choity. They are young and unmarried. I also appreciate that he wants to cultivate her father. But I do not understand what your interest is. Is Choity's mom exceptionally beautiful?"

"Chhi, chhi. What are you saying? If I had married in time, I would have had a son and a daughter-in-law of their age."

"Then why did you go with Roop like a tugboat?"

---

[48] Cantillation of the Name.

"Because the appointment was taken for me. I wanted to understand the strength and weaknesses of our applications. The lawyer advised me that if no document enlisted in the rule can be produced, we should produce the records of bank accounts, LIC policy, or even a private employer's certificate. Next Monday is our hearing before the Assistant Registrar. Just five more days."

"I could not attach the specified documents with the application as I do not have them. My migration papers were destroyed in the flood. I did not have any fixed assets till you made me buy this flat. My job in Tezpur began as an ad hoc engagement without any letter of appointment. After a year, the Committee adopted a resolution in a meeting to regularise the ad hoc teachers. We were asked to note down the status on the register. After two years, I was given my first increment. As I continued as a contractual employee, I did not receive any pension, and so I do not have a pension payment order book. The school forwarded my State Bank account number to the PF Accounts office, and my PF amount was remitted directly to the bank at Guwahati. Now tell me which document I should present to the Registrar?"

"When we lived in Tezpur, I stayed in a party dormitory, and you stayed in a working women's hostel, sometimes in a private ladies' mess. I shall ask a party colleague to get me a residence certificate. You can write to your friends and acquaintances. This certificate should be from 1965 or before.

"Is there anybody still alive who can give us a certificate?"

"Let us try. By the by, my grandson is coming on the evening flight. You have seen him two years back. You can take his help without any hesitation. He will go to Tezpur with me and visit your school. You had an account in the local cooperative bank of tea garden workers. Can you get me the account number of that bank?"

"Let me see. The account was closed in 1993 before I shifted to Guwahati." Aparajita checked an old diary and found the account number in which she used to save one-third of her salary for the days after superannuation. Rabi took down the number and bade her adieu.

6.7 Hearing before the Panjikaran officer

Roop accompanied Rabi dadamoshai and Opu madam in an autorickshaw to the Assistant Registrar's office for their hearing. This was a democratic country where no person could be detained unless he had been told the imputations against him and given a reasonable opportunity to defend himself. A magistrate with judicial authority could examine the viewpoints of both sides and decide if a prima facie case existed, if he could be granted bail, and if he should be sent to police custody for interrogation or to judicial custody till the judicial process was over. The Assistant Registrar was not a judicial magistrate. Therefore, he could not decide the issues like bail, police custody, or jail custody. But before he finalised the citizenship status of individuals, he wanted to offer the affected persons reasonable opportunity to defend themselves. That was the background of this personal hearing.

"What will happen if he rejects our application for citizenship? Shall we become Bangladeshis or Pakistanis?" asked Opu, like an adolescent girl.

Rabi tried to remove her fear by saying, "I don't think those countries will agree to accept us as their citizens."

"Wah! That will be fine! We shall be able to spend the last few years of our lives here only. All this blablabla does not really mean anything. I knew it all through."

Roop was about to tell her that if their names were not enrolled, police would arrest them as infiltrators or illegal migrants any time they wanted. Before he could say it, the autorickshaw driver took a sudden turn and applied the brake with considerable noise.

"We have reached. Please get down," he said in a hoarse voice.

Roop held Opu by the hand so that she did not stumble at the puddles on the way. Rabi showed the hearing notice to the front office staff to report their arrival. He requested if their hearing could be held together because the old lady had no one to help her but her neighbour. The request was granted considering her age and fragile health.

The Assistant Registrar checked the details of their cases from the laptop provided by the State Coordinator with specially developed application software. The details of Rabindra Guhathakurta appeared on the screen at a click of the mouse. The officer read out the biodata of the individual recorded from the statement given by him in his application. The officer pointed out a gap in history from 1947 to 1957. Rabi clarified that he went to the U.K. in 1947 to do post-graduation. Thereafter, he studied labour law and company management and got a diploma in the subjects. He joined a British tea firm in London, worked for five years, and then returned to India to see his ailing mother in Calcutta.

"But you have not submitted any proof for this."

"I was a British subject at the time I left India. The return ticket for my voyage got destroyed in the course of time. I can only give you the copies of the certificates issued by the University of London if that helps."

"We are not considering your fitness for a job. We have nothing to do with your academic certificates. Your birthplace was Barishal of East Bengal. You are to produce a document establishing your date of entry in India and the state of Assam before 1965 and another document as proof of your sustained stay in Assam. That's all."

At this stage, Aparajita Debi mentioned in an agitated voice, "Mr Guha was a freedom fighter. He took part in the revolution of 1942. He was lynched by the British S.P. and kept in prison for three years. How can you say that he is not an Indian?"

As Opu became emotional and started sobbing, Rabi felt embarrassed. He intervened and said, "Opu, will you please calm down. I do not want any benefit in lieu of my participation in the freedom movement or even any sympathetic consideration because of that. We fought to remove the fetters of Bharatmata as our holy duty. We never thought that the old story should be recounted to secure the citizenship of our country. We thought the citizenship of India was our birthright. If the parliament of the country has framed laws for citizenship under which today we are treated as non-citizens, we cannot blame the officer. He has no way but to follow the sections of the Act and paragraphs of the Rules. Sir, you please carry on."

The officer said further that Rabi babu had not even submitted any document to prove his prolonged stay in Tezpur. The photocopy of the membership card of the Communist Party of India issued in 1959 by the Assam state committee cannot be taken as proof of residence.

"I used to stay in a dormitory in the party office. There was no official allotment order."

The officer was feeling helpless. He said in exasperation, "Rabi babu, only God can save you." Then he looked at Roop and asked him, "Do you have any proof that he was a freedom fighter? Was he recognised as such by the Govt of India? Does he get the pension for freedom fighters?"

Roop replied, "Will you kindly look at this scanned image of a Tamra-Patra[49] bearing his name?" He handed over his mobile to the officer. The officer looked at it, zoomed in on the photo and then said, "Can you send a copy of the forwarding letter of the MHA to us?"

"I shall send you the copy if the letter is available at our house. His brother, my grandfather, had brought his sacrifice to the notice of the Ministry of Home Affairs. As he was an officer of the Central Secretariat Service and posted in Delhi, he could pursue the file assiduously. My senior grandpa was not interested in these official recognitions. Finally, when the MHA conveyed the decision, he could not refuse the honour given by the state. The memento was kept in our house in Kolkata. He did not agree to take the pension from the government. He could not imagine that someday a government letter would be crucial to settle the issue of his citizenship."

"For the time being, Mr Guha, I am holding you as a D-voter. If additional documents are submitted by you within fifteen days, we shall review your case before preparing the final list. Let us now hear Mrs Aparaita Nandy."

Opu protested mildly, "Sir, please do not address me 'Mrs'. I am unmarried."

---

[49] A copperplate bearing the state insignia, on which the name of the recipient and his contribution in freedom struggle are inscribed.

On hearing this, the officer expressed surprise but apologised at the same time. He began to go through the narrative of Aparajita Nandy from the laptop. At the end of his perusal, he questioned Aparajita, "Miss Nandy, you said you had a Pakistani passport when you left Sandwip, and immigration formalities were observed at Akhaura before you entered India. But you have not submitted proof of surrendering the passport to the Collector's office at Silchar. What did you do with your passport?"

"Sir, at Silchar, we stayed in a refugee colony by the Surma river. One night when we were asleep, a flash flood swept the low areas of the valley, and our hut was inundated. Water entered the trunk containing our documents, cash money and spare sarees. The documents and notes were reduced to paper pulp. I went to the office of the D.M., but the staff refused to give me a receipt for the passport as the names of the holder were not legible. But I am sure the immigration office at Agartala has the record of our migration."

"The rule requires the applicant to submit the proof. You have not submitted the same. The stories of why your family had to leave Sandwip or how your parents died are of no relevance to us. We need strong documentary evidence."

"Believe me, officer, everything I said in my statement is true."

The officer smiled wryly.

Rabi said, "She has been teaching in a school at Tezpur since 1963. Is that not enough evidence?"

"We shall examine that part. But that will not establish if she had migrated legally. Let me see what evidence she has given for her stay in Assam since 1955." The Assistant Registrar critically perused the narrative for the second part and opened the attachment of the scanned copies. He felt completely frustrated when he could not find any residential certificate of the municipality of Tezpur or Silchar, or even a telephone bill or an electricity bill in her name.

"At Silchar, we lived in an unauthorised refugee colony. The municipality did not collect tax, nor did they provide the standard civic amenities. At Tezpur, nobody was ready to give part of their house on rent to a single woman. I stayed either in a lady teachers' mess or in a working women's hostel. One of the mess members used to collect the monthly charges by rotation. Similarly, the manager of the hostel used to collect the charges on a register. No receipt was issued to the residents or members. The residents had no direct interface with the municipal authorities. Who will give us the certificate of residence?" retorted Aparajita Debi.

The officer thought for a minute and said, "Did you not have a bank account in any nationalised bank? You can give us a certificate from the bank manager."

"I was a newcomer in Tezpur. I did not know any account holder to introduce me. At last, Mr Guha took me to the Tea Garden Workers' Co-operative bank, and on his recommendation, I could open an account to keep my monthly savings. I had closed the account in 1993 after I transferred the amount to SBI, Maligaon. The staff of the cooperative bank had taken back the passbook and chequebook, and I have no records with me. Mr Rabi Guha visited Tezpur last week. But the staff were all new, and they refused to issue a certificate to him."

"Yes, they said if the Registrar or the State Coordinator wanted the information, they would provide it, but not otherwise. They are afraid to issue any certificate that may be used for enrolment of an outsider as a citizen," said Roop.

The officer had a brief smile on his face. He said that it was not the job of the Registrar to call for records from public bodies to help the applicants out of the way. He asked Ms Nandy if she could produce a certificate from her school regarding the period she worked there. He was prepared to give due weightage to it. Aparajita was at her wits' end. She only had a letter from the headmistress of her school conveying the date of her superannuation. This letter did not mention the date of her entry, nor did she ever get a proper letter of appointment. The visit of Roop and Rabi did not bear any fruit. The present headmistress did not know Aparajita personally and refused to issue a certificate. Nobody wanted to earn the wrath of the local people.

"Ms Nandy, if you are not able to produce any certificate from any authority, it will not be possible for us to include you in the list of citizens. I am sorry."

Rabi began to argue that it would be totally unfair to deny citizenship to an educated old lady like Aparajita Debi, who worked as a teacher for thirty long years. The contribution she made to the upbringing of several generations of students should not be forgotten.

"A lady who lived all through in India except for eight years, considering herself a genuine citizen of this country, cannot be denied her citizenship," contested Rabi.

"The government rose from its slumber after seventy years to determine the citizenship of the entire population of a state. How can one obtain or secure various documents after reaching the age of seventy or eighty? What assistance is the state providing to the applicants who are old and infirm, to the poor and illiterate, or to the specially enabled? The government is asking people to produce records more than fifty or sixty years old, although the government did not preserve its own transactional records older than five years. If a person produces a border pass of 1951, how will the government verify it? So, the government will not accept such documents. Sir, I request you to be humane. You cannot throw an old lady of 85 years to prison or a *ghuspetia* camp, ignoring her spotless life in this country? The absence of a few papers cannot be a crime more heinous than fraud, dacoity, rape, or murder. In such cases, the state bears the responsibility of proving the charge by collecting evidence and producing witnesses. The state could not issue a birth certificate to all the newly born babies under the highly efficient British raj or the fledgling new government of the country. But in the question of citizenship, the state demands proof from its own people. What will happen if the mother asks the child to give the proof of its birth!"

The Assistant Registrar was getting impatient. He gestured that the hearing was over.

"Mr Guha, we are govt officers, not members of the Parliament, nor members of the judiciary. We are bound by the laws and rules framed by the legislature and interpreted by the judiciary. We can neither change the rules nor interpret them. The wise men have prepared the list of documents that need to be submitted by the applicants. If submission of such documents is difficult for anybody, the judiciary is there to grant him relief. The hands of public servants are tight. We cannot go beyond the letters of the rule. We cannot even interpret the rule based on the spirit of the law. However, you can take a printout of today's proceeding from the office and approach the Foreigners' Tribunal suo motu. The FT is the judicial authority to decide if you are a foreigner."

Rabi could not but agree with what the officer said. He stood up to leave. "Thank you, sir. In the circumstances, I think submitting the letter of the MHA in my case is just a formality. It will not help you to decide. I will rather request you not to give me any favour out of the way. Kindly keep us together in the same bracket. Namaskar."

While Roop went to collect the copy of proceedings from the office, the two old persons waited for him, sitting on a bench in the corridor. Some local people looked at them with derisive smiles on their faces. They wanted to ensure that none of the forty-lakh people excluded from the draft list got their way into the final list.

Opu told Rabi in a low voice, "Rabi dada, one day you had taught me to love the land from Hindukush to Kanyakumari, from Sindh to Manipur as our country, as our *desh*, named Bharatbarsha. You believed in what you said and joined the Indian National Congress at the age of seventeen to free our country from foreign rule. You also joined the revolutionary group of Troilokya Chakrabarty. I was an ordinary girl, but like most people educated in schools, I too was exposed to the concept of nationalism. I received a big jolt when Muslims and Hindus of India were recognised as separate nations by the British, and East Bengal was declared as part of a separate country called Pakistan. We came over to India, treating India as our motherland. We went through a long period of distress, poverty, and misery. But we continued to sing 'Jana Gana Mana Adhinayaka Jaya Hey'[50] in all solemn public events. I promoted the spirit of patriotism in the minds of my students and exhorted them to the service of the Indian nation. My lectures used to inspire them, and many of them joined the All India Services to serve the country and protect its integrity. My students believed in me that one's country was to be revered higher than any other being. What will they think of me now?

Today I am being declared a non-citizen, no longer an Indian. From today, I will not be invited by the children of our Resident's Society to join the flag-hoisting ceremony on the fifteenth of August[51] or the twenty-sixth of January[52]. I cannot believe that I shall not sing

[50] The national anthem of India, composed by Tagore.
[51] The Independence Day of India.
[52] The Republic Day of India.

Jana Gana Mana or Vande Mataram once again in my life. What kind of life will that be? How can I not feel proud when an Indian receives a Nobel Prize or wins a medal in the Olympics or when ISRO would send an Indian to the moon?"

Rabi was listening to her monologue silently. Each word toucbed the depth of his heart and made him speechless.

Roop came out with a computer printout and saw the two old friends sitting mutely with moist eyes. He called an App-cab over his phone and helped them return to their housing with him.

Chapter Seven

7.1 Sagar receives a letter from Opu

When Sagar was enjoying the evening tea with her husband, Satya wanted to know about her sister-in-law, who was known to be in Silchar in 1961. If she were still alive, she must be facing the ordeal for her citizenship now.

"If she listened to the proposal of my father, she would not have faced this day," Sagar said with pungency in her voice.

At that moment, Padma came to deliver a letter. It was an inland letter. The address was written by a trembling hand. Satya could not read hand-written stuff because of poor vision. Sagar put on her reading glasses and looked at the name of the sender before opening it. She exuded surprise.

Satyabrata asked, "Who has written it, Sagar? Does anybody still write a letter in pen and paper?"

"Your sister-in-law, Opu. We have just taken her name, and her letter is in our hands. What a coincidence!"The letter bears our old address of Russa Road and has been redirected. Mr.Sarkar bought the flat from us, if you remember. He is a true gentleman! She began to slice open the letter.

Satya said, "I never saw my only sister-in-law in my entire married life. I do not even know how she looks."

"What a pity! Not to have seen the tall and beautiful 'Ms Aparajita Nandy'! You see, she is still unmarried."

"Why? Why didn't she marry?"

"I really do not know. After my uncle died in Silchar, she probably left the place after a year or so. A letter written by me came back undelivered. But she never informed us where and how she was living. She had passed M.Sc., and therefore, it should not be difficult for her to eke out a living or to get a nice husband. Let me go through the letter and find out why she has decided to break her silence now!"

Dear Didi,

I do not know if you still remember me. After all, it had been nearly seventy years since we last met. I was only fourteen years, and you were eighteen. After appearing for your intermediate examination, you spent some days with us in Sandwip before going to Barishal. You had been my childhood icon, my inspiration. I never forgot you.

Since 1946, we lived an accursed life, my parents and me, and yes, our grandparents too. But luckily, you were away from Sandwip, untouched by those tragic events. You did not even know what exactly had happened with us in 1955 when we were about to leave Sandwip. You never came to see us in Silchar as we lived in a *bustee*[53].

You wrote me a long letter when my father died. The letter is still with me, one of my few treasures. But even then, neither the senior uncle nor you came to stand by my side. After a year, I left for Tezpur.

I spent my life working as a teacher. After retirement, I settled in Guwahati. I was also happy in my own way, having no encumbrances or liabilities. Someday I would coolly pass away. That would be the ideal end for me.

But that wish is not going to be fulfilled. I wrote you a letter two years ago, giving you some hint of my apprehensions. I did not receive any reply. This is my last attempt to contact you.

Meanwhile my apprehensions have come true. They have decided that I am not a citizen of this country. I am one of the forty lakh people whose names have not been enlisted in the Citizens Register. I am not surprised, as even freedom fighters, men from the services, and a family member of the ex-President share the same anguish. After a few days, I shall appear at the hearing before the Assistant Registrar. If I fail to clear this hurdle, I may have to spend the remaining days of my life in jail or in a camp. If you send a reply and confirm your address, I shall give it to the jail authorities to send the information on my end to your son. I may not have ever seen him, but he is my only heir.

Your once-beloved sister,
Opu.

---

[53] Slum

When Sagar finished reading the letter, her voice choked, and her eyes gave out droplets of tears. The happiness of her life seen in juxtaposition with the pathos of her sister's life hurt her like a sting. What was Opu's fault that she spent her life in such distress, in lifelong loneliness and now waiting to spend her last days in jail!

Satya was also brooding sadly over the course of the life of her sister-in-law. But everything was not lost yet. Something could still be done to save her from confinement. Her case could be fought in court. He called out, "Debu, Debu!"

Having returned from court, Debabrata Ghosh, a senior advocate, was relaxing for a while in his bedroom before entering his chamber for the second innings. The loud call from his nonagenarian father, bearing a mark of unusual excitement, made him spring to his feet, and he replied, "Yes, Papa, what is it?"

Satya drew his attention to the letter lying on the centre table. "That letter is from your Opu mashi."

Deb looked at her mother, sitting quietly with moist eyes, looking towards the darkening evening sky. He picked up the letter and went through it. Before he could ask, Satya told him that she was his aunt, a relation by blood from his mother's side. Satya had seen her father on the days of his marriage but never saw his sister-in-law. The two branches of the same family drifted apart from each other in the cyclonic storm of Partition. That letter was like an SOS message, and their family must do everything possible to save her from the humiliation of imprisonment.

Deb asked her mother, "Ma, how is it that in my life of sixty-five years, I have never met my aunt? When she lost her father, you could have brought her to our family."

"My father did ask her to live with them, as did she in Barishal in her childhood, but she ignored the proposal. There may have been many incidents she took to her heart without knowing the full facts. There must have been failures from my side, too, maybe outside my knowledge. If we had met, these wounds could have healed."

"Let me see. What is the full name of Opu mashi?" Without waiting for the answer from her mother, Deb turned the backside of the letter and found the name and address of the sender. Ms Aparajita Nandy. The name seemed to be familiar. He had heard the name recently. But when and in what context? He needed to concentrate hard to dig out the reference from the recycle bin of his memory.

"Can you go to Guwahati and bring her here?" asked Sagarika.

"Oh yes. I will immediately ask my junior lawyer in Guwahati to contact her and ascertain the position of her case. I shall go to Guwahati by the weekend after taking his briefing on the last hearing. Let me send him the address of my yet-to-see aunt."

Deb took a photo of the sender's address and forwarded it to Mr Sahadev Pal on WhatsApp with his brief instructions.

7.2 Roop reminds Sagar of Banaripara

Roop decided to go back to the USA. He would come back when the litigation comes up before the Foreigners Tribunal. On his way to the airport, he visited the house of Debabrata Ghosh firstly to brief him personally about what had happened in the departmental hearing and secondly to collect the parcel from Shefali aunty for her daughter, Choity.

Roop was lucky to get two busy persons together at home — one a doctor and the other an advocate. When he entered the house, he found two more people were already there. They were Noor and Sahana. They were talking to two old people, Satyabrata and Sagarika. Since the marriage of Debabrata with Shefali, members of the two families mixed like family friends. Shefali had come back from her clinic, where she was working as a consultant after retiring early from the government health service. Noor would retire from his college that week. They were planning to visit the USA, where their son was studying. Shefali had told them that Roop would come to see them that day before taking his return flight.

Shefali welcomed Roop and introduced him to her parents-in-law as a friend of Choity. Noor began talking to Roop as Debabrata had not yet reached home after the court.

"So, young man, how are things in Guwahati? Is your grandfather alright?"

"Uncle, things are not working the way we expected. I have come to take some advice from Ghosh uncle."

As Satyabrata looked at Noor inquisitively, he told him that the grandpa of this young man lived in Assam for a long period and was facing trouble for citizenship. Sagarika remembered that her sister was also facing the same crisis. But she did not mention her name as the family problems were not discussed before outsiders.

"Did he come from East Bengal?" she asked.

"Yes, ma'am. We are originally from the Barishal district. The district is known for Mukunda Das, Troilokya Chakrabarty, and Mahatma Aswini Kumar Datta."

"Wow! It seems you are in love with the *desh* of your forefathers. But do you know that Barishal is the hometown of the most famous Bengali poet of the post Rabindra era?" asked Sahana, the Khasi journalist.

Roop remained silent. Nazrul was born in Churulia near Asansol. Bishnu De and Buddhadeb Bose were from East Bengal; Sunil Ganguli, too. But he did not know if any of them hailed from Barishal. Noor understood the problem. He said that Roop should not be faulted for not knowing the birthplace of Jibanananda Das. He did not hear the name from his grandpa. Barishal became proud of the greatest romantic poet of modern times after they had left the district.

"It seems you have never visited your ancestral place. Do you know that Barishal is famous also for its paddy, guava and the B.M. College? What is the name of your village?" asked Sagarika, trying to find out something.

Roop knew the name of the place, but he feigned as if the name had temporarily slipped from his memory. The old woman might again surprise him with some information not known to him.

"Uncle," Noor addressed Satyabrata. "His love for Barishal is so genuine that his face glows when he speaks of it. I marked it when I met him for the first time."

"Yes, young men who hear of the beautiful riverine land that was once theirs romanticise the pre-partition times when everything was hunky-dory. On the other hand, most people born in West Bengal have no idea of Bangladesh, her towns, villages, and rivers. Only the people who have witnessed both the parts, before and after the partition, are torn between the emotions of love and hate."

Sahana added further, "The development of roads and the flourish in academic activities are truly remarkable but unknown to the present generation of Indian Bengalis. Both the states restricted the free interchange of ideas, culture, and literature. Lack of knowledge about the other half has created an artificial rift between the two sisters. Bangladesh is gradually emerging as a liberal nation. On the other hand, West Bengal is gradually losing its pre-eminent position among the states of India, and the Bengali literature of Kolkata is losing its earlier supremacy.

Noor, the professor of history began to say, "The Germans and the Vietnamese solved their problem of an artificial divide. The Koreans, the Chinese, the Kashmiris, the Punjabis, and the Bengalis have not yet found a solution to their problems."

Feeling bored by the pedantic lecture from Noor, Roop became busy doing justice to the fish fry without taking part in the discussion. His mind was extremely disturbed. *'Is there no way to save his dadamoshai?'*

Noor was keeping a watch on Roop. He said in a bid to continue the discussion, "There is no solution in near future. Someday two Koreas may decide to merge as the two Germanys did. But Bangladesh is an independent country. She will never give up her independence to merge with West Bengal and be happy as a federal state of the Republic of India. Some forces may work to foment the sentiment of Bengali nationalism, but the huge bloodshed and the prolonged human suffering during the partition and its aftermath will not inspire the Indian Bengalis in favour of such a move. Nor will the mighty Republic of India ever allow such secession."

Roop was all attentive to the ice cream served by Shefali. Suddenly, he began to blurt emotionally, "The Bengalis who migrated from Bangladesh or erstwhile East Pakistan are being harassed in the name of citizenship registration. They have no sympathy for the victims of the partition. They have been following the two-nation or three-nation theory and proving Jinnah right by treating the total population of East Bengal as foreigners from the twenty-sixth of January of 1950. The Bengalis who are unable to submit such records or certificates as are acceptable to Government officials are being labelled as foreigners. The people born to migrant East Bengali parents, who do not possess birth certificates or other documents, may find it difficult to remain outside a jail. Every Bengali speaking individual residing in states other than West Bengal is now looked upon as a suspected Bangladeshi."

There was a sound of a jeep stopping at the gate. In his early career, Deb had purchased a Jonga Jeep auctioned by the military stores' department of Fort William. He got it repaired and painted in a local garage and designed its interior to his requirement. He used to carry about fifty-sixty law books, gazetteers, records of Supreme Court judgments, etc., from his house to High Court. It was a small library having select reference books required for citation in the current cases. Deb used this old jeep for his transit to the High Court. He had a big Toyota car for family use. The old Jonga made enough sound to declare Deb's arrival. Before Debabrata could press the doorbell, Shefali had opened it. She rebuked Deb in a muffled voice for being late, "Roop has been waiting for long. Don't you know that he is to catch a flight?"

Sagarika and Satya got up from the sofa. They do not remain present when their son discusses a case with his client. But today, Sagarika got up reluctantly, more as a compulsive convention than as a genuine gesture of gentility. Roop stood up and said, "Madam, we are Guhathakurtas from Banaripara."

Sagarika's eyes sparkled. 'Really!? I know some Guhathaurtas of Banaripara. Please meet me when your consultation is over."

Debabrata was not apologetic for being late. Indians, when in India, believe in the eternity of time. Most Hindus and all Buddhists and Jains also believe in rebirth to enjoy or suffer the leftover consequences of their deeds of the present birth.

But Indians in the Western countries are quick to adapt themselves to the Western philosophy of life. Life is only one for an individual, and the existence of an immortal soul is questionable. Therefore, one has no time to waste, and every moment of it must be used for achieving the goals of this life. Roop was to go to the airport to catch a flight for Delhi and then to catch the flight for New York after an interval of nineteen hours. He had already gone into the American mode and, therefore, came straight to the subject.

"Good evening, sir. The hearing is over. The authorities will not relent in view of his age or background as a freedom fighter. At one point, the officer wanted to see the verified communication of the Ministry of Home Affairs offering the *Tamra-Patra* to the senior grandpa. But from his briefing, it became clear that they would finally go by the rule and not use their discretion. Our application was practically rejected, although no rejection letter was issued. A computer-generated unsigned report of the day's proceeding was handed over to us... here it is."

Deb went through the photo of the print-out, which indicated that in the day's hearing, the applicant appeared but could not submit any of the listed documents. Therefore, his name could not be included. He should either file an application with the Foreigners Tribunal to determine his status or surrender himself to the police station within fifteen days. Deb asked him about the decision given to Rabi babu's neighbour. Roop waved his hand dismissively. He and his dadamoshai visited Tezpur to get a certificate from the school for his neighbour. They also went to a cooperative bank where she had an account for thirty years. The staff of the bank did not recognise his grandpa, who was once their union leader. Nobody agreed to issue a certificate on his own. They were simply afraid of reprisal.

Deb took out two *vakalatnama*[54] forms and got them signed by Roop. He agreed to fight on their behalf in the Foreigners Tribunal. Deb advised him to write a letter to the MHA to testify to the authenticity of the letter they issued in the late sixties. Perhaps he could use the lie-over time in Delhi. Roop stood up to bid farewell. The GPS-guided cab had already stopped at the gate.

Shefali hurriedly brought a packet from her bedroom and gave it to Roop to hand it over to Choity. Roop kept it inside the hand-baggage. Noor, Sahana, Shefali, and Deb wished him a safe flight.

Roop said to Deb, "Sir, I don't know if your mother hailed from Barishal. She may know some people. I will meet her when I come back. She may excuse me this time. Bye."

[54] Letter of engagement of a lawyer to plead a case on behalf of somebody.

7.3 Deb meets his Opu mashi

At night, Deb received a call from Sahadeb Pal, his junior advocate at Gauhati High Court. After the court, he went to Saraswat Abasan and met Ms Aparajita Nandy. As she lived alone in the flat, Sahadeb faced difficulty getting the door opened. One old man came out from the opposite flat, and at his intervention, she agreed to open the door and allow him in. When Sahadeb told her that he was sent by Mr Debabrata Ghosh of Kolkata, she could not recognise who Mr Ghosh was. At one point, she said she did not know anybody in Kolkata. As he was not able to satisfy her, the old man from the opposite flat came to my rescue. He said he knew one advocate of Kolkata of the same name, so the lady might speak to him in his presence. Then the old lady depicted the crisis in her life. She had always considered Bharatmata as her *Deshmata* or motherland since her school days before the partition. During the riot in Noakhali, their house in Sandwip was set on fire, but they still did not leave their *desh*. Their island was declared to be a part of Pakistan at the time of independence. Only after the death of her old grandparents could they leave Sandwip for India. But now, in 2018, she is being asked to show records and prove the date when she had legally crossed the border. From her rambling talk, it could be gathered that her application for citizenship was not accepted at the stage of the draft list. And then, she was given a chance to appear personally before the dealing officer. Yesterday the hearing was held, and her case was again turned down for the non-compliance of statutory requirements. She was asked to approach *suo motu* the Foreigners Tribunal for a decision, or she might be arrested. The local police advised her that she must not move out of the city till the case was disposed of by the Tribunal.

Hearing the summation from Sahadeb Pal, Deb briefed his parents about the status of the case of Opu mashi. The state had already spread the noose, loosely though, around her neck. She would not be allowed to escape their clutches. He asked her mother to send a reply to her sister. He would dash to Guwahati on Sunday and prepare a strategy to save her. Sagar wrote a letter to Opu, informing her of Debu's visit to her place on Sunday. Deb dropped the letter at the GPO for quick despatch by air-mail.

Deb flew to Guwahati on Sunday in the morning. Sahadeb picked him up from the airport and reached the Saraswat Abasan. Opu was quite excited to learn from the reply sent by her Sagar didi that her nephew was coming to visit her. She didn't know how old or young he was. Did he look like his mother? She asked Rabi to be present and meet her nephew. When Deb entered her flat with Sahadeb, Opu wondered why his nephew had come with the lawyer who had visited her four days ago. Debabrata wondered why Rabi babu was present here; he did not tell Roop about his plan to visit Guwahati. Sahadeb wondered why Aparajita Debi was hesitating to accept his senior as her nephew; Rabi Guha wondered why Mr Ghosh, the lawyer, came from Kolkata to see Opu on his own. Of course, Opu told him that her nephew would visit her that day for the first time.

"Is he really the nephew of Opu? Does it mean that his mother is Sagarika?"

Everybody had their head reeling for a few seconds. They all sat on whatever sitting place they could get in the room.

"Are you Debu?" Aparajita conjectured. "Are you the son of Sagarika Ghosh?"

"Yes, I am Debu, Debabrata Ghosh, son of Satyabrata and Sagarika Ghosh. I am your nephew, and you are my one and only Opu mashi."

Deb came forward and touched the feet of Aparajita with a bow. The aunt clasped him to herself. Both wondered why they had never met each other earlier. After shedding a few drops of tears, Aparajita collected herself and Rabi and Sahadeb heaved a deep sigh of relief, having been satisfied with their queries.

"Mr Guha, is she the neighbour for whom you came to our house?"

"Yes, I didn't know that you were her nephew."

All of them had a hearty laugh.

Opu brought a small box containing her certificates and old letters of their Sandwip and Silchar days. She inherited some of them from her parents. Among all stuff was a group photo of the Nandy family when Opu was barely five years old and Sagar was nine. The two sisters were in the front row, clinging to each other. There were a few letters from Sagarika. Deb recognised the handwriting of her mother. In one letter, Sagarika had mentioned her three-year-old daughter, Bratati, and her newly born son, Debabrata.

The two lawyers began to draft an application for the Tribunal. Opu was intermittently calling up from her memory some events of her childhood and sharing them with her newfound nephew. Had he not been a sixty-five-year-old man, she would have caressed him like a darling boy.

But the foreboding of an impending catastrophe gradually changed the ambience of the room into one of seriousness. The lawyers sat together, scrutinising the previous submissions. Rabi was assisting the lawyers with various information, but when they were scratching their heads for a suitable expression, he would quickly prepare tea for them. Deb was taken aback at two things about Rabi babu; first, his agility at this age, and secondly, his knowledge of the contents of various containers in Opu mashi's kitchen!

Two drafts were prepared, one for Ms Nandy and another for Mr Rabi Guha. It was decided that the headmistress of the school and the manager of the co-operative bank would be called upon to give witness for Aparajita Debi, while the membership card of the undivided Communist Party of India and the letter of the MHA accompanying the *Tamra-Patra* would be cited as the evidence in favour of Mr Rabi Guha. The lawyers sent letters to the Secretary of the Bangali Girls' High School and the Secretary of the Co-Operative Bank, seeking information on Aparajita Nandy.

After his return, Deb briefed his parents about Opu mashi. Sagarika and Satya were amused to hear the details of his first encounter with his aunt.

"Opu mashi was quite thrilled to see me. She took out some old letters and a group photo that featured mom. She gave me all these mementoes. She has endorsed her flat in my name. She was apparently in a mood of resignation from worldly interests and preparing herself for spending her last days in an Indian jail. Unless some old student came forward to defend her, it would be difficult to save her. She does not have the freedom to leave the city and contact anybody in Tezpur or Silchar.

"Then how shall we meet her?" Sagarika asked her husband.

"If Muhammad cannot come to the mountain, the mountain shall go to Muhammad. We shall go to Guwahati. Debu, you will book our tickets by train. I cannot travel by air."

Deb did not mention to them anything about Opu mashi's neighbour, considering that part unnecessary and redundant. But Sagarika wanted to know much more about her sister. All her queries finally culminated in one question—*Why did she remain unmarried?*

Obviously, Deb had no answer.

Shefali, however, hedged a guess when she went to bed with Deb.

"Roop said his senior grandpa was her neighbour. You have come to know that Mr Guha was a trade unionist in Tezpur, where Opu mashi was also working as a teacher. Now the fact has come out that he was a close friend of Opu mashi for many years. Both also remained unmarried. The question is, why did they not marry?"

"I see. They might have met for the first time at Silchar. There was no possibility of their meeting each other earlier, but why did they not marry in so many years? Strange!"

After reaching Delhi, Roop approached the North Block Enquiry Office to get entry into the Ministry's office to explain his problem. He met the Under Secretary of the Ministry of Home Affairs under whose seal the letter was issued to Mr Kabindra Guhathakurta about fifty years ago, at the time of awarding the *Tamra-Patra* for Sri Rabindra Guhathakurta. The Officer expressed his lack of authority to issue another letter on a subject closed long ago. Roop was directed to meet his boss, the Deputy Secretary, with a letter explaining the background and the need for an authenticated copy of the original letter. Roop approached the officer with his letter, and the officer marked it to the section officer and asked Roop to come again the next day. Roop got the air ticket validated for a flight after two days. The next day, the dealing assistant prepared a file on his computer, connecting the scanned copy of a fifty-year-old guard file with a long note and put it up through the S.O. and the U.S. to the D.S. After the file moved back and forth two or three times with queries and answers, the D.S. ordered the Assistant to put up a draft reply. So Roop had to go again on the third day. The draft reply was corrected by the S.O., examined by the U.S., and approved by the D.S. At the end of the day, the reply was printed, but it was to be sent by post to the address of Mr Rabi Guhathakurta. Roop requested the Deputy Secretary to mark a copy of the verification letter to the State Coordinator of Panjikaran in Assam, for necessary action. Roop had to spend two days extra in New Delhi before he flew for New York.

The time for submission of the application before the Foreigners' Tribunal had come near.

As the replies to their letters did not reach till then from the school and the bank, the lawyers decided to file their petition to the FT so that Opu debi could get bail from the Tribunal till the disposal of the case. They would later submit a supplementary affidavit when fresh evidence was available. Meanwhile, Rabi babu received the letter sent by the MHA.

Chapter Eight

8. 1 Concerns of the young Indians in America

After landing at New York Airport, Roop rang up Choity with a view to handing over the packet her mother entrusted to him. They decided to meet at Wall Street McDonald's.

"So, Roop da, you went all the way to Kolkata to engage *my* lawyer father to fight the case for *my* grand aunty!"

"Your grandaunt? What do you mean?" Roop managed to ask with a hung jaw.

"Mom told me that you gave two vakalatnamas to my father, one for your senior grandpa and the other for his neighbour, Aparajita Nandy. My father went to Guwahati yesterday to trace out his aunty. Then it came to light that the aunt of my father was the neighbour of your grandpa. Therefore, you may withdraw the *vakalatnama* for her. My granny will now fight the case for her sister."

"I see! This is like a Greek drama. Some new facts getting unfolded at every turn. Will you now take your precious packet and relieve me?"

"Yes, it is precious indeed! All my original documents are here, even my birth certificate."

"Why did you get all the original documents here?"

"I shall apply for U.S. Citizenship. Never know when some agency will bring a charge that before independence, my grandparents lived in some village that is now in Bangladesh, and therefore, our allegiance to India is doubtful. After all, the laws of citizenship can be modified at any time by the ruling party by a simple majority."

"Yes, even the constitutional provisions can be amended by them, so long as they enjoy the two-third majority in the Lok Sabha and a simple majority in the Rajya Sabha. When this is done, it will be in the name of the security of the state, but everybody knows that such laws are used against politically inconvenient people.

You know, four years ago, I thought of going back to India. I had a tiff with Shri on this issue. But now, seeing the illogical harassment of our grandparents, I am also worried for myself. It will certainly be better if *we* take American citizenship and simultaneously enjoy the benefits of OCI[55]."

Choity smiled at Roop's use of the word 'we' but did not object to it. She said, "By the way, do you remember Babul? I met him again in a program of the Bengali Association. He said his father opposed adopting the citizenship of another country. His mother is a close friend of my mom, and she has no objection to adopting the citizenship of a first world country."

"I had met them in your house. Mr Noor Rahaman is a patriotic Indian. He is Indian by choice. But under the 1985 Amendment, he may not get through the citizenship test. Sahana madam is a Khasi by birth. Shillong was a part of Assam at that time. Her father settled in Guwahati when Meghalaya became a separate state. Now she is not recognised as an Assamese citizen. She is asked to take the citizenship of Meghalaya. But she has no land property there and no permanent address. Both are now in West Bengal, residing for more than thirty years and accepted as Bengali in the Bengali society."

"I don't understand one thing. Our country is India. There is only one citizenship. How can a state determine the citizenship of an individual who may be moving from one place to another, from state to state? Will not Mrs Rahaman be treated as an Indian citizen if neither Meghalaya nor Assam agree to give her citizenship in their respective states?"

"If they are not treated as Indians, their son will also be disqualified. His passport can be confiscated. To escape such a possibility, he should adopt the citizenship of U.S. or Canada or Australia, as early as possible."

"Roop da, when will you again go to India?"

[55] Overseas Citizens of India. enjoy all fundamental rights except the right to vote.

"Maybe in three-four months, or a little later, when the Tribunal fixes the date for hearing. They have a big list of pending cases."

"Please tell me before you purchase a ticket. I may go to see my grandaunt and also meet your senior grandpa, the living freedom fighter.

After bidding her goodbye, Roop returned to the University and met his professor. Shri was in her cubicle. Hearing the voice of Roop, she popped her head up to see if Roop had come back to his cabin. Of late, she was in two minds about whether to continue her friendship with him. Roop was so good-looking and attractive. They had been friends for four years. Roop was a typical Bengali middle-class boy and had inherited a strong sense of morality. Shri liked his morality but disliked him because of his other values, especially his nagging love for his motherland. She always doubted if Roop would finally take up the citizenship of the United States. She was clear in her mind that she would not leave the U.S. for any other country in the world, least of all India. She would marry Roop only if he became a citizen of America. She would not allow anybody to take advantage of her American citizenship and marry her, only to use her as a stepping-stone for acquiring citizenship. Most of her friends were like that. But not Roop. He had already spent the number of years required for the purpose of registration, but he was still ambivalent about losing his Indian identity.

She met Roop in the canteen during the break for lunch. "Hi Roop, how are things in India? Could you solve the problems of your grandfather?"

"No. The problem has further aggravated. The local population is so much brainwashed against the immigrant Bangladeshis that anybody speaking in Bengali or having origin in East Bengal in their remote past is in a dire problem. During the early years after freedom, people of one side continued to cross over to the other, treating that side as their own country. The state did not provide a boundary wall or barbed wire fencing along the border. The border police, inadequate in number on either side, were unequal to the task of preventing trans-border ferrying. They became part of a corrupt machinery to facilitate free trade and cross-migration in lieu of handsome gratification. The minority people, who were persecuted on one side of the border, were hell-bent on crossing over to the other side where the people of their religion were in the majority. They hoped that the majority of people of their community would embrace them and help them resettle. Their all hopes were belied as destitute refugees from East Bengal were forced to go to the jungles of Andamans and *Dandakaranya* and driven out from Marichjhampi at gunpoint by the police. The people who entered Tripura considered themselves luckier than those in the refugee camps of West Bengal. They could assimilate with the migrant Bengali population already living there. The refugees who went to Assam were branded as foreigners by the Assamese speaking people. Laws were enacted to deport these foreigners. They did not find their names in the NRC of 1951. Now the government of Assam is ferreting them out, as in the game of foxhunting, after fifty, seventy years of their stay in the state. People like my senior grandpa and the grandaunt of Choity are caught in this cleft-stick situation."

"Grandaunt of Choity!" Shri exclaimed, drawing the attention of the people at other tables. "How did you find out Choity's grandaunt in Assam in these few days? Oh, you must have gone together. I see." Shri got up in a huff. Roop did not call her back in order not to create a scene in a public place.

8.2 Sagar learns of Rabi's visit to their house

Sagar was feeling chest pain as if it was the onset of a heart attack. '*What did Noor say? Rabi Guhathakurta had come to this house two weeks ago! Rabi da in this house and she could not know! How strange it was that the person she loved in her youth and for seventy bygone years she wanted to meet for once, did visit her house, sat in this drawing-room but she could not even know, let alone talk to him*!' She was in terrible anguish. She prayed every day to get one chance to apologise to him, but presently that opportunity came, only to tantalise her, and slipped away.

Doctor Shefali was in her room for some rest. In fact, she had requested Noor to pay a visit and meet her mother-in-law in the afternoon. She was keen to meet him after the abrupt departure of Roop. She would not tell her why. For one week, she was pestering Shefali to know when Noor Rahaman would again visit their house. Finally, Shefali requested Noor to find a little time for her mother-in-law, and Noor obliged without wasting any time.

After Satya went out for his afternoon walk, Shefali took Noor to Sagarika's room. Sagar asked him to sit on the single sofa in front of her bed. As Shefali knew that her mother-in-law wanted to get some confidential information, she left the room discreetly.

But after Noor had spoken for a few minutes, Sagarika felt an uneasiness in her chest, and Noor called Shefali di immediately to attend to her. Fortunately, for Sagar, her daughter-in-law was an experienced doctor, and she was at home. She immediately took charge of her and pushed an injection that saved her life.

Questioned about the talk that he had with Sagarika, Noor said that aunty wanted to know who the grandfather of Roop was. Roop had told her that he belonged to the Guhathakurta family of

Banaripara, and since then, aunty was seized by this question. As she was in Banaripara for a few years, she knew many members of this clan. It seemed she knew a freedom fighter too and wanted to cross-check his name from him. When Noor told her the name of Rabi Guha Thakurta, she was surprised. "I asked her, Aunty, do you know Rabi babu? Roop said his senior grandpa was a freedom fighter."

'She said, "Ay, Rabi da was a freedom fighter. I gave him the first bouquet of flowers when he was released from jail. We lived in the same place for nearly two years."

"Aunty, do you know that he came to this house only two weeks ago?"

"What? You mean you have seen him here, in my house?" Aunty said, almost in disbelief.'

Noor told Shefali, "When she knew that he had come to this house a few weeks ago, she was completely overwhelmed and began to crackle. She was asking herself, whining, 'He didn't come to see me. How could that be? Then what did he come here for?'"

Shefali requested Noor not to repeat this narrative to anybody, especially to her father-in-law, lest he might also face an emotional upheaval and the family be plunged into a tragedy. The old man lived his life like a Buddhist monk, practising self-restraint and containment as principles of worldly happiness. He did not deserve to receive a shock and meet a tragic end.

Satya was walking on the wide pavement outside his house. After completing a round of the Institute of Culture, with a walking stick in hand, he returned to the gate of his house. He was surprised to see an ambulance stopping there.

"Is this the house of Dr. Shefalika Ghosh?" the ambulance driver asked.

"Yes." Satya went in and found her daughter-in-law taking care of her mother-in-law, and Mr Rahaman was rushing out to guide the ambulance staff to come in with a stretcher. Satya asked, "Shefali, what happened to Sagar? Why did you call the ambulance?"

"Nothing to worry about, papa. She had a minor attack. I have pushed an injection. There is no crisis now. But let her be in a nursing home for two, three days."

Noor and Shefali accompanied Sagarika to the nursing home at the end of the road. Satya could not make out what caused the sudden problem for Sagarika. Nor did Debabrata. Sagar returned after three days.

After four months, Sahadev communicated to his Senior that the hearing was fixed by the Tribunal for a date after twenty days. He took the credit for fixing both the hearings on the same day, one after another.

It was a tough decision to allow Sagarika to travel for a full day by train, barely four months after her recovery. Sagar was insisting on her going to Guwahati so obstinately that Satyabrata could not prevail upon her. After all, this would be the only chance for the two sisters to meet each other after their long separation. He condescended when Doctor Shefalika volunteered to travel with them. Nobody saw the mischievous smile Shefali stole on her lips behind others. She could not help herself from prying into the affair of her mother-in-law.

8.3 Forays made by Noor and Sahana

A few days passed. One day Noor rang up Debu da to say that Sahana was given an assignment by her House to cover the pitiable living condition of the non-citizens in Assam. She was visiting the jails of Assam at different locations. Noor accompanied her on this trip. If the tribunal fixed the date of hearing for Rabi Guha and his neighbour, Debu da might inform him. He would like to attend the hearing at Guwahati.

Sahana had taken permission from the competent authority to visit the Female Ward of the Sanitpur Central Jail, which was presently functioning also as a Detention Centre. She had earlier visited the Goalpara (Matiya) Illegal Migrants Detention Camp. This camp was under construction on a war footing. Built for three thousand inmates, this camp would be one out of the six detention camps to be constructed in Assam to meet the exigency arising from the *panjikaran* drive.

This state would be able to hold the maximum number of eighteen thousand detainees in these camps after two years. But about four million people were excluded from the draft list. If the government conceded to enlist fifty per cent of them by conducting a review liberally, about 2 million people would still be outside the final list.

When Sahana presented the narrative to Noor in a hotel room at Tezpur, Noor intervened by saying, "You have not added the unknown number of people who have been excluded because they were not allowed to fill the form for citizenship as they came after twenty-fifth of March 1971. They were *suo motu* treated as illegal migrants or infiltrators. Some of them will be pushed back to Bangladesh, while most of them will be arrested as soon as the detention camps are ready. The declared non-citizens have lost the right to property. Driven out of their homes, they are hiding in places like abandoned go-downs or jungles. Thousands are living in shanties on arid fields under plastic sheet covers to protect their body from sun and rain.

Not allowed to live in towns, they are passing their days in hunger, in most unhygienic conditions, having no access to drinking water and health care facilities.

They are not citizens, so they do not have any constitutional rights. They are not citizens, so they do not have the right to civic amenities. They are not Indians, so they do not deserve any compassion. They are passing the time to be caught by the police whenever they want. They will not run away. Many are working on the Matiya camp project. When the camp is ready, they will jostle to enter the camp as inmates to get proper shelter and food. Who cares for citizenship?"

"Obviously, the government cannot hold so many people in camps or jails in one state. They will open many more camps in other states also," said Sahana.

"If all the states open six such camps in each state, they will hardly be able to accommodate half a million people, whereas Assam alone is going to have more than two million detainees, and the process of registration of citizens has not yet begun in other states."

"This will prove to be an ill-conceived and self-defeating project if the government launches it for the whole country. If the total detainees sum up to a minimum of 10 million people, will the state keep them in lifelong captivity? If all such people branded as foreigners or illegal migrants are let loose on bail, how will they earn their bread and live a civilised life? Without any land to till or job to support their families, they will be effaced from this earth slowly but surely."

Sahana made many despatches on the state of suspected and declared foreigners detained in different jails. It could be said that the detainees' lot was not worse than that of the convicted criminals so long as they were kept in a regular jail. The systems in jail were regulated and well-established. A camp being a new construct, it could not be said if a camp would be a better place than a jail. The life of the inmates was abominable in all jails as the prisoners did not have any human dignity. The weak ones were often abused physically by the stronger fellow prisoners.

The prospect of such a demeaning life for the grandpa of Roop saddened Noor. After retirement, he had enough time to spare. If Rabi babu, the veteran freedom fighter, needed his help, he would gladly render his services for him.

Noor did not know that the neighbour of Rabi babu was lately discovered to be the aunt of Debu da. Therefore, he was surprised to receive a call from Debu da to help Aparajita Debi. The lady had received a notice for a hearing from the Foreigners Tribunal of Gauhati. The hearing was scheduled after a week. The school where she worked as a Maths teacher or the bank where she had a savings account for thirty years were called upon to issue a certificate in her name, but they did not reply, nor did they confirm their appearance as a witness in favour of Aparajita Nandy. Since Noor was spending time in the tea gardens surrounding the Tezpur town, he might find some time to visit the Bangali Girls' High School on D.B.Road and persuade the headmistress to issue a service certificate for her and to appear as a witness for her in Gauhati Tribunal. Secondly, he could also visit the Co-operative Bank and persuade the manager to certify the opening and closing of her account. This would rescue an old customer from sheer peril.

Noor was shaken by the stories of languishing humanity reported by the press. The story of Sanaullah Khan exposed the hollow claim of the politicians that everything was hunky-dory, fair and fine. He made up his mind to visit the school where Aparajita Debi had worked as a teacher.

Noor had worked as a lecturer in Baruah College for some years before shifting to Kolkata. Many of his students were then teaching in schools. When the headmistress stood up to honour her professor, he felt confident in obtaining the certificate of employment from her. But he did not know how much ostracised the people in authority were to issue a certificate. Therefore within a few minutes of a warm reception, he found his old-student-cum-present-headmistress standing like a stone wall. She flatly denied that any Ms Aparajita had ever been a Maths teacher in the school. Noor still insisted that as the lady retired about twenty-five years ago, only some senior teachers might know her. The headmistress asked an assistant teacher to consult the teachers in the staff room. Most of the young teachers shook their heads when a more-than-fifty-five-year-old teacher said that when she was a student in this school, one Nandimani used to teach them maths. She was also the prayer teacher. The headmistress asked her not to guess but be specific about Aparajita Debi. The senior teacher failed to recollect the first name of Nandimani. This was not unusual as many teachers were known to the students by some nickname given to them by the older batches. These nicknames got carried forward by word of mouth from year to year.

Noor came back, disappointed.

In the evening, he narrated his failed mission to Sahana. She had gone to the Sonitpur Central Jail and was able to collect a lot of information on the female detainees. "Did you go to any person other than the headmistress? You had got a lead from the senior teacher, but you did not follow it up. This is the problem with professors. If something is not written in a book or a journal, or some data are not published by a government agency, they cannot see a thing before their eyes and arrive at a fact."

Sahana went on to describe how she entered the Female Ward in the jail and took a clandestine interview of an inmate. She was captured three years ago by the Karnataka police at Yaswantpur railway station and handed over to the Assam police as her ticket was from Guwahati. This woman belonged to a Hindu farmer family of Jessore, but after her marriage, she was with her in-law's family in Sylhet. The woman gave birth to two children. Gradually reduced to the stature of landless labourers, they were looking for work as daily wage labourers. The agent of a big labour contractor in Guwahati allured them to come to India, where many bridge construction projects were going on. As Sylhet was earlier a part of Assam, her husband could also speak in Assamese. He came to Assam with his family in 2001 and worked at Bogibeel. When the contract was over after twelve years, the contractor brought them to Guwahati to work on building construction projects. They stayed in a *bustee* of Bengalis for three years. The verification committee and local police worked in tandem and targeted the slums where Bengalis of India and Bangladesh lived. Finally, one day the family had to flee from Guwahati. But when the train reached the terminus, she got separated from her family and could not explain her problem to the GRP[56] in a language known to both sides. Finally, she was sent back to the GRP at Guwahati by the return train.

[56] Government Railway Police, the police of the state government deployed on the Indian railways.

The Border police booked her as a terrorist infiltrator from Bangladesh, having links with anti-Indian terrorist groups. When she was produced before a magistrate, she was ordered to be in jail custody. After spending a night in Guwahati, she was dumped in the Sanitpur jail of Tezpur. During these years, she was neither interrogated by any investigating agency nor produced before a court for bail. The jail officials told her that she was a Bangladeshi and that if the Bangladesh government did not take her back, she would have to remain there for her whole life. She did not know where her husband and children were. She observed silence about them lest they would also be caught and imprisoned. Sahana concluded, "She has no money and no lawyer. She is in a state of despair. The superintendent sometimes sends for her in his official flat and asks her to make him happy."

Noor had a soft heart. He was moved by the suffering of the woman. A girl from a farmer family in Bangladesh came to India to change her lot and get a better deal, finally got imprisoned as an infiltrator and compelled to stay with hardened criminals for three years of her life. Nobody knew when she would be freed and in what condition. Most likely, she would then be reduced to a street beggar. Noor became concerned for Rabi babu and his friend, who might face the same fate if no evidence was produced on their behalf. At night, Debu da called him again. He told Noor that Aparajita Nandy was his aunty, and therefore, Noor should leave no stone unturned to collect the testimonial for Aparajita Nandy.

The next morning, he reached the school and asked the clerk about Nandimani. The clerk was a Muslim and wanted to help Mr Rahman. He could remember the surname and said, "You mean Nandy Didimani? Is she still alive?"

"Oh, yes." It now occurred to Noor that the students called Ms Nandy 'Nandimani' as it was difficult to pronounce 'Nandy Didimani'.

"Is her first name Aparajita?"

"Sir, wait a minute." The clerk opened a steel almirah in which many old attendance registers were kept in bundles. The registers for the year 1993 and the previous thirty years showed the name of Aparajita Nandy in the roll of teachers. "Here is Aparajita Nandy, M.Sc. She was here from 1963. I had joined three years before her retirement and knew her as Onko ma'am. Sometime back, the secretary received a letter from a lawyer concerning a teacher. He collected the particulars himself and did not disclose the name of the teacher. He kept the letter with himself. Sir, what do you want to know about her?" Noor told him that the old lady was called upon to prove her citizenship. If the school issued a certificate that she worked here from 1963, she would be saved from jail. The clerk took Noor to the headmistress. She was visibly annoyed with the clerk but could not refuse to issue a 'To whom it may concern' certificate to her once-upon-a-time professor.

Noor felt confident that he had something with him to defend Opu mashi. He had to reach the Tribunal office before 10 a.m. tomorrow. Meanwhile, Sahana had also returned from the bank. The manager told her that he would give the required information if the Tribunal called him to depose. At night, they tried to inform Debabrata of the school certificate over the phone, but the signal was too feeble.

8.4 Preparations for hearing in the Tribunal

The relatives of Aparajita Debi had already begun their preparations to be present in Guwahati at the time of the hearing. Roop had picked up the *Tamra-Patra* from his Kolkata residence on the advice of Debabrata Ghosh and reached Guwahati two days in advance before the hearing. The letter of the MHA was already received by his Rabi dada.

Deb reached by the morning flight of the next day. After checking in his hotel, he went to the flat of his Opu mashi. Sahadeb had filed a supplementary affidavit incorporating new materials like the letter of MHA, but it did not contain an unambiguous reply to the correspondence. It said that records older than five years were weeded out following the Manual of Office Procedure, only the name of Rabi Guha as one of the recipients of *Tamra-Patra* could be verified from the guard file of the year 1966. Debabrata, Sahadeb, Rabindra and Roop sat together to prepare their arguments and counterarguments. Opu sat on the divan listening intently to their discussion. Deb was checking on his mobile phone to see if the train of his family was running on time and if his parents were all right. At noon, Noor rang up Deb to confirm that he could obtain the certificate for his Opu mashi. But what would happen to Rabi babu and his neighbour?

"You mean you have collected the certificate for my Opu mashi? That is great. Roop has got a letter for his grandpa from the MHA. You come to the Tribunal office directly by ten," said Deb. It was the turn of Noor to be surprised at Deb's show of indifference towards Rabi Guha's neighbour.

The lawyers mentioned the school certificate in a fresh supplementary.

Choity had joined her family in Kolkata. She checked from Roop if the hearing of his senior grandpa would also take place on the same day.

Thammi was collecting information on Roop. Why did he come again to India within six months? Choity was escorting her grandpa and grandma on their train journey to Guwahati, accompanied by her doctor mother. Everybody was excited at the prospect of seeing Ms Aparajita Nandy. Satya, Shefali, and Choity were brimming with simple curiosity, while Sagarika was in a complex mood of penance and expectation. Penance because she had not maintained any contact with her younger sister and expectation to meet Rabi da, her love-at-first-sight after nearly seventy years. She could gather from Choity that Roop came with her from the U.S. to stand beside his senior grandfather during the hearing in the Tribunal. They reached Guwahati at four p.m., Right Time.

Deb received them at the station and took them to his hotel. A room was reserved for the Rahaman family. But when would Noor and Sahana come? The evidence would be vital for Opu mashi.

Rabi entered the flat of Opu in the afternoon with a flask of tea. Ever since Malati left the job of maid, Rabi used to cook lunch for her in his kitchen and prepared tea for both in the morning and evening because her Parkinson's problem had accentuated.

After the hurly-burly of visitors in the morning, she felt mentally exhausted. After taking lunch with Roop and Rabi da, she slept for two hours in her flat. In the afternoon, Opu sat by the open window. She was waiting for Rabi dada. Talking to Rabi dada over a cup of tea for one hour was the most precious time for her. Her face glowed up as she heard Rabi stepping in.

The refracted rays of the setting sun entered the flat through its westside window and filled the interior with magical chiaroscuros. The two persons were face to face with two cups of tea, entranced.

"Rabi dada, it has been more than a year that I have not seen the sunset on the Brahmaputra with you. I do not know if I shall have the chance once again."

"Why do you talk like this, Opu? We can go to the riverside tomorrow."

"Tomorrow is our hearing. I do not know if they will take me to some prison from the court itself. They may not arrest you as you were a freedom fighter. There will be *hungama* if they do. Shall we be separated? That will be the most dreadful thing for me. Can't we be together in a jail?"

"Why are you becoming so weak and pessimistic? A reputed lawyer from Kolkata will appear for us. He is your own nephew. He will make an all-out effort for you. Roop has told me that the entire Ghosh family reached Guwahati this afternoon by train. You can understand how deeply they are concerned for you."

"Don't tell me all that!" Opu burst out like the Vesuvius. "Nobody in this family knows me or has ever seen me. Even my sister, my childhood icon, did not meet me after she left for Barishal. I was hardly fifteen."

"Kanak aunty was very fond of you."

"True, but when we passed through the harrowing time between 1946 and 1962, they did not stand by us except writing a few letters. I don't know why they are making such a show now."

"What happened to Kanak aunty and Suresh uncle?"

"I don't know. After moving from Silchar to Tezpur, I did not give my address to anybody as I did not have one."

Rabi remained silent. He felt there was a big communication gap between the two branches. The head sir and Kanak aunty were, according to him, broad-hearted persons. At one point, he was angry with Sagarika for walking out on him but when he came to know that Sagarika got his letter only after her marriage with Satyabrata Ghosh, his anger gradually dissipated over the years. Maybe she had no choice at that point in time. But he wanted to meet Sagarika at least once to free himself from the vow. He could not ask her address from Opu, as he never disclosed to her that he had a relationship with Sagarika. When he learnt from Roop that Choity's grandparents were coming to Guwahati, he felt excited at the prospect of meeting Sagarika once again.

"What happened? What are you thinking, Rabi dada?"

"I am feeling guilty for not keeping any track of Kanak aunty. She was stitching one *aasan* for me and another one for my wife. I don't know what happened to those *aasans*."

"She had sent one aasan for me when my father went to attend didi's marriage. She wanted that I should sit on that aasan during my marriage rituals. That wish of her remained unfulfilled." Then suddenly, in a spurt of emotion, she began to charge Rabi. "Why didn't you marry me, Rabi dada? I waited for your 'yes' for my whole life."

Rabi had no answer. He remained quiet. Darkness pervaded the earth unnoticed. After some time, he got up and went out, shutting the door.

In the afternoon, Roop had gone out to take a stroll on the bank of the river Brahmaputra. His mind was, however, occupied by the revelations during the prolonged conference. Earlier, when he visited Guwahati, he did not take much notice of Aparajita Debi. He only knew that his senior grandpa took care of the solitary, old woman, being the next-door neighbour. The man enjoyed playing the role of a good Samaritan all through his life. But after attending the day's conference, he learnt many facts relating to his senior grandpa and his soulmate, Opu. He could realise that the two persons had a deep relationship that could be described as metaphysical. No one knew exactly when this relationship began. He learnt that the father of Aparajita Debi had offered her hands to her Rabi dada, and she had also given her consent, but finally, they decided not to marry, nor to enter a modern live-in relationship but to live for each other.

'*How is it possible to spend the whole life in such a surrealistic relationship*?' he asked the question to the setting sun.

After dinner, Roop lay on a folding cot placed transverse to the charpoy of his senior grandpa.

"May I ask you a question, dadamoshai?"

"Yes, my grandson, you have grown up. You can ask any question."

"Dadamoshai, do you love Opu ma'am?"

"Yes, Roop. I have loved her since I met her in Silchar. But she fell in my love much earlier when she lived in Banaripara. I did not take notice of her at that time as she was barely twelve. We were separated quickly by the tide of events. I went to jail for three years, and she went back to Chattagram to continue her studies."

"Then why did you not marry her when both of you were at Silchar?"

"Grandson, we are not the authors of our life stories. The Great Author who is writing it enjoys providing many twists and turns, surprises, and irony in its course. Who could ever think that the young men and women of East Bengal, who took part in the Quit

India movement and were incarcerated for the freedom of the country, would now face the charge of being illegal migrants or foreigners in independent India? Just like the course of a river, an individual's life is not a straight line. There are many turns and twists, curves, and cascades in our lives. If you wait for one more day, you may get some answer to your question."

"No problem, dadamoshai. Please have a good sleep tonight, as tomorrow will be a busy day."

8.5 Hearing in the Foreigners Tribunal

The tribunal office was located on the backside of a shopping complex constructed by the city development authority. It was quarter to ten, when Roop reached the place in a cab with his senior grandpa and Nandy madam. Roop was not sure how he should address her. It was confirmed that she was the girlfriend of his grandpa, his dear dadamoshai, and she should be given the status of grandma. *But as they were still not married would it be correct for him to address her as grandma*? He knew that Bengali society was full of confusions and contradictions as distinguished from the American society, and so he decided to play safe. The issue would probably be settled today, with the judgment of the Tribunal on their citizenship.

Roop took them to the hall where the hearing would take place, made them seated comfortably in the waiting room and came out on the foyer. It was so stuffy inside. One by one the court staff, lawyers and petitioners came. Sahadeb Pal, advocate accompanied his senior, Mr Debabrata Ghosh. Roop saw that Ghosh uncle had come with his mother, Mrs. Sagarika Ghosh, but she was not quite comfortable to get down the cab. Roop went ahead to assist her. Sagarika was pleased to see him and extended her right hand to take his support. Sagarika held the arm of Roop without any hesitation; he was the grandson of Rabi da. He was like her own grandchild.

Rabi da was in London for many years. Did he marry after returning to India or before? Whom did he marry? He must be happily married and must've forgotten the trivial promises he made in his early youth.

She needed to take brief rest after three/four steps. She held the arm of Roop firmly and asked him, "Roop, has your grandfather already arrived?"

"Oh yes. Senior Grandpa and Nandy madam came with me. Granny, do you know my grandfather?'

"Yes, I know the Guhathaurtas."

"Perhaps you do not know that my dadamoshai died seven years ago. His elder brother Rabi is my Boro dadamoshai."

"I know Rabi da. Who are the members of his family?"

"I am the one in third generation from his family. Perhaps you know that he did not marry."

Sagarika was shocked. She stumbled at the threshold of the hall. If Roop had not held her firmly, she would have fallen on the floor. Opu looked at the entrance door, hearing the swish of an averted fall. She could recognise her Sagar didi instantaneously and stood up to welcome her. Sagarika tried to restore her balance and then quickly cast a glance around the room and focussed her sight on a grey-haired, tanned-skin old man sitting erect by the side of, yes, she must be her cousin, Opu!

The two old ladies hugged each other, uttering various unintelligible sounds as mark of primitive emotion. During this time, Sagarika kept her gaze on Rabi who was standing behind Opu. After releasing her sister, Opu followed her gaze, and then introduced him, "He is Rabi dada, Mr Rabi Guha. We are sailing in the same boat." "I know him. He is the son of Biren kaka. He was in London. How did you find him here?" asked Sagarika.

Before the conversation could proceed further, two groups of people entered the place – the Member, the government pleader and an executive magistrate in the first group, followed by Choity, Shefalika and Satyabrata. Debabrata asked Shefali to monitor the location of Sahana on her smart phone, as the presence of Noor is important for Opumashi.

In a few minutes, the business of the tribunal started with the case of Ms. Aparajita Nandy. She stood in the witness box, undaunted. Sahadeb Pal, the local advocate led the petition on her behalf. The proceeding went on with examination and cross-examination by both sides. While Sahadeb harped repeatedly on the sentimental aspect of her evacuation and subsequent struggle in life, the government pleader was focussed only on the legal requirements. He would not give up an inch of space to Aparajita so long as she did not fulfil the statutory conditions. Arguments continued for long, but the lights of hope for Ms. Nandy flickered off one by one. She could not cite any documented proof for her legal immigration, or for her long stay in Assam. Her passport was destroyed in floodwater, then how would she prove her date of entry into post-partition India. Debabrata pointed out that the government could have easily verified the facts if they had acted in time. Even at this stage the issue of passport in her name by the government of Pakistan was a verifiable matter. Even if the Bangladesh government failed to connect the records, the Indian immigration office of Akhaura-Agartala border could be able to confirm her entry in 1955. The Tribunal member however did not agree to direct the State Coordinator in this regard. He accepted the submission of the deputy magistrate that it was impractical to take up verification of lakhs of refugees. The G.P. pointed out that under the Citizenship Rules, the applicant-refugees were to submit their required testimonials.

The Member however agreed to accept other proofs issued by some government agency, reputed employer, bank or post office or LIC etc. But unfortunately, no such certificate could also be submitted by the petitioner. Debabrata argued that the agencies were threatened by some organisations against issuing certificates to refugees. Ms. Nandy's banker stated that they would issue a certificate, only when the Registrar or State Coordinator called for such certificate.

"Do you want to say that even the school where she claims to have worked, refused to issue a service certificate?" questioned the Member. Debabrata began to fidget, his eyes searching for Noor in the audience.

Noor and Sahana had already entered the hearing room stealthily. At this juncture, Noor stood up and said, "Excuse me, sir, here is a certificate for Aparajita Debi from the headmistress of the school. I have personally brought it from Tezpur just now."

"Who are you?" roared the G.P.

"He is Mr Noor Rahaman, a retired professor. He was deputed by me to approach the headmistress personally for the certificate." Mr Ghosh collected the original certificate from Noor and gave it to the Member.

There was glee among the audience. The executive magistrate and the G.P. were seen conferring in a whisper. The G.P. said that a certificate issued 'To whom it may concern' and 'based on records and in good faith' was not acceptable as the present headmistress did not know her. She was needed to affirm personally for whom the certificate was issued. "We shall examine her to see if her certification is satisfactory and tenable."

Debabrata urged the tribunal to call the headmistress of the school to appear before the tribunal to testify the certificate. Again, the G.P. stood up to object that this was not the practice in the tribunal. The petitioner was to produce the witness. Debabrata argued that the tribunal had enough power to frame its rules and should extend its authority to help the old and the infirm, the poor and the downtrodden, the illiterate and the specially enabled so that justice was delivered correctly to all.

The Member gave seven days' time, when his Opinion would be communicated.

"Next case" he announced, "Mr Rabindra Guhathakurta."

Rabi came to the witness box after helping Opu come out of it. After the initial formalities, Sahadeb Pal began to examine the petitioner, bringing out the strong points for him. Without losing time he came to his role in freedom struggle and wanted to impress upon the Tribunal that the petitioner was a freedom fighter. "He was incarcerated for three years in Barishal jail for taking part in the August Kranti movement."

The Member asked Rabi about his sacrifice and Rabi replied to him succinctly.

Opu was listening intently to the statement made by Rabi. Opu said in a whisper, "Why are you understating your heroic act for the country?" Rabi stopped his statement thinking that he had probably disclosed more than what was warranted.

Both the Member and the lawyers could hear what Opu said. Debabrata took the cue and asked, "Mr Guha, did the Govt of India recognise your sacrifice for the freedom of this country?"

Rabi did not know what to say. He never asked for any recognition. But his younger brother Kabi was unstoppable. He pursued the government by providing all records from Barishal Town library, Banaripara police station and Barishal court to issue a Tamra-Patra in his elder brother's name. But Rabi had never kept it with him. Roop was sitting at the rear with Choity, engaging her in small talk. Debabrata called Roop to show the Tamra-Patra to the Member. To the surprise of Rabi, Roop took out the Tamra-Patra from his long side bag and kept it before the member. The copperplate bore the state insignia and a text lauding the role played by Sri Rabindra Guhathakurta in the freedom struggle. The Member was profoundly impressed to see a Taamra-Patra for the first time in his life.

The government pleader was however indomitable. "How does this plate of copper help prove his citizenship?"

"Mr Guha, do you have any letter from the Central government testifying to the award of the Tamra-Patra that was given fifty years ago. How do we connect the Tamra-Patra with you?"

"Can I connect myself to anything on this earth? One officer signed a letter fifty years ago. I have never seen him. Today, you are asking me for a letter from the present office bearer to authenticate the signature of the old letter. It is not practical. How shall I convince you of the genuineness of a copper plate? Perhaps, it has no value today other than the value of the metal."

"But this letter was issued by the Ministry only four months ago when I approached them for verification." Roop stood up and produced a copy of the letter given by the Deputy Secretary of the MHA addressed to the State Coordinator of ANRC.

The G.P. looked at it without showing any respect and commented that the letter did not testify to the old letter. It merely stated a historical fact that once upon a time, a Tamra-Patra was given to one Rabindra Guhathakurta. The connection between the recipient with the deponent was not established by the MHA.

The Member pulled an aggrieved face, made a tch-tch sound between his tongue and lips and showed his helplessness.

The G.P. came back once again. He pointed out that there was a time lag in the story of the petitioner. He had left Barishal in July 1947. But he claims to be in Assam from October,1957.

Sahadeb Pal again examined the petitioner to bring out the story of his life during these years. But the G.P. pooh-poohed the story of his voyage to London as a copy from the life-story of Col. Suresh Biswas, the adventurer. There was no proof that he was in London in or around August 1947, he said emphatically

Rabi did not know what to say. He could produce the diploma certificates of the University of London. But he did not have them with him.

Suddenly, the senior Mrs. Ghosh got up in the audience and said, "Here is a letter he wrote from London in October 1947."

She displayed an airmail letter from her handbag. Choity took the letter and gave it to the Member. The Royal mail carried the insignia of the crowned side-face of the sixth George and the addressee as 'Mrs Sagarika Ghosh, care of Mr Satyabrata Ghosh, Near Patra Market, Krishnagar, Nadia, West Bengal, India'.

The name of the sender was written on the letter,

Rabi Guha, A53/2/F South Street, London, U.K.

The Member saw the cover page and commented, "We should be satisfied. What do you say?"

The G.P. smiled mischievously and returned the letter to Debabrata, saying, "I don't want to read the letter in court. After all, it is your mother's treasure."

Red-faced at the awkward development, Debabrata returned the letter through Choity. In the audience, Shefali elbowed Sahana and exchanged meaningful glances.

Only Noor made a comment to Satyabrata, "Uncle, it is good luck that aunty brought the letter with her. This is called premonition."

"But we came to attend her sister's hearing! I do not even know that Rabi babu is also facing the same charge on the same day."

"Both are your son's clients. I, too, didn't know that the freedom fighter's neighbour was Debu da's Opu mashi."

Meanwhile, the G.P. resumed his interrogation, "Well, Mr Guha, you submitted your party membership card as proof of your continuous long stay in Assam. But unfortunately, documents issued by a political party are not admissible. If we make an exception in your case, this may open a floodgate, and political parties will issue cards giving false dates of issue. Can't you submit some other document about your place of residence?"

"I thought about it but could not find any solution. I lived in the party commune attached to a party office. Wholetime workers are allotted a charpoy in the dormitory and are served rice meals twice a day from the community kitchen. Everybody was equal. Who will give me a residential certificate? I cannot issue a certificate for myself, can I?"

The G.P. spoke again in a pseudo-sympathetic tone, "Mr Guha, if you produce a certificate from an M.P. or a state minister, we would reconsider."

The Member adjourned the sitting for a week, leaving no doubt in the mind of the audience as to the final Opinion of the tribunal. Debabrata asked Sahadeb to get ready to make an appeal to the High Court.

Chapter Nine

9.1 A family reunion

It was already one-thirty p.m., and everybody was hungry. In the morning, Roop had seen that at one end of the Complex, there was a Punjabi *dhaba*[57]. He took the help of Choity to herd the group slowly to the Dhaba. The ambience was typically Punjabi, with a tandoor in front to prepare roti and a *sigree* by the side for other veg and non-veg preparations. One amiable-looking *Sardarji*[58] in a blue turban was sitting at the cash counter. But the other workers were mostly Biharis.

The group was absorbed within itself. Noor introduced himself to Opu mashi, proudly taking the credit for the certificate from her school. Opu was overwhelmed that an unknown person had come forward to help her at this critical hour, and he was a Muslim. She looked at him gratefully and wanted to know how he managed to get the certificate. Sagarika and Rabi found the slot opportune to break the ice.

He wondered aloud, "Didimani, how could you produce that seventy-year-old letter at the right moment?"

"I had received only two letters from you, and this one is the second one. I brought both the letters with me. It was just providential that the Government Pleader asked for proof of your being in London, and I remembered the letter in my bag."

"Thank you. But it is a bigger surprise for me that I am seeing you here today!"

---

57 An wayside eating joint.

58 A Sikh, who defends his religion, besides the weak and oppressed people.

As the group entered the dhaba, everybody was eyeing for a seat close to their person of choice. When the dust settled, it was seen that Choity sneaked herself between Rabi and Sagarika, Shefali and Satya were on two sides of Opu; Roop and Noor and Deb and Sahana were on two other sides of the table.

"Papa, do you know who is sitting on your right? She is your sister-in-law," said Shefalika.

Satya and Aparajita smiled at each other. Aparajita said, "Jamai babu[59]!"

"How sweet to hear this call from you, Aparajita!"

"Opu, not Aparajita. I shall call you Satya da." Satya extended his hand, and Opu allowed him to touch her trembling fingers. "How nice it would have been if I could touch this hand when we were youthful!"

Seeing a big family enter his restaurant, the Sardar himself rushed to the table after the customers had taken seats and the waiter had served them normal drinking water. Sardarji wanted to know what they would like to have. On behalf of the group, Roop and Choity placed orders for palak-paneer, mixed vegetables, butter chicken, dal-makhani, dahi, and tandoori roti.

Opu said, "Grandson, will you get me a half plate of plain rice? It is difficult for me to chew thick roti."

Her request immediately found support from Satya and Sagarika. Roop ordered two plates of rice and reduced the number of rotis. He also added some bottles of cold drinks as everybody was thirsty. The Punjabi Sikh owner went back to his seat after conveying his instructions to the cooks and head bearer. The group felt relaxed and began to chirp.

Choity started by asking Rabi, "Dadu, did you really fight with the British police? Were you a revolutionary in disguise!"

"Hmm. Who told you all this?"

"Earlier, I heard the story from Roop da, but today it is confirmed in the court. Why do you not tell us the event elaborately?" Rabi was trying to avoid Choity, as he wanted more to hear from Sagarika.

"Why don't you tell her, Rabi dada? Are you sorry for what you had done that day?" said Opu.

---

[59] Husband of one's sister.

"I am not sorry. But today, I am not proud either. You see, so many revolutionaries laid down their lives, but what has happened to the ideals, they had championed? Now love for the country is not talked about. I am worried because, in the present panjikaran exercise, love for India, the sacrifices made for the country, endeavours made to maintain the integrity of the new India, and service given to the countrymen have absolutely no place. There is no emotional content. Very few freedom fighters are now alive. Maybe by 2025, the entire tribe will be extinct. I was kept in jail for three long years without trial. I was detained in a jail full of criminals Finally, a chargesheet was filed with the charge of 'attempt to murder'. If the S.I. had succumbed, I would have been hanged within three months. But all those sufferings have no value today. I never asked for anything in return, any post or money. I kept serving my motherland and her exploited working class in my own way. But the government will now brand me as an outsider, a foreigner - because I did not keep any record of my entry to Assam in 1957, because I did not purchase any property, or stay in a leased or rented property. Because I did not join the party in power, nobody will oblige me today by issuing a certificate. But I do not lament my fate. Just think of any person who came to this side of the border to settle here permanently and serve this country with love and loyalty but is being relegated to prison because some certificates or testimonials are not available with him. Just think of this lady who taught in a school for nearly thirty years. But now, the situation is such that nobody is coming forward to confirm it. How can an exercise of this nature take place in a charged atmosphere of hatred against a particular section of people?"

Sahana said, "Here, the society is so divided and fragmented that many government functionaries are biased against the Bengali speaking people, even before it has been established that they are illegal immigrants."

Satya commented, "Who is a foreigner? Debu's mother is a citizen, but her sister is a foreigner? The people who migrated from East Bengal between 1947 and 1949 to West Bengal, though initially called refugees, got citizenship of India automatically by the Constitution, but the Bengalis who reached Assam during the same period were called infiltrators from East Pakistan and not counted as citizens in

1951. Those who were Indians one day, how did they become non-Indians after a date without doing anything? When did they eschew their Indianness?"

Food was already served. Shefali chose to serve it personally to the oldies by her side.

Opu asked her, "Are you Debu's wife? What is your name?"

"Yes, Shefali is my name."

"I am Aparajita, sister of your mom-in-law."

"Yes, these days, I am hearing a lot of you. You were the learned lady of Sandwip."

Opu felt happy that she had been called the learned lady in front of Sagarika. Shefali also introduced Sahana as the journalist-wife of Noor bhai.

Opu smiled at them and asked, "Why did you go to Tezpur? Only to visit my school?"

"No," Sahana said, "I went to visit the Sonitpur Jail to make a report on the condition of the female detainees. I interviewed a female intern. She used to be in Guwahati three years ago. The family ran away from Guwahati, but she was caught at Yaswantpur railway station and sent back to Assam police. She has been living in prison for three years with no hope. There has been no investigation, no trial. She does not know where her husband and children are. Absolutely hopeless."

"What is her name?" asked Opu.

"Malati. I think she is around thirty-five."

Opu suddenly began to weep. Tears ran down her cheeks. "A Hindu Bengali girl, just like us! She was born in Jessore. Was it such a crime to be in India, that she must spend years in jail with criminals?" Opu said punctuating her words with sob.

Sahana and Shefali wondered at the unexpected show of emotion. Rabi commented, "Malati was her maid a few years ago."

Satya looked at Rabi and then asked Sagarika. "Sagar, will you tell us when you first met Rabi babu?"

Everybody became silent. Was Satyabrata doubting Sagarika at this age? Sagarika had already produced Rabi's letter to her in the court. She had no way to deny her once-upon-a-time relationship with Rabi.

But Sagarika was a gutsy lady. She maintained an expressionless face and narrated how, one day, Haru da announced the bail of Rabi Guha when she was discussing some matters of the girls' school with Biren uncle. Biren Guha was the father of Rabi Guha.

"Next day, he was received at the school ground by the people of Banaripara. His four friends also joined the programme. A stage was erected before the school building. I had not seen in my life such overwhelming spontaneity with which the crowd brought him to the school ground. He was carried by his friends on a chair. People were shouting Vande Mataram as well as Rabi Guhathaurta zindabad. Haran Mukherjee was on the dais. They asked my father, the head sir, also to come on the stage. I was given the task of conducting the programme. The familiar sedan chair of my father's office stopped where I was waiting with a large bouquet. He came down from the chair, unsure to look at me. I handed over the bouquet to the man standing before me and said, '*I salute you, our valiant freedom fighter. Please come onto the dais. I am the teacher-in-charge of the new girls' school.*' Then Haran babu came forward and embraced him. Others also embraced him one by one. I began to conduct the function with a welcome speech. I remember that I addressed him as the morning sun of liberation. All other speakers narrated the incident of the ninth of August and described how he faced the police torture and yet kept on shouting Vande Mataram. He delivered an impromptu speech, thanking everybody. He hoped that freedom would be achieved soon."

Sagarika closed her narration by saying, "That was how I met Rabi da for the first time. Let me add that I saw him for the last time when he came to Nabadwip to attend my marriage. He left India and went to London. I do not know why. This letter somehow reached my *sasurbari*, despite carrying an incomplete address. My father-in-law read this letter and wrote to Biren kaka, giving him the address of his son."

The Sardarji came to the table with an extra plate of onion and cucumber, cut into round pieces and enquired about the quality of the food. He wanted to be sure that some preparations were not unduly hot. Choity and Sahana thanked him profusely.

"Thank you, madam. You told us about the reception given to Rabi babu when he was released on bail. But we want to know about the action that led to his imprisonment. We know Mr Guha will not narrate the story of his valour, but will you give us an eye-witness's account of the event?" Noor said to Sagarika.

Before a fumbling Sagarika could say anything, Aparajita began to say, "Among the eye-witnesses, only I am present here." After casting a winning glance at her Sagar didi, Opu said, "Rabi dada already described the outline of the event in the court. But he did not describe his role. Kanak aunty, Sodu aunty, Kabi, and myself had taken a position on the roof of their house to have a clear view of the meeting. But within fifteen minutes, everything went topsy turvy. From a rickshaw, two policemen began to announce through a *chong*[60] that the D.M. had clamped section 144, prohibiting any gathering of more than five persons, and therefore, the assembly of men in the school ground was unlawful.

But the speech had already begun. The sub-inspector of the police station came with fifteen-twenty lathi wielding policemen and began a lathi charge on the crowd to disperse them. The speakers began to shout new slogans given by Gandhi ji. Rabi dada and his friends formed a human ring around the leaders on the stage. Azharuddin Daroga became mad with anger. He jumped on the stage and began to kick the leaders down the platform. Then he took out his revolver and fired once in the air. He threatened to fire at anybody going near him. Rabi dada was undaunted and challenged the Daroga to fire at him. As Haran babu took out a letter from his pocket and began to shout at him, the Daroga grabbed him by the collar and raised the butt of his revolver to crush his head, but Rabi dada quickly delivered a punch at his unguarded diaphragm. It was a massive blow with full body weight, and the huge Azharuddin Daroga slumped like a dead body. On the ground, many people were writhing in pain. The policemen rushed to rescue their officer. Rabi dada and his friends ran behind the school building."

[60] Funnel-shaped device to enhance the volume of speech, used when microphone was not available in remote areas.

Rabi knocks out the armed Daroga of the British Govt.

"Then what happened?" asked Noor.

"I can't describe that. A British police officer came with many armed policemen. They began to beat the local inhabitants indiscriminately. When Rabi dada and his friends were caught, the British officer began to beat them mercilessly. Rabi dada continued to shout Vande Mataram till he was half-dead. Then the police packed them on two cycle vans and left for the district town. His body was totally smeared in blood."

As Opu stopped here in a choked voice, tears rolled out at the recollection of the incident.

Rabi looked at her and said, "Satya da, your sister-in-law ran a mile behind the van, shouting at the police for my release. She went back from the ferry ghat at the end of her futile chase, crying and sobbing."

Everybody became silent for a few seconds till Shefalika observed that Opu had not eaten anything till then. Her fingers were just groping aimlessly for the rice on her plate. She said, "Opu mashi, your fingers are trembling. May I help you?" She began to spoon-feed her like a child. Opu looked at her with gratitude in her eyes.

Sahana commented, "Who feeds you on other days, Opu mashi?" Opu looked at Rabi coyishly. Choity and Roop burst into laughter.

The Sardarji came back and asked the ladies with great humility if the quality of food was alright. When most of them commended the quality of cooking, he felt confident and asked in chaste Bengali, "Madam, apnara ki Kolkata theke berate esechhen (Are you tourists from Calcutta)?"

His sudden switch to Bengali immediately befriended him to the group. Very soon, he learnt that they came to attend their hearing at the Foreigners Tribunal, as two members of the group had failed the citizenship test.

"My name is Balwant Singh. We have also come from Pakistan. Some of my grandpa's brothers were butchered in a train when they left for Amritsar on the fourteenth of August. My father was only ten and my grandfather forty when they crossed the border on foot after a month. All the Hindus and Sikhs of West Punjab were either killed or were forced to quit. Since the Punjabi Muslims of East Punjab were treated exactly the same way, the refugees of either side were rehabilitated on the enemy's property. But the number of refugee Hindus and Sikhs was much more in number, and many of us spread out to other states. In Guwahati, we started small businesses of different types and prospered gradually. We were also asked to apply before the Panjikaran officer. I was born in a Guwahati hospital, but my father was not. They asked him for various documents, but he left this world this year at the age of 79 with a regret that he could not have the citizenship certificate before his death. He was deeply hurt that he was asked to prove that he was an Indian. His elder son, my elder brother, had joined the army and participated in the Kargil War. He got a Vir Chakra posthumously. And here, they were going to declare his father a non-citizen, a persona non-grata, because he did not have a proof of entry in Assam many decades ago. When we wrote to the government that we would return the Chakra if our father's name were not included, the Registrar conveyed the inclusion of my father's name in the list. I got the benefit consequentially." Sardarji ended his tale with a smile.

When the group came out of the restaurant, uncertain about their next move, Sagarika came close to Opu and asked, "Opu, why did you remain unmarried?"

"I don't know. Rabi dada accepted the proposal made by Papa but he kept me waiting."

"Didn't you ask him why?"

"I did. He said he was bound by a vow to somebody."

At the same time, Satyabrata was talking to Rabi. He wanted to know why Rabi had disappeared from Nabadwip all of a sudden and then why did he leave the country without anybody's knowledge. Rabi understood that Satya da was unhappy with him for writing the letter to Sagarika. He would be more suspicious if his questions were not answered. Rabi needed to be a little away from the crowd to explain what caused the mental anguish that forced him to leave the country. He took him aside for a talk.

Satya repeated his question to Rabi, "Why did you run away from Nabadwip in the first place and then finally from the country?"

"Satya da, those days I was under severe mental strain. The final hearing of my case was going on. I had to be present in the court for the whole day. If the case lingered up to fourteenth or fifteenth of August, the judgment might have gone against me. The incident of Didimani happened simultaneously, and I could not stand by her.

I hope you are aware of the circumstances in which Didimani and her family came to Nabadwip. She was threatened by a local Muslim gangster to marry her after three days.. Panicked, the headmaster moshai left Banaripara with his family under the cover of darkness. The gangster came to know of this within one hour of their departure, and his men burnt their abandoned quarters at night. The communal flare-up during the next few days made many Hindus homeless. We, too, had to leave our ancestral home after the first week of July. A letter from the head sir reached us just before our departure. It was an invitation card for Didimani's marriage.

After we reached Kolkata, I was asked by my father to go to Nabadwip to attend the marriage. Headmaster moshai had specifically requested my presence. My father thought that the request of Suresh da should not be dishonoured. Nabadwip was a new place for him.

The presence of a reliable young person would be of great help to him. Sagarika was my friend. I thought she would be happy to see me in her marriage. I went to Nabadwip on the day before her marriage. The next morning the head sir sent me to Bowbazar of Calcutta to buy a piece of jewellery. You know all that. It was a risky job to carry big cash or an expensive ornament on a crowded train. Bowbazar was still a riot-prone area of Calcutta. However, I could come back in time safely.

In the evening, I was taking a stroll outside the marriage venue. I saw our Haru da of Banaripara approaching to attend the marriage of Didimani. He told me that most of the Hindus of Banaripara had vacated their houses after the murder of Badal Majhi. Shah Jahan had found out that Haru da was the person who helped Sagarika to flee. Haru da was forcibly converted to Islam. Only on that condition, he was allowed to continue there. He had nowhere to go. Our evacuation had made people like him completely helpless. They could not put up a fight against the Muslim goondas and had to surrender meekly.

I was so upset by these incidents that I decided to lodge a protest with the British Government against their decision to partition the country. The British government was a secular one. The Anglican Church was officially recognised as the religion in the United Kingdom. But they did not practise discrimination against people belonging to other religions, nor did they take political and economic decisions based on religious considerations. Then how were they working on a bill that would divide their Indian Empire into two countries based on religion? The British Parliament was going to give a deadly blow to the unity and integrity of their Indian dominion. They were also deceiving their own people by reneging secularism as state policy. I decided to immediately go to London and lodge a protest before the bill was passed. I had estimated that preparation of the draft, the introduction of the bill in two houses, debate on various clauses and passage of the bill would take at least six months after the third of June. Without wasting any time, I left Nabadwip for Calcutta, reached Howrah station at night, and spent the night on a bench of the station. Without going home, I roamed outside the Dock area during the day. A cargo ship was scheduled to leave on a voyage to Dover. I intercepted a *khalasi* of the ship in a liquor shop. When he boozed out, I wore his dress and boarded the ship at midnight with his drunk colleagues, who were the firemen of the boiler. You know the rest."

Satya was critically examining the narrative of Rabi while listening with rapt attention. Unable to detect any hole, he asked, "What kind of protest you wanted to make in London when the bill for freedom was to be tabled?"

"Like that of Bhagat Singh. Violent, but not even a bruise to anybody. At Trafalgar Square, I would burst a cracker that would cause enough sound. I would raise slogans against the partition of India and distribute handbills. Copy of the handbill would also be posted to newspaper offices well in time."

"Why did your mission fail?"

Rabi grinned, mocking himself. "Satya da, if God is not willing, we cannot achieve success in any endeavour. The British government had advanced the date of granting freedom to India and Pakistan to the fifteenth of August 1947. After the third June proposal of Lord Mountbatten, the Labour Government was set to draft the India Independence Bill on a war footing. The bill was passed into an Act without any debate on the eighteenth of July, only a day after my voyage began. I shovelled coal to the ship's boiler for nearly a month and reached Dover on the thirteenth of August. I was detained by the immigration authorities for a day and magnanimously released on the afternoon of the fourteenth to enjoy and celebrate. I did not know if the celebration was for the partition of India or for her independence! I had no opportunity to raise my fist in protest. The people of India and Pakistan were celebrating the event on the streets of London before the India House when their countrymen were engaged in a bloodbath in Punjab and the world witnessed the streaming of an uncountable number of refugees to Tripura, Assam, and West Bengal from the eastern Pakistan."

Satya knew that Rabi had answered his question squarely. "Sagarika was your friend. You came to Nabadwip to attend her marriage. You had even undertaken a trip to Calcutta at considerable risk of your life. But why did you write her a letter from London?"

"You see, Satya da, I had left for abroad without anybody's knowledge. I reached London after twenty-five days and found that my voyage had become meaningless. Then I wrote a letter to my mother, giving her my whereabouts, but I did not get any reply from her for a month. Maybe I had made some mistake in writing their new address in Calcutta. Then I wrote two-three letters to my friends, including Didimani. I requested them to contact my parents and inform them about my well-being."

Satya had one more question, 'Were you in love with Sagar before her marriage?' but civilised social behaviour demanded self-restraint from him. Being an epitome of gentlemanliness, Satya thanked Rabi and bade him adieu.

9.2 Sagarika meets Rabi

Coming out of the restaurant, Roop was assisting Sagarika in coming to the gate, and Choity was holding the arm of Opu. Sagarika slowed down to enhance the gap with Opu. Satisfied that they were outside the reach of hearing of Opu and others, Sagarika lowered her voice and told Roop, "I want to talk to your grandpa separately. Can you arrange it? We shall go back tomorrow morning. I do not know if I shall meet him ever again."

Roop replied, "Don't worry, thammi, let my grandpa and Opu ma'am return to the Abasan, and I shall take you out from your hotel with the help of Choity."

When all others went to their respective rooms in the hotel, Roop decided to spend the time in the lounge, reading some magazines. Very soon, Choity came down after changing her dress and sat in the lounge to give him company. The two had become friends, and the recent happenings in their families had provided enough fodder to them for rumination. During their gossip, Roop disclosed that his father would join the post of GM of North Frontier Railway by the end of this month. Then, his father would be in a position to look after boro dadamoshai. Roop would also come to Guwahati to stay with his parents.

"Won't you go back to the University?" Choity asked.

"I will. But not before the marriage."

"Marriage? Whose marriage?"

"Marriage of those who are still unmarried."

"What do you mean?" Choity was not feeling sure if Roop was going to propose her.

Roop tried to cover up the slip of the tongue, but he made a further mess when he said, "Marriage between those who are willing to marry."

"It seems you are in a hurry to get married."

"I am. I do not have any idiosyncrasy to remain unmarried for a political cause."

"That's good. But whom are you going to marry? Shri has got a new friend, you know."

"Yes, an American-African. She never liked the Indians. I would marry somebody who has a love for India and the Indians." Choity became thoughtful as she did not know what to say.

Then he changed the subject and disclosed that Sagar thammi wanted to meet 'Rabi da'. But how would she go on an *abhisaar*[61] without raising the eyebrows of her husband? Choity did not see any problem and said she would find some excuse to take her out.

Accordingly, after spending an hour with Roop in the lounge, Choity entered the room of Satya and Sagar and asked her grandma if she would like to meet her sister at her flat, where she and Roop were presently going. She gladly wanted to accompany them. On reaching the Saraswat Abasan, Roop took Sagarika to the flat of her Rabi da. Rabi was somewhat taken aback to see both Choity and Sagarika at the door of his spartan room. He quickly put on a kurta over his vest. He offered them two chairs at the dining table to sit on and switched on the fan of the sitting space. The ladies surveyed the place with their eyes roaming at all corners.

Choity asked Roop, "Where does my mashi-thammi live?"

"She lives in the flat opposite to this one. But she must be in her siesta now. We shall visit her after half an hour," he said.

"Can we sit in your flat for some time?" Sagarika asked Rabi. "Sorry, we have come without an appointment."

"You live in a big house in a posh area of Kolkata. Will you feel comfortable in a *bachelor's* single-room apartment?" Rabi said, emphasizing the word 'bachelor'.

"Let me find out the source of your happiness in living like this for a whole life." Sagarika was unstoppable.

Roop and Choity exchanged looks, and Choity said, "Roop da, it is very hot today. Can we have some ice cream?"

Roop said, "Why not? There is an ice cream parlour just near the main road. Let's go and have a scoop."

"Thammi, you tell him the stories of your Banaripara days and see if he too has any story to share. We'll be back in a few minutes," Choity pranked at her own grandma.

---

[61] A lover's secret trip to meet the beloved.

"Don't forget to bring ice cream for me, naughty girl."

The two angels vanished in a moment.

Rabi was watching her. Sagar was presently a poor replica of the young Didimani of Banaripara, whom he knew. At the age of over eighty-nine, she became a fat old woman with wrinkles furrowed on her forehead.

"I heard from Deb that you fell ill recently and were hospitalised. Why did you take the trouble of a long train journey to come to Guwahati?"

"What do I do, Rabi da? God is not permitting me to die before I get your pardon."

"Pardon? For what?"

"Why didn't you marry for your whole life?" Sagarika posed a counter-question.

"Because it just did not happen. What can be done by small humans if God did not want it?"

"But there must be some earthly reasons, some causal connection with our actions. Rabi da, you forgive me, please. It was all my fault."

"What is your fault? What are you saying all this, Sagar?"

"Rabi da, why are you kidding me? I know what I have done. I walked out of the commitment and got married. I have been simmering within myself for my whole life. You had vowed to marry me and no other woman. Yes, I remember every word that you said. Also, you won't marry before the country became free. No one knew of these vows you had taken, especially the one involving the two of us. But I failed to wait for you. Rabi da, please excuse me.

When your final hearing began, Biren kaka and you shifted to some relative's house in Barishal town to attend the court every day. I was praying for you to God. At the same time, my mind was weaving a *baluchari*[62] saree of our future married life."

"Yes. But the weaver of India's destiny was also working on a tapestry of a different kind," said Rabi. "When the Cabinet Mission failed to achieve consensus, Lord Mountbatten forwarded the proposal of partitioning India to the Secretary of State."

---

[62] A brand of saree woven at Bishnupur in West Bengal, picturesquely depicting mythical stories in tapestry.

"Yes." Sagarika continued, "The moment the demand for Pakistan was conceded by the Viceroy, the voice and temper of the Muslims changed in East Bengal. As you were busy in the court, you were not aware of the rapid changes in the countryside. Next Monday, a group of Muslim boys in lungi entered the school when I was teaching in a class. Their leader, Shah Jahan Mian, entered the classroom and asked me to marry him on the next Jumma day. He said that this land would go to Pakistan, and Muslims would have the sole right to enjoy the land and its women. He said he liked me for my beauty and wanted to marry me as his third wife. He graciously gave me a clear three days' time to make up my mind. He stated that I must give my consent wilfully. If I did not, he would get my father killed, and me raped. The girls in the class were stunned, and I came back running to our quarters.

Papa was shocked at the audacity of the Mollah. He went to the Officer-in-charge of the police station to lodge a complaint. The officer only expressed his helplessness in the absence of a government with a political will to govern.

On Tuesday, I sent a small letter to you through Haru da. I thought that only you could save me from Shah Jahan. I began to wait for a reply. Haru da said your judgment would be delivered in a day. In the afternoon, he said that the hearing was adjourned. There was still no reply from you. Through Haru da, you had advised me to ask for more time from the lecherous Mollah. On Thursday, the Muslim goondas threatened my father by showing a dagger, and I began to pray for his life. There was no reply to my letter.

Papa said he had already sent a letter to our maternal uncle living in Nabadwip. It was expected that Nadia district would remain a part of India. We must run away from Barishal and escape to Nadia. On Friday, Haru da came back early. The judgment was reserved for the next day. I lost all hopes. Papa's life was now in danger. Should I not agree to forsake my religion to save the life of my father? I decided to surrender to Shah Jahan in the evening.

Biren kaka came back at about four p.m. and met my father in school. Papa discussed his course of action with Biren kaka. It was decided that we should leave Banaripara by boat at dusk when the Muslims would be engaged on Friday namaaz. Haru da was asked to fix a boat with a Hindu boatman. As the sun set, Kabi went out on a cycle to see if any lackey of Shah Jahan was keeping watch on our house. We left the house one by one. In the swiftly enveloping darkness of the dusk, we left Banaripara in a small boat under the care of Badal Majhi and his son Kajal. They rowed the boat silently and avoided the Barishal ghat on Kirtankhola. Instead, they took the boat by the network of narrower waterways with forests on both sides. This was a dangerous route, but the spirited duo preferred that unfrequented route to avoid the eyes of Shah Jahan's men. Badal and Kajal gave us a lot of courage for two days, keeping watch on crocodiles in the water and tigers in the jungle. They also caught fish from the river and cooked food for us. We finally reached Khulna after three nights. Before this journey by the river, I did not know what fear for life was. We transhipped to a steamer sailing for Budge Budge. When we reached the big jetty close to Calcutta, we heaved a sigh of relief. This was a Hindu majority area in south Bengal. We reached Nabadwip by another boat in the afternoon on the fourth day.

Later we came to know that at night Shah Jahan came to our quarters and set it ablaze. He unleashed his goons to hound us out from the adjacent districts.

Papa consulted my maternal uncle, who had given us temporary shelter. They felt that the Mollah would continue to chase us until I got married. They arranged for my marriage without losing any time lest Shah Jahan's men might reach here to abduct me. Till the transfer of power, the police would not have come to our rescue. Without getting you by my side during this crisis, I could not say 'no' when Papa asked for my consent to marry Satyabrata. Ma, however, was still hoping for your appearance every day. You came only on the evening before the marriage.

You were trying to talk to me, but I did not give you any opportunity. I felt like a jilted lover and would not allow you to come near me. The next day, Papa sent you to Calcutta for some work. After you returned, I was made to wear a new necklace and led by my relatives to the marriage site. I did not meet you after that. I went through the rituals with a feeling of vengeance against you.

The marriage ceremony was over by seven. I was seated on a chair decorated like a throne, and the guests were coming to me to give me gifts and blessings for a happy married life. When the rush of guests lessened, I found our very own Haru da slowly approaching with a packet containing a saree, a rolled encomium from the students and lastly, a simple looking, closed envelope. I kept it in my vanity bag. Later, Haru da said that the letter was given by you on the fateful Friday morning. As he became busy arranging for our escape, he forgot to deliver it to me on that day. Believe me, I got this letter after the marriage ceremony was over. And I had no way to retract my steps." Sagar began to sob.

"Yes," said Rabi. "It was perhaps my destiny. I was happy in the beginning that you had successfully escaped from the grip of that rogue. But I expected you to wait for me till the independence. Papa said on the eve of our departure from Barishal that he had received a letter from Suresh da. Your marriage was fixed at Nabadwip, and we were all invited. I was shocked to learn that you changed your mind."

"Yes, that was my fault. As we fled from Banaripara with no belongings, fearing for our lives, I tried to forget the past. It was because I came to Banaripara that I could not pursue higher studies. The local people who persuaded me to join the school did not protect us. Finally, the hero of the locality did not protect me with his strong arms. I thought it would be better to erase the Banaripara episode from my memory and turn over a new leaf, to begin a new life altogether.

To speak the truth, when Papa sent the letter of invitation to Biren kaka, I had thought it was but a mere formality to inform him about my marriage. I did not expect you to turn up at my marriage as an invitee. If Biren kaka had come in your place, I would have been much happier. My own uncle, Sisir kaka, came all the way from the troubled Sandwip, and that gave me immense happiness. When I saw you on the day before my marriage, I felt anger flowing like burning oil through all my veins. I did not like to look at your face. I saw you again in the evening. 'What a shameless fellow! He will watch the marriage of the girl who was betrothed to him,' that is what I thought of you at that moment.

Your letter was in my handbag. I found time to go through it the next morning when Satyabrata went to the terrace for free-hand exercise. Here is that letter."

Sagarika took out a letter from an ordinary envelope and began to read.

"Dear Sagar,

I am extremely worried about your safety in view of the Shah Jahan incident. I am also astonished to see the extent of their meanness!

Unfortunately, I am stuck in the District Court. Since I am out on bail, my movement is restricted by the court order. I cannot also break the vow and marry you before the independence of the country. Please understand my situation and hold on for a few more days. If the situation does not permit you to stay here, please leave Barishal as quickly as possible and hide with your family members in some safe district. As soon as I get released from court attendance, I shall join you. Send your address to the postmaster of Banaripara. He knows me.

The country will get her freedom maximum in six months, and we shall marry on the day of her Independence.

Rabi.

07.06.47"

As I read it, the truth came home to me, and I realised that you were also in a difficult situation. If you had jumped the bail, you would have been taken into custody, and the judgment would have gone against you. In the circumstances, there was no alternative for us but to leave Banaripara. But could I not wait for you at the new place of settlement? My father had become somewhat impatient, but I should have stood firm. On reading your letter, I realised that I had committed a big mistake. I asked the son of my maternal uncle to locate you. After half an hour's search, he reported that the invitees from Banaripara were missing. 'He must have left at night without taking any food at your marriage,' said my mother angrily. 'How can he digest so much insult from you?'

After the eighth day ritual at my maternal uncle's house, when I went back to my in-laws' house at Krishnagar, Biren kaka came to see me one day. He regretted that he could not come to my marriage as he was busy settling down in Calcutta after leaving the disturbed district of Barishal. The situation might have gone out of control after the partition became effective. Biren kaka was talking to me in the presence of my father-in-law. He gave him his address and requested him to ask his son to be in touch with them in Calcutta. When he got a chance to talk to me alone, he told me that you did not return home after your trip to Nabadwip. Sodu aunty wanted to know if I had any information about you. I told him that I did not have any talk with his son and had no information about his whereabouts. Biren kaka was surprised to hear my words and left for Nabadwip to meet my parents. For three months, nobody knew if you were alive. When I got your letter from London, I felt relieved, and my father-in-law wrote to Biren kaka about you.

During these months, I was extremely worried about you. If something untoward happened to you, I would not be able to forgive myself. I know it was a big shock to you, and that was why you left the country without returning to your family from Nabadwip. For your disappearance, I was held guilty by your family members in their silent trial. You made a vow not to marry any woman if you didn't marry me. True to your word, you didn't marry. You led a lonely life like an ascetic. In fact, I didn't expect you to remain unmarried all these years. You had ample reason to marry any woman of your choice because I married before the day of independence, and you were therefore free."

Rabi was listening to Sagarika without interruption. At this point, he contested, "Was I? Could I break the vow without your consent? No, that was not possible. I could not interpret my situation in my own way and declare myself free from the vow. You were to free me, Sagar."

"You are free from your vow right from this moment, Rabi da. Forgive me. Your whole life is wasted for me. This gesture of mine has no real meaning for you. Forgive me."

"It is upon me to attribute a meaning. I am so happy today that God has kindly ordained this meeting with you. Now I shall be able to marry."

"What!? Are you joking, Rabi da!"

9.3 Resolution

Roop and Choity came back after an hour. Enough time was given to Sagarika granny. She had no future. They were more interested in Aparajita. They were eagerly looking for some positive development in respect of her. Roop already received some hints from his sr. Grandpa on the previous night.

They pressed the doorbells of both the flats. Roop entered his grandpa's flat and called Sagar granny to come over to the flat of Opu thammi and have ice cream together. They brought ice cream for the three old people. Roop handed over one to Rabi and stayed back with him. Opu opened the door of her flat, but she was surprised to see Choity and Sagar didi at the door instead of Rabi dada. She controlled her exclamation and asked them to come in.

Handing over the ice cream cones to the two old ladies. Choity said, "Mashi-thammi, have it quickly before it begins to melt."

Opu was fumbling with the cone as her grip was not sure. Choity helped her in opening the wrapper. Opu said, "I have never eaten a cone. In childhood, I ate ice cream in Chittagong that had a stick with only flavoured ice around it. Nothing like this! What about you, Choity?"

"Don't worry about me. I had a tutti-fruity and Roop da, a kesar-pista," said Choity.

"You know, thammi, we saw a Marriage Registrar's office on the way. Roop da asked me if I would accompany him to that office. I said, 'What for?' He said, "Why do young men and women visit that office?"

Everybody broke into laughter. "I have no objection if you visit that office with the grandson of Rabi da," said Sagarika. Choity blushed and became busy reading an old newspaper while sitting on the balcony

"Didi, you must have eaten such cones earlier?"

"Yes, Opu, many times."

"Must be. You are married. You have a husband, a son, a daughter-in-law, and a granddaughter too. Although you did not earn money, there are many people to get you cones, kesar-pistas, tutti-fruity, and what-not."

Sagarika looked up to Opu and said, "I thought those who were in service as you and earned a lot of money could buy anything they wanted. Until Debu got established, we were spendthrifts for the best part of our life. I did not have any freedom in spending. Now, of course, Satya gives me enough pocket money from his pension, but now I do not know what to buy or how to spend."

"Didi, you don't know how lucky you have been! You left Banaripara fearing abduction by a Muslim goonda, but within a month, you got such a handsome husband as Satya da. He was in government service in Calcutta. Although Rabi da was there in Banaripara, you did not consider marrying him. He did not have a job. How would he have supported you? In fact, the Partition worked in your favour. Your marriage and settling down in India right before independence and later buying a house in the city of Calcutta would not have happened but for the partition.

Contrast this with what I faced in my life. I escaped with my parents from the island in the darkness of night during the Noakhali riots. Our grandparents lived on the island through the days of the partition, terrorised by the Muslim goondas. After the death of both the grandparents, we left our homeland, but not before I lost my virginity. We came to Assam via Tripura and became known as refugees. My parents died, and I was still unmarried. Rabi dada helped me in getting a job at Tezpur. You know how the society looks at an unmarried woman and how she is treated by her colleagues or neighbours, at the workplace, in a market, or at social gatherings."

"Opu, why didn't you marry before you left Sandwip?" asked Sagarika.

"All the Hindu families were living in uncertainty. They could not think of taking additional responsibility."

"But you could marry when you migrated to Silchar."

"Who will marry a ravished, gang-raped woman, didi?"

Choity was shocked to overhear this. She pretended to be watching the pedestrians walking on the road outside. Sagarika lowered her head. She remembered why her father suffered a stroke in 1965.

Opu continued to say, "Didi, I missed you all through my bad days. My father left this world with a grudge against the senior uncle. After your marriage, he did not go back to Sandwip and work out a planned exit for all. After the trauma of 1946, our grandparents became mentally unstable, if not imbalanced and physically infirm. It was neither possible for them to cross the sea nor possible for us to leave them behind. For eight years, we lived at the mercy of our Muslim neighbours. Papa loved all of you. But he took it to his heart that sr. uncle left the grandparents to his charge alone, and he could not leave the island till they were no more. Finally, when sr. uncle enquired about the money realised from the sale of land, he did not know how to tell him that a good amount of that money was spent in buying a tenement in a refugee colony, and more than fifty per cent of the balance currency notes were destroyed in floodwater.

Consequently, he went into a shell, hoping for better days to come when he would be able to pay fifty per cent share to his elder brother. But he never saw better days. First, mother died of snakebite, and later, he succumbed to the head and spinal injuries incurred during the Bengali language movement in Cachhar."

"Yes, I learnt of their deaths from your letters. But when my father died, and I wrote to you, I did not get any reply from you. Maybe, you had already shifted to Tezpur, and you did not give me your address. If you had given, and we had exchanged some letters, we could have produced them before the Tribunal as evidence."

She also informed Opu how the news of the death of Shakticharan and Nayantara in 1954 had hurt them. Her father used to break into a cry, '*I could not do anything for them!*' He was suffering within himself as he could not stand by the side of his brother before or after they left the homeland. He had spent all his savings on her marriage and had to take up a new job immediately for his survival.

"Papa often said that Sisir had come to India as a refugee. The amount he received from the sale of family property must not be adequate for him to buy a plot of land in any township in India. He wrote to Sisir uncle to come over to West Bengal from Silchar. They could stay with him. But Sisir uncle did not give any reply to his offer. My father could not take time off from his duty as headmaster to make a long journey to Silchar. Sisir uncle might have been hurt for that.

But Papa was also not keeping good health those days. Often, he met Shamsul Haq, who introduced himself as his classmate at Sandwip school. He gave many updates on Sandwip, including the heinous crime committed on his niece and the suicide of Amina bibi on account of that. The parents of Amina went to court, seeking justice as the suicide was sparked by the action of her husband. The case caused a stir in the Muslim community of Noakhali. The Muslim women began to raise their voices against the misdeeds of their menfolk. The intention of Mr Haq was not clear, but his vivid description of the crime committed on you took a heavy toll. Papa was in a state of shock, and at night, he suffered a cerebral attack followed by paralysis of his left side. He used to love you too much, Opu! Even after his partial recovery, he used to say, 'Now what will happen to Opu! Will she ever get married? She will never be looked upon with respect in the society.' "

"Didi, I must have been born in an inauspicious moment. Now I shall have to go to jail for the remaining days of my life. I was a science student, and I never believed in fate or stars, but I do not understand why things always go against me. Without committing any sin in my whole life, why do I have to go to prison? I left Pakistan and came to India to become her citizen. If the authorities considered me an illegal entrant, or if they wanted me to follow a specific procedure, why did they not apprise me of what I should do in the circumstances? I was allowed to serve as a teacher, and the Education department did not consider me a foreigner. They engaged me as a head examiner for ten consecutive years. The headmistress gave me the duty to lead the prayer session in the morning. And they knew that I was born in Sandwip and that I migrated in 1955. Did I ever suppress any information or make false declarations? After seven years of stay in Silchar, my name was included in the voter list of Assam. Everybody said that the inclusion of one's name in the voter list was proof of one's citizenship. In the nineties, when the photo identity card for the voters was made compulsory by the Election Commission, I obtained this card at Guwahati after settling down in this flat and applying for inclusion of my name in the electoral roll of Guwahati. But when the registration of citizens under ANRC came up, the lawmakers stipulated that the details of the 1967 electoral rolls were to be produced. Do they expect one to preserve the details of voter slip of that year and search out the name from the illegible bunch of papers of election offices in 2015?"

"Don't give up, Opu. Remember our grandpa used to say, 'Aparajita does not surrender'."

"What should I fight for, didi? I have no husband, no family. Now they say, I have no country. My whole life is spent futile like this. I am neither a housewife nor a nun, neither a woman enjoying earthly pleasures nor a woman aspiring for sainthood. I loved a person, but he did not know of this. After many years when I met him again, he said his heart was mortgaged to another. Having been ditched by her, he decided not to marry any woman. Perhaps he held all women as basically deceitful. What do I do in this situation? I, too, remained unmarried. I could not marry him, but I remained betrothed to him for life. If we had been married, I might have lived with him in the same detention camp. They would have allowed us to meet during visiting hours. Then the life in the camp would have been more bearable."

"Who is your friend, Opu thammi? Is he Roop's sr. grandpa?" asked Choity, raising her head from the newspaper. She had sneaked in silently, unable to resist the feminine temptation of hearing the secret stories of other women.

It became clear to Sagarika that because of her, Opu could not marry Rabi da.

"Rabi da is so smart and handsome even at this age that it was only natural to fall in his love at a young age. But could you know who the woman was in his heart?" she asked.

"No, I never asked him. The lady is already married for many years. What is the point of fighting with her? If Rabi da is still engrossed in her love, what can she do? The problem is with Rabi dada. If he gives his word, he never goes back on it. He gave his word to Papa to take my care. Since then, he has kept me guarded from wicked men like a caring husband."

Sagarika kept on listening without uttering a word.

At that moment, the door opened and Rabi entered, saying, "It is going to be five, Opu. Will you not go to the riverfront to see the sunset from a cruise?"

Choity was looking at the ninety-two-year-old cameo. Opu gave him a smile that could be worth many a kingdom. Only Sagarika sat silently. She felt that Rabi da belonged to her till half an hour ago. But then he decided to walk over. He would marry Opu as early as possible. She remained uncertain if she should be happy for Opu or be sorry for herself.

"Today, my didi has come to meet me. They will go back to Kolkata tomorrow. Let me spend some time with her. She has come to see me all the way from Kolkata. We shall go for the cruise safari tomorrow."

"Okay, then let me go for a walk."

"Wait for a minute, Rabi da. I have a gift for you," Sagarika stopped him.

She opened her carry bag and took out an aasan, beautifully embellished. The name of Rabi was embroidered in the left corner in golden coloured threads. "The gift is from my mother. You might have seen her working on it in our Banaripara quarters. But she had no time to give it to you by her own hand."

Rabi remembered the affectionate face of Kanak aunty. He asked, "How did the head sir and aunty spend their last days?"

"After my marriage, Papa did not have any savings. But he never let me know of his financial distress. He had joined a new school in Midnapore. He had a cerebral attack in sixty-five and became paralyzed. He lost his job after three months. My parents rented a single room tenement in Jadavpur and spent their last days in penury. I helped them buy medicines. If I could continue to work as a teacher after my marriage, I could have helped them adequately. After the death of my father, I brought my mother to our house and looked after her till she died at the age of seventy. I found this *aasan* in her trunk. She had woven the second one for your wife. I could not see it there."

Rabi took the *aasan* with great reverence for Kanak aunty and bade farewell to Sagarika.

9.4 How would this story end?

Newspapers carried the stories of humiliation and suffering of many people who could not convince the registration officers that they fulfilled the legal criteria. There were stories of suicides committed by women who could not prove their relationship with their living husbands, not to speak of those whose husbands had either died or forsaken or divorced them. Children of refugee parents could not prove who their parents were. Sahana's report on yesterday's proceedings in a Foreigners Tribunal involving a ninety-two-year-old man who was once awarded a *Tamra-Patra* by the government of India for his significant sacrifice in the freedom struggle shocked the conscience of many readers. The lackadaisical reply given by the Home Ministry was shredded into pieces by the lawyers appearing for the government. The attestation letter merely informed the name of the recipient and did not testify to the original letter. The story of an old unmarried lady teacher of a Tezpur girls' school was more heart-rending, as, in her old age, she could not move from door to door and office to office to collect some certificates and testimonials. She retired at the age of sixty-two, and today she is over eighty-five. All the officers and administrators have changed. Who will now issue a testimonial based on personal knowledge? If a record is produced, who will attest the same before the court, linking the record with the petitioner?

After the story of a poor Bangladeshi woman named Malati was published, the government issued orders to review the status of the under-trial prisoners in Assam and release the detainees not produced before a court in one year. It was expected that the reports published in the newspapers would bring some change as the PMO ritually put-up important news items in a folder to the PM.

Whatever be the true reason behind it, the government stepped up the passage of the Citizenship (Amendment) Bill in 2018. When the new bill becomes an Act and is implemented, Hindu refugees or illegal migrants might be granted citizenship or refugeeship. But there are many vested interests standing in between, and the non-citizens are keeping their fingers crossed.

Roop and Choity stayed back for a day before catching the flight for Kolkata. The Ghoshes and the Rahamans left already by a train. Roop went to the Marriage Registrar's office in the morning with his sr. grandpa and asked for the notice form. The Registrar thought Roop was the groom, and the old man must be his guardian, but he got the surprise of his life when Roop told him that the old man was the proposed groom. He was unmarried, just like the proposed eighty-five-year-old bride. When the names were written in the form, the Marriage Registrar looked askance at the newspaper lying in front of him and wanted to know if they were the same persons.

The Marriage Registrar said, "I am not fussy about rules, but in this case, the lady should come to my office with her Aadhar card and sign the notice before me."

"Okay, she will come to your office in the afternoon. You may satisfy yourself that she is still alive. But in that case, I would request you to solemnise our marriage today. If the marriage is not completed before our next hearing, which is just six days away, it may not materialise at all. Most likely, the police will take us into custody. We have waited for our whole life to marry each other. Kindly do not quote rules to foil our last wish."

"I'll see," the Registrar said condescendingly. "But are you Indian citizens?"

"We were born in British India. Until the Tribunal declares to the contrary, we whole-heartedly believe ourselves to be Indian citizens. We are permanent residents of this country and unquestionably loyal to the presiding deity of Bharatbarsha. What else can I say?"

Before they came out of the office, Roop had a short discussion on the side with the Registrar and obtained two blank forms from him. It was the turn of Rabi to be surprised.

"Roop, for whom did you take that form?" Roop smiled coyishly but did not give a reply.

As they returned to the housing complex, Roop asked Rabi if he had proposed to Opu ma'am and if she had given her consent.

"Grandson, have you proposed to Choity, and has she given you, her consent?'

They looked at each other mischievously and then burst into a roaring laughter. They were standing before the door of the flat. Rabi told Roop to leave him alone for a few minutes. He must discuss an urgent matter with Opu.

"Okay, then let me go to Choity and finish my urgent discussion with her. I shall come back with her after lunch. Roop went out before Rabi entered the flat of Opu.

"Why are you laughing so loudly, Rabi dada? What gives you such surfeit of joy?"

"Let's go in. I will tell this in a closed door." Rabi drew the latch. He came to the middle of the drawing-room and knelt before Opu like Walter Raleigh before Queen Elizabeth I. He held her hand and said softly, 'My darling! May I kiss your hand? Will you marry me?"

Opu was flabbergasted by the histrionics. She allowed him to kiss her hand and embrace her. But then she started fuming in rage.

"Why are you doing all this drama? Have you forgotten your age? Just now, before entering my flat, you were laughing like a mad man. Every neighbour could hear that. What will they think of you? No one has ever seen you taking a drink. How have you gone tipsy today?"

Rabi began to sing in Bengali, "Your love has made me drunk. O my darling!"

"Stop this nonsense. Tell me clearly what has happened. Why are you behaving like this? This does not become you."

"Believe it or not, I am going to marry you today."

After a few moments, Rabi said in a composed voice, "I have come to take your consent." He produced an official form from his pocket. "I got this form from the Marriage Registrar. You will go with me to his office in the afternoon and sign the form before him. He wants to see you."

"Why?"

"To see that you are alive. To see that you are voluntarily marrying me, not being coerced to do so."

"But before I agree, I must know what suddenly changed the situation? What happened to your vow?"

"I am free from the bondage. I can now marry a woman of my choice. It is such a relief!"

"How did you get this freedom? Who is that woman?"

"Guess. She may be known to you."

"I see. Is she Sagar didi? She was the only aged lady you met yesterday, and you met her after seventy years."

The silence of Rabi confirmed her deduction.

"Oh, that is why she was carrying your letters! Now everything is clear to me. She came here not to stand by me but to see you, her ex-lover!" Opu said sarcastically.

Opu began to weep silently, later breaking out in despair, "I have never done you any harm, didi. Why did you do this to me?"

"Opu, don't blame her unnecessarily," Rabi tried to console her. "She never knew that you had developed an interest in me at an early age. At the time of making the vow, I did not know either that you were in love with me."

"Kalachand[63], why didn't you give me a better deal? What sin did I commit that I suffered so much?"

"I do not believe that Kalachand has no other work but to play with your destiny. It is certain that human beings do not control the course of their life except in a small measure. Time has no beginning or an end. It only has a long infinite middle. We are positioned at a certain point where the history of creation is poised to meet the future of creation before it becomes a part of the past. We are too small and insignificant to understand the real meaning of the moment. With our limited knowledge and cognition, we never realize what is correct to do at a given moment.

"Why didn't I share my treasured secret with her when didi and I strolled on the sea beach of Sandwip during the vacation? Maybe, in that case, my life would have been different."

"What could you do? God has not given us the faculty of prescience. We are left to play our roles without any script. Unlike a film director, the Great Director of creation provides only the setting and introduces the living beings on the floor. Thereafter,

---

63 Lord Krishna is also called by this name; the name is popular in Chittagong and Comilla.

He allows the actor to play his role to his best understanding of a given situation."

"Is not everything the *playful activities* of Kalachand?"

"Those who believe that Kalachand controls all the movements of all microcosms and macrocosms pass the buck to him for all their failures and misdeeds. If He directs the actors for all actions, He must accept the blame for their failures and misdeeds. But we know that human beings make some decisions individually or collectively and choose the path of goodness or evil or loiter in some unknown grey area. God has endowed some creatures with a high level of consciousness, cognitive faculty, decision-making ability, and creativity. They enjoy limited autonomy under the overall suzerainty of the Supreme Being. The more the endowments are, the greater is the responsibility. Sometimes He punishes us by inflicting natural calamities. These can be reduced if we live in harmony with nature. But we cannot escape from our sufferings if these are the outcome of our actions or caused by the actions of other people. The Partition of India is one such event in our lifetime, and this citizenship registration in Assam is another. Some groups of human beings are trying to impose their supremacy over other groups. The Hindus of East Bengal or the Bengalis in Assam are suffering at the hands of more powerful groups. I think God is watching the drama and enjoying the tragic spectacle. Maybe He has some satisfaction through the purgation of His excess emotion of pity.

In our life, we suffered for years as refugees. Many could not withstand the suffering. No political leader is ever tried by a Court of Justice and held responsible for whatever happened. Neither Jinnah nor Nehru nor Mountbatten was tried for partitioning a country. The movers of the present citizenship drive, isolating about two million people of Bharatbarsha, as non-citizens or as non-statal beings of India, Bangladesh, or Pakistan, will never be. There is no justice for the suffering humanity, whether they were refugees of 1947 or the people of Indian origin declared non-citizens in 2018.

As individuals, we remained unmarried for nearly our whole lives. We would face captivity for the remaining years of our life. The order will be pronounced in the next hearing. Goalpara

Illegal Migrants' Detention Centre will receive us. Hurry up, Opu. It is time for us to get married. We must foil their design to deny us the happiness of being a married couple. Those who remain passive to the turn of events are contented with their lot and do not move forward. But there are people who try to steer the situation in their favour. They take the game forward. God feels happy to watch the new initiatives. We shall make the detention camp our home. We may live on different floors of the tower but will be permitted to meet each other on fixed dates. We shall know that we are there, living in the same building and that we will meet on the next date."

Rabi visualises that Opu and he, having been declared aliens, are reaching the Detention Centre as their final destination.

"And when we leave this world, we shall be known as husband and wife," remarked Opu.

Now take your lunch and have some rest. We shall go to the Marriage Registrar's office at four p.m. The Registrar has agreed to waive the notice time. Roop and Choity will join us there and be the witness."

"Okay, Rabi dada," agreed Opu. "Please take that aasan with you. I shall take mine with me. Kanak aunty had foreseen this day and gave us these gifts with her blessings. We shall sign the papers sitting on the pair of aasans given by her. Rabi dada, then we shall go to the Brahmaputra and see the setting sun."

"Yes. But do not call me Rabi dada anymore. Call me Rabi, only Rabi."